COMMERCIAL EXCELLENCE

HOW THE WORLD'S BEST COMPANIES DRIVE CONTINUOUS PROFITABLE GROWTH

CASTALIA HOLDINGS

Originally Published by Castalia Holdings

ISBN 9798331403034 (Hardcover edition with dust jacket)
ISBN 9798326121769 (Casewrap hardcover edition)

Contents

Introduction

The concept of Commercial Excellence has gained substantial momentum in recent years, particularly within manufacturing sectors, such as chemicals and oil & gas. Following two decades focused on Operational Excellence, these industries are now poised to build upon the foundation of continuous improvement, data-driven decision-making, and efficiency that they developed during the operational focus era, and that can now be adapted to analyze customer data, predict market trends, and optimize pricing strategies.

Commercial Excellence requires a strategic approach that prioritizes quick wins that can serve as catalysts for broader transformation efforts. Communicating these early successes will inspire and motivate teams, reinforcing the value of the transformation journey.

Gathering customer data enables companies to tailor their products, services, and marketing efforts to meet customer demands, and helps the organization to respond swiftly to market changes and customer needs. Once companies have established a reliable understanding of the market and customer behavior, they can align customer mix with product mix to balance supply and demand and maximize profitability.

Managing the salesforce and distributors effectively is an important element of achieving Commercial Excellence. Many companies that excel in engineering and manufacturing can fall short commercially because of their passive management of distributors and the poor discipline of their client-facing sales teams. The most successful companies foster discipline within their sales teams and maintain a "deep bench" of potential distributors that can be called upon to ensure sustained performance. Engaging closely with customers allows companies to check their progress and fine-tune their Commercial Excellence planning to swiftly address any issues.

Major strategic shifts require major cultural adjustments. Clear and consistent messaging and training across all levels of the organization will reinforce the new attitudes that are required to underpin the transformation's success. The shift from planning to execution also requires a different mindset and skill set. Whereas planning involves analysis and decision-making, execution demands focus, determination, and adaptability.

Embarking on the journey toward Commercial Excellence is a significant endeavor. This book aims to inspire and motivate, providing practical tools to drive real change. Your journey will require a substantial and ongoing commitment, and a willingness to adapt and evolve, but I am sure that you will find your investment to have been worthwhile.

I urge you to embrace the principles of Commercial Excellence that you will find in this book with enthusiasm and determination. Your achievements will not only transform your organization, but they will also inspire others to strive for excellence in their own fields. Ultimately, your success will be measured not just by financial gains but by the positive impact that you can have on the people and the world around you.

Greg

Chapter 1

An idea whose time has come

> « Il y a quelque chose de plus puissant que la force, que le courage,
> que le génie même: c'est l'idée dont le temps est venu »

> — *Émile Souvestre*

Raising the Bar for Industrial Manufacturing

Industrial manufacturing companies have long been the backbone of global economies, producing essential goods and materials. However, in recent years, these companies have increasingly been compared to top service providers, highlighting the need to match the convenience, transparency, and innovation of leading service-oriented businesses. This shift in benchmarking underscores the growing expectation for industrial firms to offer experiences and services similar to those provided by tech giants and customer-centric companies. As these companies strive to stay competitive, understanding this comparison is crucial for growth and sustainability.

Traditionally, industrial companies focused on efficiency and quality. Their primary objectives were to optimize production processes, minimize costs, and ensure the highest quality standards for their products. However, the rise of customer-centric models in the service sector has redefined these standards. Companies like Amazon and Google have set high expectations for customer experiences, support, and personalized services, prompting industrial firms to adopt similar engagement and satisfaction levels. This transformation requires a fundamental shift in how industrial companies operate, prioritize customer needs, and leverage technology.

To meet these elevated expectations, industrial companies must adopt customer-centric strategies using advanced analytics and digital technologies. For example, General Electric's Predix platform offers real-time data analytics to improve customer operations, demonstrating how industrial firms can adopt service-provider attributes. Predix enables predictive maintenance, operational efficiency, and enhanced decision-making capabilities, providing a competitive edge in the industrial sector. By leveraging such platforms, companies can gain deeper insights into customer needs, preferences, and pain points, allowing for more tailored and responsive solutions.

Transparency and communication are crucial in bridging the gap between industrial firms and leading service providers. Today's customers demand clear, timely, and accurate information about products, services, and company practices. Siemens' MindSphere platform connects industrial machinery through the cloud, enhancing transparency and trust through data sharing. This initiative not only improves operational efficiency but also builds stronger customer relationships by providing real-time insights into machinery performance, maintenance schedules, and potential issues. Such transparency fosters trust, accountability, and long-term loyalty among customers.

Innovation is essential for industrial companies to remain agile and responsive in a rapidly evolving market. ABB, for instance, integrates artificial intelligence (AI) and machine learning (ML) into its offerings, allowing adaptable solutions for evolving customer needs. AI and ML enable predictive analytics, automation, and smart decision-making, enhancing the overall efficiency and effectiveness of industrial operations. By embracing these advanced technologies, industrial companies can stay ahead of the competition and continuously innovate to meet changing market demands.

Digital transformation is central to this evolution. Honeywell's Forge platform exemplifies this, providing digital solutions that optimize performance and reliability across various industrial applications. Forge integrates IoT, AI, and data analytics to deliver actionable insights, streamline operations, and improve asset performance. By adopting such digital platforms, industrial companies can achieve higher levels of operational excellence, reduce downtime, and enhance customer satisfaction. As industrial companies adapt to new market expectations for Commercial Excellence, they can rise to the challenge by embracing customer-centric strategies, transparency, innovation, and digital transformation.

Benchmarking Against Leading Technology Companies

Industrial firms are increasingly compared to technology companies, reflecting the expectation to adopt innovative practices, agility, and customer-centric approaches. Historically, industrial companies focused on operational efficiency and product quality. However, the rise of technology giants like Apple, Google, and Amazon has set new standards in innovation, customer engagement, and rapid adaptability. These companies excel in leveraging data, fostering continuous innovation, and maintaining a relentless focus on the customer experience. Industrial firms must emulate this agility to stay competitive and relevant in the modern market.

One key area where industrial firms can learn from technology companies is in innovation and agility. Technology firms rapidly develop and deploy products, pivoting quickly in response to market changes and customer feedback. Siemens' MindSphere platform, an industrial IoT system, exemplifies this approach. MindSphere enables seamless data integration, real-time analytics, and remote monitoring, allowing companies to innovate and adapt swiftly. By leveraging such platforms, industrial firms can enhance their operational agility, improve decision-making, and respond more effectively to market dynamics.

Industrial firms are also expected to leverage data for decision-making and enhancing customer experiences. GE's Predix platform uses big data analytics for real-time insights and predictive maintenance, helping industrial clients optimize performance and reduce downtime. By harnessing the power of big data, companies can gain valuable insights into customer behavior, operational inefficiencies, and market trends, enabling them to make data-driven decisions that drive growth and competitiveness.

Customer-centric approaches are hallmarks of technology companies. These companies place the customer at the center of their business models, using data to tailor products and services to individual needs. Honeywell's Forge platform offers connected solutions that enhance operational efficiency and customer satisfaction, demonstrating how industrial firms can integrate customer-centric strategies into their operations. By prioritizing customer needs and leveraging digital tools to deliver personalized experiences, industrial companies can build stronger relationships, increase customer loyalty, and drive long-term success.

Digital transformation is a critical component in bridging the gap between industrial firms and technology companies. This transformation involves adopting digital tools and platforms to streamline processes, enhance product offerings, and improve customer interactions. ABB integrates AI and ML into its products to create smarter, more adaptable solutions that meet the evolving needs of their customers. By embracing digital transformation, industrial firms can achieve higher levels of efficiency, innovation, and customer satisfaction, aligning themselves with the benchmarks set by leading technology companies.

Customer Expectations for Convenience

Customer expectations for convenience have evolved significantly in recent years, impacting all sectors, including industrial companies. Customers now demand the same level of convenience from industrial firms as they do from service providers and technology companies. This shift requires industrial companies to reevaluate their customer engagement strategies and adopt practices that enhance convenience, mirroring the standards set by leading service-oriented businesses and tech giants.

Historically, convenience was not a primary focus for industrial companies. The emphasis was on product quality, operational efficiency, and cost-effectiveness. However, the rise of companies like Amazon, which revolutionized the retail experience with seamless purchasing processes and swift delivery, has redefined customer expectations. Customers now expect industrial firms to provide similar levels of convenience in their interactions, whether they are ordering parts, accessing support, or managing services.

To meet these heightened expectations, industrial companies must prioritize enhancing customer interaction. This involves streamlining processes and adopting digital tools that facilitate easy and efficient customer engagement. For instance, Caterpillar has made significant strides in this area by launching its Cat® App, which allows customers to manage their equipment remotely, schedule maintenance, and access real-time data. This mobile-friendly approach ensures that customers can interact with the company conveniently, mirroring the user experiences provided by top tech firms.

Another critical aspect of convenience is providing real-time support and accessibility. Customers today expect immediate responses to their inquiries and quick resolution of their issues. Industrial companies can achieve this by leveraging technologies such as Artificial Intelligence (AI) and chatbots to offer 24/7 customer support. For example, Siemens has integrated AI-driven customer support systems that provide instant assistance and troubleshooting, ensuring that customers receive timely help without the need for prolonged waiting periods. This approach not only enhances customer satisfaction but also aligns industrial firms with the service standards of leading technology companies.

Seamless integration and automation of processes are also essential in delivering convenience. Customers expect industrial firms to offer automated solutions that simplify their operations and reduce manual interventions. Honeywell's Forge platform exemplifies this approach by providing an integrated suite of applications that automate various industrial processes, from maintenance scheduling to performance monitoring. By automating routine tasks, Honeywell ensures that customers can focus on more strategic activities, thereby enhancing overall convenience.

Personalization is another cornerstone of convenience that industrial companies must embrace. By leveraging data analytics and customer insights, industrial firms can offer personalized experiences that cater to the specific needs and preferences of their customers. General Electric (GE) utilizes its Predix platform to gather and analyze data from customer interactions, enabling the company to tailor its services and product recommendations. This personalized approach not only improves customer satisfaction but also fosters loyalty by making customers feel valued and understood.

As customer expectations for convenience continue to rise, industrial companies must adapt to remain competitive. By enhancing customer interaction, providing real-time support, integrating automation, and offering personalized experiences, industrial firms can meet and exceed these expectations. The examples of Caterpillar, Siemens, Honeywell, and GE illustrate how industrial companies are already making significant strides in this direction. Ultimately, the ability to deliver convenience comparable to that of leading service providers and tech firms will define the future success of industrial companies in the global market.

The Demand for Transparency

Customers increasingly demand greater transparency from industrial companies. This expectation encompasses not only clear and honest communication but also detailed insights into operations, sourcing, and sustainability practices. Meeting these demands is essential for industrial firms seeking to achieve Commercial Excellence, as transparency fosters trust, enhances reputation, and drives customer loyalty.

Historically, transparency was not a primary focus for industrial companies. The emphasis was traditionally on operational efficiency and product quality. However, in an era of heightened consumer awareness and digital connectivity, transparency has become a critical component of business strategy. Customers now expect the same level of openness from industrial firms as they do from consumer brands and service providers. This shift is driven by the increasing availability of information and the growing importance of corporate social responsibility.

Transparent communication is fundamental to building trust with customers. Industrial companies must ensure that they provide clear, accurate, and timely information about their products and operations. For example, BASF, a global leader in chemicals, regularly publishes detailed sustainability reports that outline their environmental impact, safety practices, and efforts to promote sustainable development. By openly sharing this information, BASF not only complies with regulatory requirements but also builds trust with stakeholders, demonstrating a commitment to ethical practices.

Transparency in the supply chain is another critical area where industrial companies must focus their efforts. Customers and regulators increasingly demand to know the origins of raw materials and the ethical standards of suppliers. Nestlé, for instance, has implemented blockchain technology to enhance supply chain transparency. By using blockchain, Nestlé provides real-time, verifiable information about the journey of their products from farm to table, ensuring that customers can trust the integrity and sustainability of their products. This level of transparency not only meets regulatory demands but also strengthens customer trust and loyalty.

Environmental sustainability is a key aspect of transparency that industrial companies must address. Customers and stakeholders are increasingly concerned about the environmental impact of industrial operations. Companies like Siemens have set ambitious targets for carbon neutrality and regularly publish progress reports to demonstrate their commitment to sustainability. Siemens aims to achieve carbon neutrality by 2030 and uses digital tools to monitor and report on their environmental performance. By transparently sharing their sustainability goals and progress, Siemens enhances its reputation and aligns with the growing demand for environmentally responsible practices.

Digital tools play a vital role in enhancing transparency. Platforms like

Honeywell's Forge provide real-time data on operational performance and environmental impact. By integrating IoT, AI, and data analytics, Honeywell enables customers to access detailed insights into their operations, monitor key metrics, and ensure compliance with sustainability standards. This level of transparency not only improves operational efficiency but also builds trust with customers and stakeholders by demonstrating a commitment to accountability and continuous improvement.

Meeting transparency demands helps industrial firms achieve Commercial Excellence by fostering trust, enhancing reputation, and driving customer loyalty. Companies like BASF, Nestlé, Siemens, and Honeywell illustrate how transparency can be effectively integrated into business strategies. By adopting transparent communication practices, ensuring supply chain visibility, committing to environmental sustainability, and leveraging digital tools, industrial companies can meet the evolving expectations of their customers and stakeholders.

Innovation Expectations

Innovation is a driving force in the industrial sector, and companies face increasing pressure to match the innovation levels of leading technology firms. This requires embracing a culture of innovation and leveraging advanced technologies to create value and stay competitive. Traditionally, industrial firms focused on efficiency and quality, but the rapidly changing market demands and technological advancements necessitate a shift towards continuous innovation.

Adopting cutting-edge technologies such as artificial intelligence (AI), the Internet of Things (IoT), and big data analytics is essential for driving innovation in the industrial sector. For instance, GE's Predix platform offers real-time analytics and predictive maintenance capabilities, enabling industrial companies to optimize operations, reduce downtime, and enhance productivity. By leveraging these technologies, industrial firms can gain deeper insights into their processes, identify areas for improvement, and implement innovative solutions that drive efficiency and growth.

Creating a culture of innovation involves encouraging creativity, risk-taking, and collaboration within the organization. Siemens' "Future Makers" program is an excellent example of fostering an innovative culture. This initiative empowers employees to develop new ideas, collaborate on innovative projects, and bring their creative solutions to life. By promoting a culture that values innovation and supports employees in their creative endeavors, Siemens ensures that it remains at the forefront of technological advancements and market trends.

Collaboration with external partners and stakeholders is another crucial aspect of driving innovation. Honeywell's partnership with Seeq, a data analysis company, enhances Honeywell's ability to analyze and interpret large volumes of data, driving smarter decision-making and innovative solutions. By collaborating with technology partners, industrial firms can access new expertise, share resources, and accelerate the development and deployment of innovative products and services.

Customer-centric innovation focuses on understanding and addressing the specific needs and preferences of customers. ABB, for example, involves customers in the product development process, ensuring that the solutions they create are tailored to meet customer requirements. This approach not only enhances customer satisfaction but also drives innovation by aligning product development with market demands. By actively engaging customers in the innovation process, industrial firms can create more relevant and impactful solutions.

Industrial companies must also stay ahead of technological advancements and continuously explore new opportunities for innovation. This involves investing in research and development (R&D) and staying informed about emerging trends and technologies. For example, Honeywell invests significantly in R&D to develop advanced technologies and innovative solutions that address the evolving needs of their customers. By maintaining a strong focus on R&D, industrial firms can ensure that they remain competitive and can adapt to the rapidly changing market landscape.

By embracing innovation, industrial firms can achieve Commercial Excellence, enhance their competitive edge, and drive long-term growth. Companies like GE, Siemens, Honeywell, and ABB demonstrate how innovation can be effectively integrated into business strategies. By adopting advanced technologies, fostering a culture of innovation, collaborating with external partners, focusing on customer-centric innovation, and investing in R&D, industrial companies can meet the increasing expectations for innovation and stay ahead of the competition.

Impact on Manufacturing Industries

The evolving expectations of customers have had a profound impact on manufacturing industries, including energy and chemicals. Traditionally, these sectors focused on efficiency, cost control, and product quality. However, the growing demand for Commercial Excellence requires these industries to adopt advanced technologies, enhance sustainability practices, and improve customer engagement. This transformation is essential for maintaining competitiveness and achieving long-term success in a rapidly changing market.

Digital transformation has revolutionized operations in the manufacturing industry. Companies are increasingly adopting AI-driven solutions, IoT, and data analytics to optimize processes, improve efficiency, and reduce operational costs. Dow Chemical, for instance, uses AI-driven predictive maintenance to monitor equipment health and predict potential failures before they occur. This proactive approach minimizes downtime, reduces maintenance costs, and enhances overall operational efficiency. By leveraging digital technologies, manufacturing companies can achieve

11

higher levels of productivity and performance.

Sustainability is a critical focus area for the manufacturing industry, driven by regulatory requirements, customer expectations, and corporate social responsibility. Companies are setting ambitious sustainability goals and investing in green technologies to reduce their environmental impact. Shell, for example, aims for net-zero emissions by 2050 and is investing heavily in renewable energy sources such as wind, solar, and biofuels. By transitioning to sustainable practices and investing in renewable energy, manufacturing companies can meet regulatory demands, enhance their reputation, and attract environmentally conscious customers.

Improving customer engagement is crucial for manufacturing companies to achieve Commercial Excellence. In today's market, customers expect personalized experiences, real-time support, and transparent communication. ExxonMobil's digital platforms offer real-time product data, enabling customers to access critical information and make informed decisions. Additionally, Solvay's innovation hubs involve customers in the product development process, ensuring that the solutions they create are aligned with customer needs and preferences. By enhancing customer engagement, manufacturing companies can build stronger relationships, increase customer loyalty, and drive long-term success.

Collaboration and partnerships are essential for driving innovation and achieving Commercial Excellence in the manufacturing industry. BP's partnership with Microsoft, for example, focuses on driving digital transformation and innovation through the use of AI and cloud technologies. This collaboration enables BP to optimize operations, improve efficiency, and develop new, innovative solutions that meet market demands. By collaborating with technology partners, manufacturing companies can access new expertise, share resources, and accelerate their innovation efforts.

The energy sector, in particular, is undergoing significant transformation to meet the evolving expectations for Commercial Excellence. Digital technologies, customer engagement, and sustainability are key focus areas for energy companies. Shell uses AI for predictive maintenance, enhancing operational efficiency and reducing downtime. BP's digital twins optimize operations by creating virtual replicas of physical assets, enabling real-time monitoring and analysis. These digital initiatives drive efficiency, reduce costs, and improve overall performance.

Customer engagement in the energy sector focuses on transparency and convenience. E.ON's app provides real-time energy usage insights, empowering customers to monitor and manage their energy consumption more effectively. By offering transparent and convenient solutions, energy companies can enhance customer satisfaction and loyalty. Sustainability drives green practices in the energy sector, with companies like Ørsted investing in renewable energy and transitioning to green solutions. ExxonMobil's investment in carbon capture technologies aims to reduce emissions and promote environmental sustainability.

The chemicals industry is also evolving to meet the demands for sustainability, innovation, and customer-centricity. Digital transformation, sustainability practices, and customer engagement are driving this evolution. BASF uses digital twins for process optimization, enabling real-time monitoring and analysis of chemical processes. Dow Chemical employs AI for supply chain efficiency, ensuring timely delivery of products and minimizing disruptions. These digital initiatives enhance operational efficiency and drive innovation in the chemicals industry.

Sustainability is a critical focus for the chemicals industry, with companies setting ambitious goals to reduce emissions and promote environmentally friendly practices. DuPont's "2030 Sustainability Goals" focus on reducing greenhouse gas emissions, increasing the use of renewable energy, and promoting a circular economy. Clariant invests in renewable energy and eco-friendly products, ensuring that their operations and offerings align

13

with sustainability standards. By adopting sustainable practices, chemicals companies can meet regulatory requirements, enhance their reputation, and attract environmentally conscious customers.

Improving customer engagement is crucial for the chemicals industry to achieve Commercial Excellence. ExxonMobil's digital platforms offer real-time data and support, enabling customers to access critical information and receive timely assistance. Solvay's innovation hubs involve customers in product development, ensuring that the solutions they create are tailored to meet customer needs. By enhancing customer engagement, chemicals companies can build stronger relationships, increase customer loyalty, and drive long-term success.

Collaboration accelerates innovation in the chemicals industry. BASF partners with HPE for data analytics, enhancing their ability to analyze and interpret large volumes of data. This collaboration enables BASF to develop innovative solutions that meet market demands and drive operational efficiency. By collaborating with technology partners, chemicals companies can access new expertise, share resources, and accelerate their innovation efforts.

By adapting to these evolving expectations, manufacturing industries can achieve Commercial Excellence, enhance their competitive edge, and drive long-term growth. Companies like Dow Chemical, BASF, Shell, DuPont, ExxonMobil, and Solvay demonstrate how digital transformation, sustainability practices, and customer engagement can be effectively integrated into business strategies. By embracing these initiatives, manufacturing companies can meet the growing demands of their customers, regulators, and stakeholders, ensuring their continued success in a rapidly changing market.

Adaptation in the Energy Sector

The energy sector is undergoing a profound transformation to meet the demands for Commercial Excellence and evolving customer expectations. This transformation involves the adoption of digital technologies, enhancing customer engagement, and prioritizing sustainability. As the energy landscape shifts, companies must adapt to stay competitive and drive long-term growth.

Digital technologies are at the forefront of this transformation, enabling energy companies to optimize operations, improve efficiency, and reduce costs. Shell, for instance, uses AI for predictive maintenance, allowing the company to monitor equipment health and predict potential failures before they occur. This proactive approach minimizes downtime, reduces maintenance costs, and enhances overall operational efficiency. By leveraging digital technologies, energy companies can achieve higher levels of productivity and performance.

BP's use of digital twins is another example of how digital technologies are transforming the energy sector. Digital twins create virtual replicas of physical assets, enabling real-time monitoring, analysis, and optimization. By simulating different scenarios and predicting outcomes, BP can make data-driven decisions that enhance operational efficiency and reduce risks. This technology not only improves performance but also enables more effective maintenance and asset management.

Customer engagement is a critical focus area for energy companies seeking to achieve Commercial Excellence. Customers today expect transparent communication, real-time support, and convenient solutions. E.ON's app provides real-time energy usage insights, empowering customers to monitor and manage their energy consumption more effectively. By offering transparent and convenient solutions, energy companies can enhance customer satisfaction and loyalty.

Sustainability is a driving force in the energy sector, with companies prioritizing green practices and investments in renewable energy. Ørsted, for example, is transitioning to green solutions by investing in wind, solar, and bioenergy projects. This commitment to renewable energy aligns with global efforts to reduce carbon emissions and combat climate change. By adopting sustainable practices, energy companies can meet regulatory requirements, enhance their reputation, and attract environmentally conscious customers.

ExxonMobil is also making significant strides in sustainability by investing in carbon capture technologies. These technologies aim to capture and store carbon dioxide emissions, reducing the overall environmental impact of energy production. By investing in innovative solutions, ExxonMobil demonstrates its commitment to sustainability and environmental stewardship. This approach not only meets regulatory demands but also strengthens the company's reputation and appeal to environmentally conscious stakeholders.

Collaboration fosters innovation and drives the transformation of the energy sector. TotalEnergies' partnership with Google Cloud, for instance, focuses on AI-driven renewable energy optimization. This collaboration leverages Google's expertise in AI and cloud computing to enhance TotalEnergies' ability to optimize renewable energy production and distribution. By collaborating with technology partners, energy companies can access new expertise, share resources, and accelerate their innovation efforts.

By adapting to the evolving expectations for Commercial Excellence, the energy sector can achieve a competitive advantage and drive long-term growth. Companies like Shell, BP, E.ON, Ørsted, ExxonMobil, and TotalEnergies demonstrate how digital technologies, customer engagement, and sustainability can be effectively integrated into business strategies. By embracing these initiatives, energy companies can meet the growing demands of their customers, regulators, and stakeholders, ensuring their continued success in a rapidly changing market.

Chemicals Industry Evolution

The chemicals industry is evolving to meet the demands for sustainability, innovation, and customer-centricity. This evolution is driven by digital transformation, sustainability practices, and enhanced customer engagement. As the industry adapts to these new expectations, companies must implement strategies that align with market demands and regulatory requirements.

Digital transformation is a key driver of evolution in the chemicals industry. Companies are increasingly adopting advanced technologies such as AI, IoT, and data analytics to optimize processes, improve efficiency, and enhance product quality. BASF, for example, uses digital twins to create virtual replicas of their chemical processes. These digital twins enable real-time monitoring, analysis, and optimization, ensuring that operations run smoothly and efficiently. By leveraging digital technologies, chemicals companies can achieve higher levels of productivity and performance.

AI-driven solutions are also being adopted to enhance supply chain efficiency. Dow Chemical employs AI to optimize their supply chain, ensuring timely delivery of products and minimizing disruptions. By analyzing vast amounts of data, AI can predict demand patterns, identify potential bottlenecks, and recommend optimal logistics strategies. This proactive approach not only improves supply chain efficiency but also enhances customer satisfaction by ensuring that products are delivered on time.

Sustainability is a critical focus for the chemicals industry, driven by regulatory requirements, customer expectations, and corporate social responsibility. Companies are setting ambitious sustainability goals and investing in green technologies to reduce their environmental impact. DuPont's "2030 Sustainability Goals" focus on reducing greenhouse gas emissions, increasing the use of renewable energy, and promoting a circular economy. By adopting sustainable practices, DuPont demonstrates its

17

commitment to environmental stewardship and aligns with the growing demand for environmentally responsible products.

Clariant, another leader in the chemicals industry, is investing in renewable energy and eco-friendly products. The company is committed to reducing its carbon footprint and promoting sustainable practices throughout its operations. By developing and offering eco-friendly products, Clariant meets the needs of environmentally conscious customers and strengthens its position in the market.

Improving customer engagement is crucial for the chemicals industry to achieve Commercial Excellence. Customers today expect personalized experiences, real-time support, and transparent communication. ExxonMobil's digital platforms offer real-time data and support, enabling customers to access critical information and receive timely assistance. This level of engagement not only enhances customer satisfaction but also builds stronger relationships and loyalty.

Solvay's innovation hubs are another example of how the chemicals industry is enhancing customer engagement. These hubs involve customers in the product development process, ensuring that the solutions created are tailored to meet customer needs and preferences. By actively engaging customers in the innovation process, Solvay can develop more relevant and impactful solutions, driving customer satisfaction and loyalty.

Collaboration accelerates innovation in the chemicals industry. BASF partners with HPE for data analytics, enhancing their ability to analyze and interpret large volumes of data. This collaboration enables BASF to develop innovative solutions that meet market demands and drive operational efficiency. By collaborating with technology partners, chemicals companies can access new expertise, share resources, and accelerate their innovation efforts.

By adapting to the evolving expectations for sustainability, innovation, and customer-centricity, the chemicals industry can achieve Commercial

Excellence, enhance its competitive edge, and drive long-term growth. Companies like BASF, Dow Chemical, DuPont, Clariant, ExxonMobil, and Solvay demonstrate how digital transformation, sustainability practices, and customer engagement can be effectively integrated into business strategies. By embracing these initiatives, chemicals companies can meet the growing demands of their customers, regulators, and stakeholders, ensuring their continued success in a rapidly changing market.

Recent Advances in Operational Excellence

Operational Excellence is a critical focus for industrial companies, driving productivity, efficiency, and overall performance. Recent advances in technologies and methodologies have further enhanced the ability of companies to achieve Operational Excellence. By adopting lean manufacturing, Six Sigma, and continuous improvement methodologies, industrial companies can streamline operations, reduce costs, and improve product quality.

Lean Manufacturing and Six Sigma are widely adopted methodologies that focus on eliminating waste and improving process efficiency. Toyota's Production System (TPS) is a prime example of lean manufacturing in action. TPS emphasizes continuous improvement, waste reduction, and optimizing production processes. By adopting lean principles, companies can identify inefficiencies, eliminate waste, and enhance overall productivity.

GE's Predix platform is another example of how digital technologies are driving Operational Excellence. Predix enables real-time monitoring and predictive maintenance, allowing companies to identify potential issues before they escalate. This proactive approach minimizes downtime, reduces maintenance costs, and enhances operational efficiency. By leveraging digital technologies, industrial companies can achieve higher levels of productivity and performance.

Sustainability is also integral to Operational Excellence. Dow Chemical's sustainability goals focus on reducing energy intensity and waste, promoting a circular economy, and enhancing environmental stewardship. By integrating sustainability practices into their operations, companies can reduce their environmental impact, comply with regulatory requirements, and enhance their reputation.

Shell's investment in renewable energy is another example of how sustainability is driving Operational Excellence. Shell aims for net-zero emissions by 2050 and is investing in renewable energy sources such as wind, solar, and biofuels. By transitioning to sustainable practices, Shell not only meets regulatory demands but also strengthens its position as a leader in the energy sector.

Customer-centric innovations are also driving Operational Excellence. Honeywell's Forge platform offers connected solutions that enhance operational efficiency and customer satisfaction. Forge integrates IoT, AI, and data analytics to deliver actionable insights, streamline operations, and improve asset performance. By adopting customer-centric innovations, industrial companies can build stronger relationships, increase customer loyalty, and drive long-term success.

Continuous improvement methodologies, such as Kaizen, are essential for driving gains in Operational Excellence. Kaizen emphasizes incremental changes and continuous improvement, encouraging employees to identify and implement small, manageable changes that collectively drive significant improvements. Dow Chemical integrates Kaizen into their operations, promoting a culture of continuous improvement and driving efficiency and quality.

Training and workforce development are also critical components of Operational Excellence. ExxonMobil's training programs support continuous improvement by enhancing the skills and knowledge of their employees. By investing in workforce development, companies can ensure that their employees are equipped with the skills and expertise needed to drive Operational Excellence.

Investments in Operational Excellence position companies for future challenges, driving growth and success. Companies like Toyota, GE, Dow Chemical, Shell, Honeywell, and ExxonMobil demonstrate how lean manufacturing, Six Sigma, sustainability practices, customer-centric innovations, and continuous improvement methodologies can be effectively integrated into business strategies. By embracing these initiatives, industrial companies can achieve higher levels of productivity, efficiency, and performance, ensuring their continued success in a rapidly changing market.

A New Focus on Operational Excellence

Over the past two decades, industrial companies have increasingly focused on Operational Excellence as a means to drive productivity and cost reduction. This focus has led to the adoption of methodologies such as lean manufacturing and Six Sigma, which streamline operations and improve process efficiency. Toyota's Production System (TPS) is a prime example of how lean manufacturing principles can drive Operational Excellence.

TPS emphasizes continuous improvement, waste reduction, and optimizing production processes. By adopting lean principles, companies can identify inefficiencies, eliminate waste, and enhance overall productivity. This approach not only improves operational efficiency but also enhances product quality and customer satisfaction.

GE's Predix platform is another example of how digital technologies are driving Operational Excellence. Predix enables real-time monitoring and predictive maintenance, allowing companies to identify potential issues before they escalate. This proactive approach minimizes downtime, reduces maintenance costs, and enhances operational efficiency. By leveraging digital technologies, industrial companies can achieve higher levels of productivity and performance.

Sustainability practices are also integral to Operational Excellence. Dow Chemical's sustainability goals focus on reducing energy intensity and waste, promoting a circular economy, and enhancing environmental stewardship. By integrating sustainability practices into their operations, companies can reduce their environmental impact, comply with regulatory requirements, and enhance their reputation.

Shell's investment in renewable energy is another example of how sustainability is driving Operational Excellence. Shell aims for net-zero emissions by 2050 and is investing in renewable energy sources such as wind, solar, and biofuels. By transitioning to sustainable practices, Shell not only meets regulatory demands but also strengthens its position as a leader in the energy sector.

Customer-centric innovations are also driving Operational Excellence. Honeywell's Forge platform offers connected solutions that enhance operational efficiency and customer satisfaction. Forge integrates IoT, AI, and data analytics to deliver actionable insights, streamline operations, and improve asset performance. By adopting customer-centric innovations, industrial companies can build stronger relationships, increase customer loyalty, and drive long-term success.

Continuous improvement methodologies, such as Kaizen, are essential for driving gains in Operational Excellence. Kaizen emphasizes incremental changes and continuous improvement, encouraging employees to identify and implement small, manageable changes that collectively drive significant improvements. Dow Chemical integrates Kaizen into their operations, promoting a culture of continuous improvement and driving efficiency and quality.

Training and workforce development are also critical components of Operational Excellence. ExxonMobil's training programs support continuous improvement by enhancing the skills and knowledge of their employees. By investing in workforce development, companies can ensure that their employees are equipped with the skills and expertise needed to drive Operational Excellence.

Investments in Operational Excellence position companies for future challenges, driving growth and success. Companies like Toyota, GE, Dow Chemical, Shell, Honeywell, and ExxonMobil demonstrate how lean manufacturing, Six Sigma, sustainability practices, customer-centric innovations, and continuous improvement methodologies can be effectively integrated into business strategies. By embracing these initiatives, industrial companies can achieve higher levels of productivity, efficiency, and performance, ensuring their continued success in a rapidly changing market.

Productivity Enhancements

Industrial companies invest in enhancing productivity through advanced technologies, process optimization, and continuous improvement methodologies. These initiatives are essential for driving operational efficiency, reducing costs, and improving product quality. By leveraging digital tools, lean manufacturing principles, and workforce development programs, industrial companies can achieve significant productivity gains.

GE's Predix platform is a prime example of how digital technologies can enhance productivity. Predix offers real-time monitoring and predictive maintenance capabilities, enabling companies to identify potential issues before they escalate. This proactive approach minimizes downtime, reduces maintenance costs, and enhances operational efficiency. By leveraging digital technologies, industrial companies can achieve higher levels of productivity and performance.

Siemens uses digital twins for process optimization, creating virtual replicas of their operations to enable real-time monitoring, analysis, and optimization. This technology allows Siemens to simulate different scenarios, predict outcomes, and make data-driven decisions that enhance operational efficiency and productivity. By adopting digital twins, industrial companies can optimize their processes, reduce waste, and improve overall performance.

Lean Manufacturing and Six Sigma are widely adopted methodologies that focus on eliminating waste and improving process efficiency. Toyota's Production System (TPS) emphasizes continuous improvement, waste reduction, and optimizing production processes. By adopting lean principles, companies can identify inefficiencies, eliminate waste, and enhance overall productivity. This approach not only improves operational efficiency but also enhances product quality and customer satisfaction.

Honeywell's Forge platform offers real-time data insights for process optimization, enabling companies to monitor key metrics, identify areas for improvement, and implement solutions that drive efficiency and productivity. Forge integrates IoT, AI, and data analytics to deliver actionable insights, streamline operations, and improve asset performance. By leveraging these digital tools, industrial companies can achieve higher levels of productivity and performance.

Continuous improvement methodologies, such as Kaizen, are essential for driving gains in productivity. Kaizen emphasizes incremental changes and continuous improvement, encouraging employees to identify and implement small, manageable changes that collectively drive significant improvements. Dow Chemical integrates Kaizen into their operations, promoting a culture of continuous improvement and driving efficiency and quality.

Training and workforce development are also critical components of productivity enhancement. ExxonMobil's training programs support continuous improvement by enhancing the skills and knowledge of their employees. By investing in workforce development, companies can ensure that their employees are equipped with the skills and expertise needed to drive productivity and efficiency.

Investments in productivity enhancements transform operations, driving growth and success. Companies like GE, Siemens, Toyota, Honeywell, and ExxonMobil demonstrate how digital technologies, lean manufacturing principles, continuous improvement methodologies, and workforce development programs can be effectively integrated into business strategies. By embracing these initiatives, industrial companies can achieve higher levels of productivity, efficiency, and performance, ensuring their continued success in a rapidly changing market.

Safety Improvements

Improving safety standards is crucial for achieving Operational Excellence in the industrial sector. Advanced technologies, best practices in safety management, and a strong safety culture are essential components of an effective safety strategy. By prioritizing safety, companies can protect their workers, reduce costs, and strengthen their reputation.

Advanced technologies enhance safety protocols and enable real-time monitoring of worker safety. BP uses AI-driven predictive analytics for risk prevention, allowing the company to identify potential safety hazards before they escalate. This proactive approach minimizes the risk of accidents and ensures a safer working environment. By leveraging AI and predictive analytics, industrial companies can enhance their safety protocols and protect their workers.

Wearable technology is another innovative solution for improving safety. Honeywell's wearable devices monitor worker safety in real time, providing valuable data on worker health, environmental conditions, and potential hazards. These devices enable companies to respond quickly to safety issues, ensuring that workers are protected and that safety standards are maintained. By adopting wearable technology, industrial companies can enhance their safety protocols and ensure a safer working environment.

Best practices in safety management drive continuous improvements in safety performance. ExxonMobil's Operations Integrity Management System (OIMS) provides a structured approach to safety management, ensuring that safety protocols are consistently applied across the organization. OIMS includes regular safety audits, risk assessments, and incident investigations, enabling ExxonMobil to identify and address safety issues proactively. By adopting best practices in safety management, industrial companies can enhance their safety performance and protect their workers.

Creating a strong safety culture is fundamental to achieving Operational Excellence. Siemens' "Zero Harm Culture" emphasizes personal responsibility for safety, encouraging employees to prioritize safety in all aspects of their work. This culture of safety is reinforced through regular training, safety campaigns, and leadership commitment to safety. By fostering a strong safety culture, Siemens ensures that safety is a core value that drives all aspects of their operations.

Training and engagement are critical components of an effective safety strategy. Chevron's safety programs reinforce safety priorities and ensure that employees are equipped with the knowledge and skills needed to maintain a safe working environment. Regular training sessions, safety drills, and engagement initiatives keep safety top of mind for employees, ensuring that they are proactive in identifying and addressing safety issues. By investing in training and engagement, industrial companies can enhance their safety performance and protect their workers.

Safety investments protect workers, reduce costs, and strengthen reputation. By prioritizing safety, companies can minimize the risk of accidents, reduce associated costs, and enhance their reputation as responsible employers. Companies like BP, Honeywell, ExxonMobil, Siemens, and Chevron demonstrate how advanced technologies, best practices in safety management, a strong safety culture, and training and engagement initiatives can be effectively integrated into safety strategies. By embracing these initiatives, industrial companies can achieve higher levels of safety performance, ensuring the well-being of their workers and the success of their operations.

Efficiency Gains

Investments in efficiency drive productivity, cost reduction, and performance improvements in the industrial sector. Advanced technologies, process optimization, and continuous improvement methodologies are essential components of an effective efficiency strategy. By leveraging these initiatives, industrial companies can achieve significant efficiency gains and enhance their overall performance.

Advanced technologies, such as AI and IoT, revolutionize operations and drive efficiency. GE's Predix platform offers real-time monitoring and predictive maintenance capabilities, enabling companies to identify potential issues before they escalate. This proactive approach minimizes downtime, reduces maintenance costs, and enhances operational efficiency. By leveraging digital technologies, industrial companies can achieve higher levels of productivity and performance.

Siemens uses digital twins for efficiency, creating virtual replicas of their operations to enable real-time monitoring, analysis, and optimization. This technology allows Siemens to simulate different scenarios, predict outcomes, and make data-driven decisions that enhance operational efficiency and productivity. By adopting digital twins, industrial companies can optimize their processes, reduce waste, and improve overall performance.

Lean Manufacturing and Six Sigma are widely adopted methodologies that focus on eliminating waste and improving process efficiency. Toyota's Production System (TPS) emphasizes continuous improvement, waste reduction, and optimizing production processes. By adopting lean principles, companies can identify inefficiencies, eliminate waste, and enhance overall productivity. This approach not only improves operational efficiency but also enhances product quality and customer satisfaction.

Honeywell's Forge platform offers real-time data insights for process optimization, enabling companies to monitor key metrics, identify areas for improvement, and implement solutions that drive efficiency and productivity. Forge integrates IoT, AI, and data analytics to deliver actionable insights, streamline operations, and improve asset performance. By leveraging these digital tools, industrial companies can achieve higher levels of productivity and performance.

Continuous improvement methodologies, such as Kaizen, are essential for driving gains in efficiency. Kaizen emphasizes incremental changes and continuous improvement, encouraging employees to identify and implement small, manageable changes that collectively drive significant improvements. Dow Chemical integrates Kaizen into their operations, promoting a culture of continuous improvement and driving efficiency and quality.

Training and workforce development are also critical components of efficiency enhancement. ExxonMobil's training programs support continuous improvement by enhancing the skills and knowledge of their employees. By investing in workforce development, companies can ensure that their employees are equipped with the skills and expertise needed to drive efficiency and productivity.

Efficiency investments transform operations, driving growth and success. Companies like GE, Siemens, Toyota, Honeywell, and ExxonMobil demonstrate how digital technologies, lean manufacturing principles, continuous improvement methodologies, and workforce development programs can be effectively integrated into business strategies. By embracing these initiatives, industrial companies can achieve higher levels of productivity, efficiency, and performance, ensuring their continued success in a rapidly changing market.

Performance Outcomes

Investments in Operational Excellence improve performance through technology, process optimization, and continuous improvement methodologies. By leveraging digital tools, lean manufacturing principles, and workforce development programs, industrial companies can achieve significant performance gains and enhance their overall operations.

GE's Predix platform is a prime example of how digital technologies can enhance performance. Predix offers real-time monitoring and predictive maintenance capabilities, enabling companies to identify potential issues before they escalate. This proactive approach minimizes downtime, reduces maintenance costs, and enhances operational efficiency. By leveraging digital technologies, industrial companies can achieve higher levels of productivity and performance.

Siemens uses digital twins for process optimization, creating virtual replicas of their operations to enable real-time monitoring, analysis, and optimization. This technology allows Siemens to simulate different scenarios, predict outcomes, and make data-driven decisions that enhance operational efficiency and productivity. By adopting digital twins, industrial companies can optimize their processes, reduce waste, and improve overall performance.

Lean Manufacturing and Six Sigma are widely adopted methodologies that focus on eliminating waste and improving process efficiency. Toyota's Production System (TPS) emphasizes continuous improvement, waste reduction, and optimizing production processes. By adopting lean principles, companies can identify inefficiencies, eliminate waste, and enhance overall productivity. This approach not only improves operational efficiency but also enhances product quality and customer satisfaction.

Honeywell's Forge platform offers real-time data insights for process optimization, enabling companies to monitor key metrics, identify areas for improvement, and implement solutions that drive efficiency and productivity. Forge integrates IoT, AI, and data analytics to deliver actionable insights, streamline operations, and improve asset performance. By leveraging these digital tools, industrial companies can achieve higher levels of productivity and performance.

Continuous improvement methodologies, such as Kaizen, are essential for driving gains in performance. Kaizen emphasizes incremental changes and continuous improvement, encouraging employees to identify and implement small, manageable changes that collectively drive significant improvements. Dow Chemical integrates Kaizen into their operations, promoting a culture of continuous improvement and driving efficiency and quality.

Training and workforce development are also critical components of performance enhancement. ExxonMobil's training programs support continuous improvement by enhancing the skills and knowledge of their employees. By investing in workforce development, companies can ensure that their employees are equipped with the skills and expertise needed to drive performance and efficiency.

Investments in Operational Excellence improve performance, driving growth and success. Companies like GE, Siemens, Toyota, Honeywell, and ExxonMobil demonstrate how digital technologies, lean manufacturing principles, continuous improvement methodologies, and workforce development programs can be effectively integrated into business strategies. By embracing these initiatives, industrial companies can achieve higher levels of productivity, efficiency, and performance, ensuring their continued success in a rapidly changing market.

Cost Savings Achieved

Operational Excellence investments capture cost savings through advanced technologies, process optimization, and continuous improvement methodologies. By leveraging digital tools, lean manufacturing principles, and workforce development programs, industrial companies can achieve significant cost savings and enhance their overall operations.

GE's Predix platform is a prime example of how digital technologies can capture cost savings. Predix offers real-time monitoring and predictive maintenance capabilities, enabling companies to identify potential issues before they escalate. This proactive approach minimizes downtime, reduces maintenance costs, and enhances operational efficiency. By leveraging digital technologies, industrial companies can achieve higher levels of productivity and performance, resulting in significant cost savings.

Siemens uses digital twins for process optimization, creating virtual replicas of their operations to enable real-time monitoring, analysis, and optimization. This technology allows Siemens to simulate different scenarios, predict outcomes, and make data-driven decisions that enhance operational efficiency and productivity. By adopting digital twins, industrial companies can optimize their processes, reduce waste, and improve overall performance, resulting in significant cost savings.

Lean Manufacturing and Six Sigma are widely adopted methodologies that focus on eliminating waste and improving process efficiency. Toyota's Production System (TPS) emphasizes continuous improvement, waste reduction, and optimizing production processes. By adopting lean principles, companies can identify inefficiencies, eliminate waste, and enhance overall productivity. This approach not only improves operational efficiency but also enhances product quality and customer satisfaction, resulting in significant cost savings.

Honeywell's Forge platform offers real-time data insights for process optimization, enabling companies to monitor key metrics, identify areas for improvement, and implement solutions that drive efficiency and productivity. Forge integrates IoT, AI, and data analytics to deliver actionable insights, streamline operations, and improve asset performance. By leveraging these digital tools, industrial companies can achieve higher levels of productivity and performance, resulting in significant cost savings.

Continuous improvement methodologies, such as Kaizen, are essential for capturing cost savings. Kaizen emphasizes incremental changes and continuous improvement, encouraging employees to identify and implement small, manageable changes that collectively drive significant improvements. Dow Chemical integrates Kaizen into their operations, promoting a culture of continuous improvement and driving efficiency and quality, resulting in significant cost savings.

Training and workforce development are also critical components of cost savings. ExxonMobil's training programs support continuous improvement by enhancing the skills and knowledge of their employees. By investing in workforce development, companies can ensure that their employees are equipped with the skills and expertise needed to drive performance and efficiency, resulting in significant cost savings.

Operational Excellence investments capture cost savings, driving growth and success. Companies like GE, Siemens, Toyota, Honeywell, and ExxonMobil demonstrate how digital technologies, lean manufacturing principles, continuous improvement methodologies, and workforce development programs can be effectively integrated into business strategies. By embracing these initiatives, industrial companies can achieve higher levels of productivity, efficiency, and performance, resulting in significant cost savings and ensuring their continued success in a rapidly changing market.

Overall Return on Investment

Investments in Operational Excellence yield significant returns through technology, process optimization, and continuous improvement methodologies. By leveraging digital tools, lean manufacturing principles, and workforce development programs, industrial companies can achieve significant returns on investment and enhance their overall operations.

GE's Predix platform is a prime example of how digital technologies can yield significant returns on investment. Predix offers real-time monitoring and predictive maintenance capabilities, enabling companies to identify potential issues before they escalate. This proactive approach minimizes downtime, reduces maintenance costs, and enhances operational efficiency. By leveraging digital technologies, industrial companies can achieve higher levels of productivity and performance, resulting in significant returns on investment.

Siemens uses digital twins for process optimization, creating virtual replicas of their operations to enable real-time monitoring, analysis, and optimization. This technology allows Siemens to simulate different scenarios, predict outcomes, and make data-driven decisions that enhance operational efficiency and productivity. By adopting digital twins, industrial companies can optimize their processes, reduce waste, and improve overall performance, resulting in significant returns on investment.

Lean Manufacturing and Six Sigma are widely adopted methodologies that focus on eliminating waste and improving process efficiency. Toyota's Production System (TPS) emphasizes continuous improvement, waste reduction, and optimizing production processes. By adopting lean principles, companies can identify inefficiencies, eliminate waste, and enhance overall productivity. This approach not only improves operational efficiency but also enhances product quality and customer satisfaction, resulting in significant returns on investment.

Honeywell's Forge platform offers real-time data insights for process optimization, enabling companies to monitor key metrics, identify areas for improvement, and implement solutions that drive efficiency and productivity. Forge integrates IoT, AI, and data analytics to deliver actionable insights, streamline operations, and improve asset performance. By leveraging these digital tools, industrial companies can achieve higher levels of productivity and performance, resulting in significant returns on investment.

Continuous improvement methodologies, such as Kaizen, are essential for yielding returns on investment. Kaizen emphasizes incremental changes and continuous improvement, encouraging employees to identify and implement small, manageable changes that collectively drive significant improvements. Dow Chemical integrates Kaizen into their operations, promoting a culture of continuous improvement and driving efficiency and quality, resulting in significant returns on investment.

Training and workforce development are also critical components of achieving returns on investment. ExxonMobil's training programs support continuous improvement by enhancing the skills and knowledge of their employees. By investing in workforce development, companies can ensure that their employees are equipped with the skills and expertise needed to drive performance and efficiency, resulting in significant returns on investment.

Investments in Operational Excellence yield significant returns on investment, driving growth and success. Companies like GE, Siemens, Toyota, Honeywell, and ExxonMobil demonstrate how digital technologies, lean manufacturing principles, continuous improvement methodologies, and workforce development programs can be effectively integrated into business strategies. By embracing these initiatives, industrial companies can achieve higher levels of productivity, efficiency, and performance, resulting in significant returns on investment and ensuring their continued success in a rapidly changing market.

The Natural Progression to Commercial Excellence

Manufacturing companies are increasingly pivoting to Commercial Excellence, focusing on profitability, customer relationships, and sales effectiveness. This shift is driven by the need to enhance operational efficiencies, improve customer engagement, and drive revenue growth. By adopting advanced technologies, optimizing pricing strategies, and enhancing sales effectiveness, manufacturing companies can achieve Commercial Excellence and ensure long-term success.

Operational efficiencies enable the shift to Commercial Excellence. GE's Predix platform and Toyota's Production System (TPS) provide stable foundations for operational efficiency. Predix offers real-time monitoring and predictive maintenance capabilities, enabling companies to identify potential issues before they escalate. TPS emphasizes continuous improvement, waste reduction, and optimizing production processes. By leveraging these methodologies, manufacturing companies can achieve higher levels of operational efficiency and productivity, creating a solid foundation for Commercial Excellence.

Customer engagement is a key focus area for achieving Commercial Excellence. Siemens offers real-time insights and personalized solutions through its digital platforms, enabling companies to enhance customer engagement and satisfaction. Honeywell's Forge platform provides connected solutions that improve operational efficiency and customer satisfaction. By prioritizing customer needs and leveraging digital tools to deliver personalized experiences, manufacturing companies can build stronger relationships, increase customer loyalty, and drive long-term success.

Optimizing sales and marketing strategies is essential for driving revenue growth and achieving Commercial Excellence. Dow Chemical uses data analytics to develop targeted strategies that maximize revenue and enhance customer satisfaction. Personalized approaches, such as tailored marketing campaigns and customized product recommendations, improve customer engagement and loyalty. By leveraging data analytics, manufacturing companies can make data-driven decisions that optimize sales and marketing efforts, driving revenue growth and ensuring long-term success.

Innovation fosters growth and drives Commercial Excellence. BASF implements dynamic pricing models that respond to market demands and maximize revenue. Siemens leverages digital twins to optimize operations and develop innovative solutions that meet customer needs. By embracing innovation, manufacturing companies can stay ahead of the competition, develop new products and services, and drive long-term growth.

The shift to Commercial Excellence ensures competitiveness and profitability. By focusing on profitability, customer relationships, and sales effectiveness, manufacturing companies can achieve higher levels of performance and success. Companies like GE, Toyota, Siemens, Honeywell, and BASF demonstrate how operational efficiencies, customer engagement, optimized sales and marketing strategies, and innovation can be effectively integrated into business strategies. By embracing these initiatives, manufacturing companies can achieve Commercial Excellence, enhance their competitive edge, and drive long-term growth.

Objective of Driving Profitability

Shifting focus to Commercial Excellence drives profitability through refined commercial practices. Enhancing customer engagement, optimizing pricing strategies, and improving sales effectiveness are key objectives for achieving profitability. By adopting digital tools, leveraging data analytics, and prioritizing customer needs, manufacturing companies can drive profitability and ensure long-term success.

Enhancing customer engagement is a critical objective for driving profitability. Siemens and Honeywell use digital tools to offer personalized solutions that enhance customer satisfaction and loyalty. Siemens provides real-time insights and tailored recommendations through its digital platforms, enabling companies to enhance customer engagement and satisfaction. Honeywell's Forge platform offers connected solutions that improve operational efficiency and customer satisfaction. By prioritizing customer needs and leveraging digital tools to deliver personalized experiences, manufacturing companies can build stronger relationships, increase customer loyalty, and drive profitability.

Optimizing pricing strategies is essential for maximizing revenue and sustaining competitiveness. BASF's dynamic pricing models respond to market demands and maximize revenue. Dow Chemical tailors pricing strategies with data analytics, ensuring that prices align with customer perceptions and market conditions. Value-based pricing, which aligns prices with the perceived value of products, is another effective strategy for maximizing revenue. By leveraging data analytics and adopting dynamic and value-based pricing models, manufacturing companies can optimize their pricing strategies, maximize revenue, and drive profitability.

Improving sales effectiveness involves adopting advanced analytics and CRM systems to streamline processes and enhance sales performance. Dow Chemical uses data analytics to develop targeted sales strategies that maximize revenue and enhance customer satisfaction. GE's Predix platform offers personalized solutions that improve sales effectiveness and customer engagement. By refining sales processes, enhancing training programs, and leveraging CRM systems, manufacturing companies can improve sales effectiveness, increase revenue, and drive profitability.

Operational efficiencies support the shift to Commercial Excellence and drive profitability. GE's Predix platform and Toyota's Production System (TPS) provide stable foundations for operational efficiency. Predix offers real-time monitoring and predictive maintenance capabilities, enabling companies to identify potential issues before they escalate. TPS emphasizes continuous improvement, waste reduction, and optimizing production processes. By leveraging these methodologies, manufacturing companies can achieve higher levels of operational efficiency and productivity, creating a solid foundation for profitability.

The focus on profitability ensures growth and competitiveness. By enhancing customer engagement, optimizing pricing strategies, and improving sales effectiveness, manufacturing companies can achieve higher levels of profitability and success. Companies like Siemens, Honeywell, BASF, Dow Chemical, and GE demonstrate how digital tools, data analytics, refined pricing strategies, and optimized sales processes can be effectively integrated into business strategies. By embracing these initiatives, manufacturing companies can achieve profitability, enhance their competitive edge, and drive long-term growth.

Revenue Growth Focus

Companies are shifting from a sole focus on Operational Excellence to a broader focus on revenue growth, leveraging efficiencies for profitability. This shift involves enhancing customer engagement, optimizing sales strategies, and adopting innovative practices to drive revenue growth. By leveraging advanced technologies, data analytics, and customer-centric approaches, companies can achieve revenue growth and ensure long-term success.

Enhancing customer engagement is a key focus area for driving revenue growth. Siemens and Honeywell use digital tools to offer personalized solutions that enhance customer satisfaction and loyalty. Siemens provides real-time insights and tailored recommendations through its digital platforms, enabling companies to enhance customer engagement and satisfaction. Honeywell's Forge platform offers connected solutions that improve operational efficiency and customer satisfaction. By prioritizing customer needs and leveraging digital tools to deliver personalized experiences, companies can build stronger relationships, increase customer loyalty, and drive revenue growth.

Optimizing sales strategies is essential for driving revenue growth. Dow Chemical uses data analytics to develop targeted sales strategies that maximize revenue and enhance customer satisfaction. Personalized marketing campaigns and customized product recommendations improve customer engagement and loyalty. ExxonMobil's customer portal offers support and information, ensuring that customers receive timely assistance and personalized experiences. By leveraging data analytics and adopting targeted sales strategies, companies can optimize their sales efforts, increase revenue, and drive growth.

Innovation drives growth and enhances competitiveness. BASF implements dynamic pricing models that respond to market demands and maximize revenue. Siemens leverages digital twins to optimize operations and develop innovative solutions that meet customer needs. By embracing innovation, companies can stay ahead of the competition, develop new products and services, and drive long-term growth.

Aligning with market trends ensures success. GE and ExxonMobil adapt their portfolios to meet changing market demands and customer preferences. GE focuses on renewable energy and sustainability, aligning with global efforts to reduce carbon emissions and combat climate change. ExxonMobil expands its range of sustainable products, meeting the needs of environmentally conscious customers. By aligning with market trends, companies can ensure relevance, enhance competitiveness, and drive revenue growth.

The focus on revenue growth ensures competitiveness and profitability. By enhancing customer engagement, optimizing sales strategies, and adopting innovative practices, companies can achieve higher levels of revenue growth and success. Companies like Siemens, Honeywell, Dow Chemical, ExxonMobil, BASF, and GE demonstrate how digital tools, data analytics, personalized marketing, and innovation can be effectively integrated into business strategies. By embracing these initiatives, companies can achieve revenue growth, enhance their competitive edge, and drive long-term success.

Enhanced Pricing Strategies

Refining pricing strategies maximizes revenue and sustains competitiveness in a rapidly changing market. Advanced analytics, dynamic pricing models, and value-based pricing are essential components of an effective pricing strategy. By leveraging data and adopting innovative pricing approaches, companies can optimize their pricing strategies, maximize revenue, and ensure long-term success.

Advanced analytics play a critical role in refining pricing strategies. Companies like BASF and Dow Chemical use data analytics to assess market conditions, customer behavior, and competitive dynamics. By analyzing vast amounts of data, companies can identify pricing opportunities, predict demand patterns, and develop targeted pricing strategies that maximize revenue. Data-driven pricing decisions ensure that prices align with customer perceptions and market conditions, enhancing competitiveness and profitability.

Dynamic pricing models respond to market demands and maximize revenue. BASF implements dynamic pricing strategies that adjust prices based on real-time market conditions, demand fluctuations, and competitive pressures. This flexible approach ensures that prices remain competitive and aligned with market dynamics, maximizing revenue and profitability. By adopting dynamic pricing models, companies can respond quickly to market changes and optimize their pricing strategies.

Value-based pricing aligns prices with the perceived value of products. GE's Predix platform gathers data on customer preferences and usage patterns, enabling the company to develop value-based pricing strategies. This approach ensures that prices reflect the value delivered to customers, enhancing customer satisfaction and loyalty. By adopting value-based pricing, companies can differentiate their products, justify premium prices, and maximize revenue.

Personalized pricing builds relationships and enhances customer satisfaction. ExxonMobil's customer portal offers customized pricing based on individual customer profiles, purchasing history, and preferences. This personalized approach ensures that customers receive tailored pricing that meets their specific needs and expectations. By leveraging data and adopting personalized pricing strategies, companies can build stronger customer relationships, increase loyalty, and drive revenue growth.

Strategic pricing drives profitability and sustains competitiveness. Siemens uses digital twins to develop customized pricing solutions that optimize revenue and meet customer needs. By analyzing data and simulating different pricing scenarios, Siemens can identify optimal pricing strategies that maximize revenue and enhance competitiveness. By adopting strategic pricing approaches, companies can achieve higher levels of profitability and success.

The focus on refining pricing strategies ensures competitiveness and revenue growth. By leveraging advanced analytics, adopting dynamic and value-based pricing models, and personalizing pricing, companies can optimize their pricing strategies, maximize revenue, and ensure long-term success. Companies like BASF, Dow Chemical, GE, ExxonMobil, and Siemens demonstrate how data analytics, dynamic pricing, value-based pricing, and personalized pricing can be effectively integrated into business strategies. By embracing these initiatives, companies can achieve enhanced pricing strategies, sustain competitiveness, and drive revenue growth.

Improved Sales Effectiveness

Improving sales effectiveness enhances profitability and customer engagement. Advanced analytics, CRM systems, and targeted sales strategies are essential components of an effective sales approach. By leveraging data and adopting innovative sales practices, companies can optimize their sales processes, increase revenue, and ensure long-term success.

Advanced analytics play a critical role in improving sales effectiveness. Companies like Dow Chemical use data analytics to develop targeted sales strategies that maximize revenue and enhance customer satisfaction. By analyzing vast amounts of data, companies can identify sales opportunities, predict customer behavior, and develop personalized sales approaches that drive engagement and loyalty. Data-driven sales decisions ensure that sales efforts are focused on high-value opportunities, enhancing effectiveness and profitability.

CRM systems streamline sales processes and enhance customer engagement. Honeywell integrates its CRM system with the Forge platform to offer real-time insights and personalized solutions. This integration enables sales teams to access critical customer data, track interactions, and develop tailored sales strategies that meet customer needs. By leveraging CRM systems, companies can optimize their sales processes, improve customer engagement, and drive revenue growth.

Targeted sales strategies optimize sales efforts and increase revenue. GE's Predix platform offers personalized solutions that improve sales effectiveness and customer engagement. By analyzing customer data and developing targeted sales strategies, GE can identify high-value opportunities, tailor product recommendations, and enhance customer satisfaction. By adopting targeted sales strategies, companies can optimize their sales efforts, increase revenue, and drive profitability.

Refining sales processes and enhancing training programs improve sales effectiveness. Siemens uses digital tools to simulate sales scenarios and develop training programs that enhance sales skills. By refining sales processes and investing in training, Siemens ensures that its sales teams are equipped with the knowledge and expertise needed to drive engagement and revenue growth. By enhancing sales processes and training, companies can improve sales effectiveness, increase revenue, and drive long-term success.

Sales effectiveness drives growth and enhances competitiveness. Companies like Dow Chemical, Honeywell, GE, and Siemens demonstrate how advanced analytics, CRM systems, targeted sales strategies, and refined sales processes can be effectively integrated into business strategies. By embracing these initiatives, companies can achieve improved sales effectiveness, enhance their competitive edge, and drive long-term growth.

Selective Customer Targeting

Selective customer targeting enhances profitability by focusing on high-value customers. Advanced analytics, personalized engagement, and targeted strategies are essential components of an effective customer targeting approach. By leveraging data and adopting innovative targeting practices, companies can optimize their customer efforts, increase profitability, and ensure long-term success.

Advanced analytics play a critical role in selective customer targeting. Companies like Dow Chemical and GE use data analytics to identify and prioritize high-value customer segments. By analyzing vast amounts of data, companies can identify customer behavior, preferences, and profitability, enabling them to develop targeted strategies that maximize revenue. Data-driven customer targeting ensures that efforts are focused on high-value opportunities, enhancing effectiveness and profitability.

Personalized engagement builds relationships and enhances customer satisfaction. ExxonMobil's customer portal offers customized support and tailored solutions based on individual customer profiles, purchasing history, and preferences. This personalized approach ensures that customers receive tailored experiences that meet their specific needs and expectations. By leveraging data and adopting personalized engagement strategies, companies can build stronger customer relationships, increase loyalty, and drive revenue growth.

Targeted strategies optimize customer efforts and increase profitability. Honeywell and Siemens refine their customer segmentation to develop

43

targeted strategies that maximize revenue and enhance customer satisfaction. By analyzing customer data and developing targeted strategies, Honeywell and Siemens can identify high-value opportunities, tailor product recommendations, and enhance customer satisfaction. By adopting targeted strategies, companies can optimize their customer efforts, increase profitability, and drive growth.

Focusing on high-value customers enhances competitiveness and revenue. BASF uses CRM systems to develop tailored solutions that meet the specific needs of high-value customers. By prioritizing high-value customers, BASF ensures that its efforts are focused on opportunities that maximize revenue and profitability. By leveraging data and adopting targeted strategies, companies can enhance their competitive edge, increase profitability, and drive long-term success.

Selective customer targeting ensures growth and profitability. By leveraging advanced analytics, adopting personalized engagement strategies, and developing targeted customer approaches, companies can optimize their customer efforts, increase profitability, and ensure long-term success. Companies like Dow Chemical, GE, ExxonMobil, Honeywell, Siemens, and BASF demonstrate how data analytics, personalized engagement, and targeted strategies can be effectively integrated into business strategies. By embracing these initiatives, companies can achieve selective customer targeting, enhance their competitive edge, and drive growth and profitability.

Optimized Product Mix

Optimizing the product mix meets market demands and improves margins. Data analytics, customer preferences, and strategic alignment are essential components of an effective product mix strategy. By leveraging data and adopting innovative approaches, companies can optimize their product mix, enhance competitiveness, and drive long-term success.

Data analytics play a critical role in optimizing the product mix. Companies like BASF and Dow Chemical use data analytics to assess product profitability, market conditions, and customer behavior. By analyzing vast amounts of data, companies can identify opportunities for product optimization, predict demand patterns, and develop targeted strategies that maximize revenue. Data-driven product mix decisions ensure that offerings align with market demands and customer preferences, enhancing competitiveness and profitability.

Customer preferences guide product development and optimization. Honeywell and Siemens engage customers in the product development process, ensuring that solutions are tailored to meet customer needs and expectations. By involving customers in the development process, Honeywell and Siemens can create products that align with market demands, enhance customer satisfaction, and drive revenue growth. By leveraging customer insights and adopting customer-centric approaches, companies can optimize their product mix and ensure long-term success.

Strategic alignment with market trends ensures relevance and competitiveness. GE focuses on renewable energy and sustainability, aligning its product portfolio with global efforts to reduce carbon emissions and combat climate change. ExxonMobil expands its range of sustainable products, meeting the needs of environmentally conscious customers. By aligning their product mix with market trends, companies can ensure relevance, enhance competitiveness, and drive revenue growth.

Optimizing the product mix enhances margins and profitability. BASF uses data analytics to identify high-margin products and optimize their product portfolio accordingly. By focusing on high-margin products, BASF can maximize profitability and ensure long-term success. By leveraging data and adopting strategic approaches, companies can optimize their product mix, enhance margins, and drive profitability.

Strategic alignment with market needs drives success. GE and ExxonMobil adapt their portfolios to meet changing market demands and customer preferences. By aligning their product mix with market needs, companies can ensure relevance, enhance competitiveness, and drive revenue growth.

Optimizing the product mix ensures competitiveness and profitability. By leveraging data analytics, adopting customer-centric approaches, and aligning with market trends, companies can optimize their product mix, enhance margins, and drive long-term success. Companies like BASF, Dow Chemical, Honeywell, Siemens, GE, and ExxonMobil demonstrate how data analytics, customer preferences, and strategic alignment can be effectively integrated into business strategies. By embracing these initiatives, companies can achieve optimized product mix, enhance their competitive edge, and drive growth and profitability.

The Holistic Approach to Commercial Excellence

A holistic approach to Commercial Excellence integrates pricing, sales effectiveness, customer targeting, and product mix. Advanced analytics, digital tools, and continuous improvement methodologies are essential components of an effective Commercial Excellence strategy. By leveraging these initiatives, companies can optimize their commercial practices, enhance competitiveness, and drive long-term success.

Advanced analytics drive dynamic pricing and optimize revenue. Companies like BASF and Dow Chemical use real-time data to develop dynamic pricing strategies that respond to market demands and maximize revenue. By analyzing vast amounts of data, companies can identify pricing opportunities, predict demand patterns, and develop targeted pricing strategies that optimize revenue. Data-driven pricing decisions ensure that prices align with customer perceptions and market conditions, enhancing competitiveness and profitability.

Optimized sales processes and training enhance efficiency and performance. Honeywell integrates its CRM system with the Forge platform to offer real-time insights and personalized solutions. This integration enables sales teams to access critical customer data, track interactions, and develop tailored sales strategies that meet customer needs. By refining sales processes and investing in training, companies can improve sales effectiveness, increase revenue, and drive profitability.

Selective targeting prioritizes high-value customers and optimizes resources. GE and Siemens refine their customer segmentation to develop targeted strategies that maximize revenue and enhance customer satisfaction. By analyzing customer data and developing targeted strategies, GE and Siemens can identify high-value opportunities, tailor product recommendations, and enhance customer satisfaction. By leveraging data and adopting targeted strategies, companies can optimize their customer efforts, increase profitability, and drive growth.

Personalized engagement builds relationships and enhances customer satisfaction. ExxonMobil's customer portal offers customized support and tailored solutions based on individual customer profiles, purchasing history, and preferences. This personalized approach ensures that customers receive tailored experiences that meet their specific needs and expectations. By leveraging data and adopting personalized engagement strategies, companies can build stronger customer relationships, increase loyalty, and drive revenue growth.

Optimizing the product mix meets market demands and improves margins. GE focuses on renewable energy and sustainability, aligning its product portfolio with global efforts to reduce carbon emissions and combat climate change. ExxonMobil expands its range of sustainable products, meeting the needs of environmentally conscious customers. By aligning their product mix with market trends, companies can ensure relevance, enhance competitiveness, and drive revenue growth.

Holistic strategies drive profitability and competitiveness. By integrating pricing, sales effectiveness, customer targeting, and product mix,

47

companies can achieve higher levels of Commercial Excellence and success. Companies like BASF, Dow Chemical, Honeywell, Siemens, GE, and ExxonMobil demonstrate how advanced analytics, digital tools, and continuous improvement methodologies can be effectively integrated into business strategies. By embracing these initiatives, companies can achieve holistic Commercial Excellence, enhance their competitive edge, and drive long-term   growth.

Chapter 2

We've been here before

"The end of all our exploring will be to arrive where we started and know the place for the first time"

— T.S. Eliot

The same, but different

For manufacturing companies, the shift from Operational Excellence to Commercial Excellence represents a natural and logical progression. After two decades of focusing on streamlining operations, reducing costs, and enhancing productivity, these firms are now turning their attention to refining their commercial practices. This strategic pivot aims to maximize revenue, enhance customer relationships, and drive overall business success. The transition is seamless, leveraging the strong operational foundations to achieve higher levels of commercial performance.

Operational excellence has provided manufacturing companies with a solid foundation. Through the adoption of advanced technologies, process optimization, and a culture of continuous improvement, firms like General Electric (GE) and Toyota have significantly enhanced their operational efficiency. GE's implementation of the Predix platform, which enables real-time monitoring and predictive maintenance, has led to substantial productivity gains. Similarly, Toyota's Toyota Production System (TPS) has minimized waste and streamlined processes, establishing a benchmark for operational efficiency.

These operational improvements have not only enhanced productivity but also freed up resources that can now be redirected towards commercial initiatives. By building on these strong operational foundations, companies can focus on optimizing their sales, marketing, and customer engagement efforts to drive revenue growth and profitability.

A key component of Commercial Excellence is enhancing customer engagement. Companies are leveraging digital tools and data analytics to better understand and meet customer needs. Siemens, for example, has developed customer-centric platforms that provide real-time insights and personalized solutions. This approach helps Siemens build stronger relationships with customers, resulting in higher satisfaction and loyalty.

Honeywell's Forge platform offers another example of this shift. By providing real-time data and insights, Forge helps customers optimize their operations, thereby adding significant value and driving repeat business. This customer-focused approach is critical for achieving Commercial Excellence and sustaining competitive advantage.

Optimizing sales and marketing efforts is critical for maximizing revenue. Companies are investing in customer relationship management (CRM) systems and advanced analytics to enhance their sales processes. Dow Chemical, for instance, uses sophisticated data analytics to identify high-value customers and develop targeted marketing strategies. This allows Dow to allocate resources more effectively and achieve better market penetration.

ExxonMobil's Chemical Customer Portal exemplifies how personalized marketing can drive commercial success. By providing detailed product information, performance metrics, and technical support, ExxonMobil builds trust and fosters customer loyalty. This level of personalization helps to drive sales growth and enhance profitability.

Innovation remains a driving force in the pursuit of Commercial Excellence. Companies are continuously developing new products and solutions that meet emerging market needs. General Electric, for example, has restructured its product portfolio to focus on high-growth areas such as renewable energy and digital solutions. This strategic alignment with market trends allows GE to capitalize on new growth opportunities and improve profit margins.

Similarly, ExxonMobil has expanded its portfolio to include more sustainable products. By responding to the increasing demand for green energy solutions, ExxonMobil enhances its market position and profitability.

Pursuing Commercial Excellence is a logical progression for manufacturing companies that have achieved Operational Excellence. By leveraging their strong operational foundations, these firms can optimize their sales, marketing, and customer engagement efforts to drive revenue growth and profitability. The examples of GE, Toyota, Siemens, Honeywell, Dow Chemical, and ExxonMobil illustrate the successful implementation of this strategic shift. This transition to Commercial Excellence enables manufacturing companies to build on their operational successes and achieve higher levels of business performance. By focusing on customer engagement, optimizing sales and marketing, and fostering innovation, these firms are well-positioned for sustained growth and leadership in their respective industries.

Enhancement of Customer Satisfaction

As manufacturing companies pivot from a focus on Operational Excellence to Commercial Excellence, enhancing customer satisfaction has become a central objective. This shift is a natural progression that builds on the efficiencies and improvements gained through Operational Excellence, enabling companies to better meet customer needs and expectations. By leveraging advanced technologies, refining customer engagement practices, and personalizing interactions, firms are striving to significantly improve customer satisfaction and loyalty.

The foundation of Operational Excellence has provided manufacturing companies with the tools and processes necessary to achieve high levels of efficiency and productivity. Companies like General Electric (GE) and Toyota have demonstrated how investments in advanced technologies and process optimization can lead to substantial gains. GE's Predix platform, for instance, enables real-time monitoring and predictive maintenance, reducing downtime and enhancing operational efficiency. Toyota's implementation of the Toyota Production System (TPS) has minimized waste and streamlined processes, setting a standard for operational efficiency.

These operational improvements have laid the groundwork for a seamless transition to Commercial Excellence. With strong operational foundations in place, companies can now redirect their focus towards enhancing customer satisfaction, ensuring that their commercial practices align with the high standards set by their operational capabilities.

Advanced technologies are key to improving customer satisfaction. Companies are utilizing data analytics, Artificial Intelligence (AI), and customer relationship management (CRM) systems to gain deeper insights into customer preferences and behaviors. For example, Siemens has developed customer-centric platforms that offer real-time insights and personalized solutions. This approach allows Siemens to tailor its offerings to meet specific customer needs, resulting in higher satisfaction and loyalty.

Honeywell's Forge platform exemplifies the use of digital solutions to enhance customer engagement. By providing customers with real-time data and insights, Forge helps them optimize their operations, adding significant value and driving repeat business. Such initiatives ensure that customer interactions are meaningful and impactful, fostering long-term relationships and satisfaction.

Personalizing customer engagement is essential for enhancing satisfaction. Companies are investing in CRM systems and advanced analytics to offer tailored interactions that address individual customer needs. ExxonMobil, for instance, uses its Chemical Customer Portal to provide personalized product recommendations, performance metrics, and technical support. This level of customization helps build trust and loyalty, which are critical for long-term customer satisfaction.

Additionally, Dow Chemical employs sophisticated data analytics to segment its customer base and develop targeted marketing strategies. By focusing on high-value customer segments, Dow can provide more relevant and effective solutions, enhancing the overall customer experience.

Continuous improvement and innovation remain vital for sustaining high levels of customer satisfaction. Companies are engaging with customers throughout the product development process to ensure that their offerings align with market needs. For instance, BASF collaborates closely with customers to co-develop new products and solutions, ensuring that they meet specific requirements and preferences.

General Electric has restructured its product portfolio to focus on high-growth areas such as renewable energy and digital solutions. By aligning its product mix with emerging market trends, the company can better meet customer demands and improve satisfaction.

The pursuit of Commercial Excellence, with a focus on enhancing customer satisfaction, is a logical progression for manufacturing companies that have achieved Operational Excellence. By leveraging advanced technologies, personalizing customer engagement, and fostering continuous improvement, these firms are well-positioned to meet customer needs more effectively and build stronger relationships. The examples of GE, Toyota, Siemens, Honeywell, ExxonMobil, and Dow Chemical illustrate how this strategic shift can lead to significant improvements in customer satisfaction and overall business success. This emphasis on customer satisfaction in the context of Commercial Excellence ensures that manufacturing companies can maintain their competitive edge and achieve long-term growth and profitability.

Increasing Customer Loyalty

The transition from Operational Excellence to Commercial Excellence among manufacturing companies is not just about improving financial metrics but also about deepening customer loyalty. This shift is a natural progression, building on the efficiencies and improvements realized through Operational Excellence. By focusing on customer engagement, personalized interactions, and innovative solutions, companies aim to cultivate long-term customer relationships, thereby enhancing loyalty.

The foundation of Operational Excellence has equipped manufacturing companies with streamlined processes and enhanced productivity. Companies like General Electric (GE) and Toyota have set industry benchmarks through significant investments in advanced technologies and process optimization. GE's implementation of the Predix platform, enabling real-time monitoring and predictive maintenance, has led to substantial gains in efficiency. Similarly, Toyota's Toyota Production System (TPS) has minimized waste and enhanced productivity.

These operational achievements provide a solid base for companies to transition smoothly to Commercial Excellence. With robust operational processes in place, companies can now concentrate on deepening customer relationships and fostering loyalty, ensuring that their commercial practices complement their operational capabilities.

A critical element of Commercial Excellence is enhancing customer engagement. Companies are increasingly utilizing digital tools and data analytics to gain deeper insights into customer preferences and behaviors. Siemens, for example, has developed customer-centric platforms that offer real-time insights and personalized solutions. This approach enables Siemens to tailor its offerings to meet specific customer needs, resulting in higher satisfaction and loyalty.

Honeywell's Forge platform exemplifies how digital solutions can strengthen customer engagement. By providing customers with real-time data and insights, Forge helps them optimize their operations, adding significant value and driving repeat business. These initiatives ensure that customer interactions are meaningful and impactful, fostering long-term relationships and loyalty.

Personalized interactions are essential for enhancing customer loyalty. Companies are investing in customer relationship management (CRM) systems and advanced analytics to offer tailored engagements that address individual customer needs. ExxonMobil, for instance, uses its Chemical Customer Portal to provide personalized product recommendations, performance metrics, and technical support. This level of customization helps build trust and loyalty, which are critical for long-term customer retention.

Additionally, Dow Chemical employs sophisticated data analytics to segment its customer base and develop targeted marketing strategies. By focusing on high-value customer segments, Dow can provide more relevant and effective solutions, enhancing the overall customer experience and fostering loyalty.

Continuous innovation and tailored solutions are vital for sustaining customer loyalty. Companies are engaging with customers throughout the product development process to ensure their offerings align with market needs. For instance, BASF collaborates closely with customers to co-develop new products and solutions, ensuring they meet specific requirements and preferences.

General Electric has restructured its product portfolio to focus on high-growth areas such as renewable energy and digital solutions. By aligning its product mix with emerging market trends, GE can better meet customer demands, improve satisfaction, and enhance loyalty.

The shift towards Commercial Excellence, with a focus on increasing customer loyalty, is a logical progression for manufacturing companies that have achieved Operational Excellence. By leveraging operational success, enhancing customer engagement, personalizing interactions, and driving innovation, these companies are well-positioned to cultivate long-term customer relationships. The examples of GE, Toyota, Siemens, Honeywell, ExxonMobil, and Dow Chemical illustrate how this strategic shift can lead to significant improvements in customer loyalty and overall business success. This emphasis on customer loyalty within the framework of Commercial Excellence ensures that manufacturing companies can maintain their competitive edge and achieve sustained growth and profitability.

Unlocking New Value

Manufacturing companies are shifting their focus from Operational Excellence to Commercial Excellence, with a clear objective of unlocking new value by enhancing customer satisfaction and loyalty. This strategic transition builds on the robust foundations laid through decades of operational improvements, enabling companies to drive growth and profitability by better meeting customer needs and fostering long-term relationships. By prioritizing customer engagement, personalization, and innovation, these firms aim to discover new opportunities and maximize their value proposition.

Operational excellence has provided manufacturing companies with significant gains in efficiency, productivity, and cost savings. Companies like General Electric (GE) and Toyota have exemplified how investments in advanced technologies and process optimization can transform operations. GE's Predix platform, which facilitates real-time monitoring and predictive maintenance, has reduced downtime and enhanced operational efficiency. Toyota's Toyota Production System (TPS) has minimized waste and streamlined processes, setting a benchmark for productivity in the automotive industry.

With these operational efficiencies firmly in place, companies are now well-positioned to shift their focus towards Commercial Excellence. This new emphasis allows them to leverage their operational strengths to better understand and meet customer needs, driving higher satisfaction and loyalty.

Customer satisfaction is at the heart of Commercial Excellence. Companies are utilizing digital tools and data analytics to gain deeper insights into customer preferences and behaviors. Siemens, for example, has developed customer-centric platforms that offer real-time insights and personalized solutions. This approach not only improves customer satisfaction but also builds stronger relationships, which are necessary for long-term success.

Honeywell's Forge platform provides another example of enhancing customer engagement through digital solutions. By offering real-time data and insights, Forge helps customers optimize their operations, adding significant value and encouraging repeat business. These initiatives ensure that customer interactions are meaningful and impactful, fostering long-term loyalty and satisfaction.

Personalized customer interactions are essential for unlocking new value. Companies are investing in customer relationship management (CRM) systems and advanced analytics to tailor their engagements. ExxonMobil, for instance, uses its Chemical Customer Portal to provide personalized product recommendations, performance metrics, and technical support. This level of customization helps build trust and loyalty, which are critical for sustained business success.

Dow Chemical employs sophisticated data analytics to segment its customer base and develop targeted marketing strategies. By focusing on high-value customer segments, Dow can provide more relevant and effective solutions, enhancing the overall customer experience and driving loyalty.

Continuous innovation is key to sustaining customer satisfaction and unlocking new value. Companies are engaging with customers throughout the product development process to ensure their offerings align with market needs. BASF, for instance, collaborates closely with customers to co-develop new products and solutions, ensuring they meet specific requirements and preferences.

General Electric has restructured its product portfolio to focus on high-growth areas such as renewable energy and digital solutions. By aligning its product mix with emerging market trends, GE can better meet customer demands, improve satisfaction, and unlock new value.

The shift from Operational Excellence to Commercial Excellence is a natural progression for manufacturing companies aiming to unlock new value. By building on their operational successes, enhancing customer satisfaction, personalizing interactions, and driving innovation, these firms can maximize their value proposition and achieve sustained growth. The examples of GE, Toyota, Siemens, Honeywell, ExxonMobil, and Dow Chemical illustrate how this strategic shift can lead to significant business improvements and long-term success. Focusing on customer satisfaction and loyalty within the framework of Commercial Excellence ensures that manufacturing companies can maintain their competitive edge, foster lasting relationships, and secure long-term profitability.

Balanced Analytical Improvements

As manufacturing companies transition from a focus on Operational Excellence to Commercial Excellence, there is a renewed emphasis on leveraging balanced analytical improvements to drive growth and profitability. This approach involves using advanced data analytics to refine customer engagement, optimize sales processes, and enhance product offerings. By integrating analytical tools and techniques into their commercial strategies, companies aim to achieve a more comprehensive understanding of market demands and improve overall performance.

Advanced analytics play a pivotal role in driving Commercial Excellence. Manufacturing companies are increasingly utilizing data analytics to gain insights into customer behavior, market trends, and product performance. For example, BASF employs sophisticated data analytics to assess the profitability of its products. By analyzing sales data and market conditions, BASF can prioritize high-margin products, ensuring that resources are allocated effectively to maximize revenue.

Similarly, Dow Chemical uses predictive analytics to monitor and adjust its product mix in real-time. By leveraging data-driven insights, Dow can anticipate shifts in market demand and adjust its portfolio accordingly. This proactive approach enables the company to stay ahead of market trends and maintain a competitive edge.

Improving customer engagement is a critical component of Commercial Excellence. Companies are investing in customer relationship management (CRM) systems and advanced analytics to personalize interactions and enhance the customer experience. Siemens, for instance, has developed customer-centric platforms that offer real-time insights and tailored solutions. This approach allows Siemens to understand customer needs better and deliver more relevant offerings, fostering long-term loyalty and satisfaction.

Honeywell's Forge platform exemplifies how digital solutions can strengthen customer engagement. By providing real-time data and insights, Forge helps customers optimize their operations, adding significant value and encouraging repeat business. These initiatives ensure that customer interactions are meaningful and impactful, driving long-term relationships and satisfaction.

Optimizing sales processes through data analytics is another critical aspect of achieving Commercial Excellence. Companies are using CRM systems and advanced analytics to streamline sales workflows and improve efficiency. For example, General Electric (GE) employs its Predix platform to gather comprehensive data on customer interactions and equipment performance. This information enables GE to offer personalized solutions and anticipate customer needs more accurately, resulting in higher conversion rates and sales effectiveness.

ExxonMobil has implemented comprehensive training programs to develop the skills of its salesforce. By focusing on both technical knowledge and customer engagement techniques, ExxonMobil ensures that its sales teams are well-equipped to navigate complex sales cycles and close deals effectively. This investment in human capital is essential for achieving sustained sales performance and commercial success.

Continuous innovation and tailored solutions are vital for sustaining customer satisfaction and unlocking new value. Companies are engaging with customers throughout the product development process to ensure that their offerings align with market needs. For instance, BASF collaborates closely with customers to co-develop new products and solutions, ensuring that they meet specific requirements and preferences.

General Electric has restructured its product portfolio to focus on high-growth areas such as renewable energy and digital solutions. By aligning its product mix with emerging market trends, GE can better meet customer demands, improve satisfaction, and unlock new value.

Balanced analytical improvements are essential for driving Commercial Excellence in manufacturing companies. By leveraging advanced analytics, enhancing customer engagement, optimizing sales processes, and driving product innovation, these firms can achieve a comprehensive understanding of market demands and improve overall performance. The examples of BASF, Dow Chemical, Siemens, Honeywell, GE, and ExxonMobil illustrate how this strategic approach can lead to significant business improvements and long-term success.

Incorporation of Behavioral Improvements

Companies are increasingly recognizing that alongside analytics, behavioral improvements are essential to driving success. This focus on behavioral changes complements data-driven strategies, ensuring that companies not only understand customer needs through analytics but also foster a culture and practices that enhance customer satisfaction and loyalty. By integrating behavioral improvements, companies can achieve a more holistic approach to Commercial Excellence, aligning internal practices with external expectations.

One of the key aspects of behavioral improvements is enhancing employee engagement. Companies are investing in training programs and initiatives that encourage employees to adopt a customer-centric mindset. For instance, Siemens has implemented comprehensive training programs aimed at fostering a culture of continuous improvement and customer focus. These programs equip employees with the skills and mindset necessary to deliver exceptional customer experiences, thereby increasing satisfaction and loyalty.

Honeywell's approach to employee engagement involves regular feedback sessions and workshops designed to align employee behaviors with company goals. By creating an environment where employees feel valued and motivated, Honeywell ensures that its workforce is committed to

61

achieving Commercial Excellence. This focus on employee engagement is necessary for maintaining high levels of customer service and satisfaction.

Creating a customer-centric culture is vital for behavioral improvements. Companies are striving to embed customer focus into their corporate ethos, ensuring that every decision and action is guided by the goal of enhancing customer satisfaction. General Electric (GE) has made significant strides in this area by encouraging cross-functional collaboration and open communication. By breaking down silos and fostering teamwork, GE ensures that all departments are aligned with the company's commercial goals and customer expectations.

ExxonMobil's Chemical Customer Portal exemplifies how fostering a customer-centric culture can lead to improved customer engagement. By providing personalized recommendations, performance metrics, and technical support, ExxonMobil demonstrates its commitment to understanding and meeting customer needs. This approach not only enhances customer satisfaction but also builds long-term loyalty.

Behavioral improvements extend to sales and service interactions, where the focus is on enhancing the quality of customer engagements. Companies are training their sales and service teams to adopt consultative approaches, emphasizing the importance of understanding customer needs and providing tailored solutions. Dow Chemical, for instance, has implemented training programs that teach sales teams to adopt a consultative selling approach. This method prioritizes listening to customers, understanding their challenges, and offering solutions that meet their specific needs.

Similarly, BASF emphasizes the importance of personalized customer interactions. By encouraging its sales teams to build strong relationships with customers, BASF ensures that its engagements are meaningful and impactful. This focus on relationship-building not only drives sales but also fosters customer loyalty.

The incorporation of behavioral improvements is a key focus for manufacturing companies aiming to achieve Commercial Excellence. By enhancing employee engagement, fostering a customer-centric culture, and improving sales and service interactions, companies can complement their data-driven strategies with practices that drive customer satisfaction and loyalty. The examples of Siemens, Honeywell, GE, ExxonMobil, Dow Chemical, and BASF illustrate the successful integration of behavioral improvements in their commercial strategies. Focusing on behavioral improvements enables manufacturing companies to build stronger customer relationships, optimize their operations, and achieve sustained growth and profitability.

The Integrated Improvement Approach

The most successful manufacturing companies often adopt an integrated improvement approach that balances both analytical and behavioral enhancements to achieve Commercial Excellence. This comprehensive strategy not only leverages advanced data analytics to understand market trends and customer behavior but also focuses on cultivating a customer-centric culture within the organization. By harmonizing these two dimensions, companies can drive sustainable growth and profitability.

Data Analytics is pivotal in informing and optimizing commercial strategies. Companies like BASF and Dow Chemical are at the forefront of using sophisticated analytics to assess product profitability and market conditions. For instance, BASF employs data-driven insights to prioritize high-margin products and adjust its production and marketing efforts accordingly. This approach ensures that resources are allocated efficiently, maximizing revenue and profitability.

Similarly, Dow Chemical utilizes predictive analytics to anticipate market shifts and adapt its product mix in real-time. By analyzing purchasing patterns and market trends, Dow can stay ahead of competitors and meet evolving customer demands. This data-centric approach not only enhances decision-making but also supports proactive commercial strategies.

Customer engagement is a critical aspect of Commercial Excellence, and data analytics play a critical role in this area as well. Siemens, for example, has developed customer-centric platforms that provide real-time insights and personalized solutions. This level of customization enhances customer satisfaction and loyalty by ensuring that products and services are tailored to meet specific needs.

Honeywell's Forge platform exemplifies how real-time data and analytics can strengthen customer relationships. By offering customers actionable insights into their operations, Honeywell adds significant value and encourages repeat business. These initiatives highlight the importance of integrating analytical capabilities into customer engagement practices to foster long-term loyalty.

Behavioral improvements are equally important in achieving Commercial Excellence. Companies are investing in training and development programs to instill a customer-centric mindset among employees. Siemens has implemented comprehensive training initiatives that promote continuous improvement and customer focus. By equipping employees with the necessary skills and mindset, Siemens ensures that every interaction with customers enhances their experience and satisfaction.

ExxonMobil's approach to fostering a customer-centric culture involves providing personalized support through its Chemical Customer Portal. This platform offers tailored product recommendations, performance metrics, and technical assistance, demonstrating ExxonMobil's commitment to meeting individual customer needs. Such personalized interactions build trust and loyalty, which are essential for sustained business success.

Optimizing sales and service interactions is another critical component of a balanced improvement approach. Dow Chemical has adopted a consultative selling approach, training its sales teams to listen to customers, understand their challenges, and provide tailored solutions. This method enhances the quality of customer engagements and drives sales effectiveness.

Similarly, BASF emphasizes the importance of relationship-building in its sales strategies. By encouraging sales teams to develop strong connections with customers, BASF ensures that engagements are meaningful and impactful. This focus on personalized interactions not only drives sales but also fosters long-term customer loyalty.

The integrated improvement approach, which balances analytical and behavioral enhancements, is essential for achieving Commercial Excellence in manufacturing companies. By leveraging advanced analytics, enhancing customer engagement, fostering a customer-centric culture, and optimizing sales interactions, companies can drive sustainable growth and profitability. The examples of BASF, Dow Chemical, Siemens, Honeywell, and ExxonMobil illustrate the successful implementation of this comprehensive strategy. This balanced approach enables manufacturing companies to build stronger customer relationships, optimize their operations, and achieve sustained commercial success.

Comprehensive Commercial Excellence

Companies' shift towards comprehensive Commercial Excellence is a pivotal move for driving overall business success. This approach emphasizes the enhancement of customer relations and the creation of value, ensuring that companies not only meet but exceed market expectations. By integrating advanced analytics, fostering a customer-centric culture, and innovating continuously, manufacturing firms aim to build stronger customer relationships and deliver superior value.

The foundation of Commercial Excellence lies in the strategic use of data analytics. Companies like BASF and Dow Chemical are harnessing the power of analytics to refine their product offerings and tailor their services. BASF, for instance, employs data-driven insights to prioritize high-margin products and adjust its production schedules accordingly. By analyzing sales data and market trends, BASF can allocate resources effectively, maximizing revenue and profitability.

Similarly, Dow Chemical uses predictive analytics to monitor and adapt its product mix in real-time. This proactive approach allows Dow to anticipate market shifts and adjust its portfolio to meet evolving customer demands. Leveraging data analytics not only enhances decision-making but also ensures that companies remain agile and responsive to market changes.

At the heart of Commercial Excellence is the goal of improving customer engagement. Siemens, for example, has developed customer-centric platforms that offer real-time insights and personalized solutions. By understanding customer needs and preferences, Siemens can deliver tailored offerings that enhance satisfaction and loyalty. This customer-focused approach is necessary for building long-term relationships and ensuring sustained business success.

Honeywell's Forge platform exemplifies how digital solutions can strengthen customer interactions. Providing customers with real-time data and actionable insights, Forge helps optimize operations and adds significant value. These initiatives ensure that customer engagements are meaningful and impactful, fostering trust and loyalty.

Creating a customer-centric culture is essential for achieving comprehensive Commercial Excellence. General Electric (GE) has made significant strides in this area by encouraging cross-functional collaboration and open communication. By breaking down organizational silos, GE ensures that all departments are aligned with the company's commercial goals and customer expectations. This cultural shift promotes a unified approach to customer satisfaction and value creation.

ExxonMobil's Chemical Customer Portal further illustrates the importance of customer-centric cultures. Through offering personalized product recommendations, performance metrics, and technical support, the portal demonstrates ExxonMobil's commitment to meeting individual customer needs. Such personalized interactions build trust and foster long-term loyalty.

Continuous innovation is vital for sustaining customer satisfaction and unlocking new value. BASF collaborates closely with customers to co-develop products and solutions, ensuring that offerings meet specific requirements and preferences. This customer-driven approach to innovation not only addresses current market needs but also anticipates future trends.

General Electric's focus on renewable energy and digital solutions exemplifies how aligning product portfolios with market demands can drive value creation. By investing in high-growth areas, GE meets customer expectations and enhances its competitive position.

The comprehensive pursuit of Commercial Excellence is a strategic imperative for manufacturing companies aiming to drive business success. By leveraging advanced analytics, enhancing customer engagement, fostering a customer-centric culture, and driving innovation, firms can build stronger customer relationships and deliver superior value. The examples of BASF, Dow Chemical, Siemens, Honeywell, GE, and ExxonMobil illustrate the successful implementation of these initiatives. Focusing on comprehensive Commercial Excellence enables manufacturing companies to remain competitive and adaptable in an evolving market.

A Change of Mindset

Improving commercial efforts is new and challenging for many executives in technical industries, requiring a change in mindset from technical to commercial and customer-focused strategies.

For many executives in technical industries, improving commercial efforts represents a novel and necessary initiative. Transitioning from a focus on Operational Excellence to Commercial Excellence requires a significant shift in mindset and approach. Leaders must embrace new strategies to enhance customer engagement, refine sales processes, and drive value creation. This change is essential for companies aiming to sustain growth and remain competitive in an increasingly complex market.

One of the fundamental changes required is the adoption of customer-centric approaches. Traditionally, manufacturing companies have prioritized operational efficiency and product quality. However, achieving Commercial Excellence necessitates a deeper understanding of customer needs and preferences. Siemens, for example, has developed customer-centric platforms that provide real-time insights and personalized solutions. By focusing on customer satisfaction, Siemens enhances loyalty and drives long-term success.

Similarly, Honeywell has invested in its Forge platform to offer customers real-time data and actionable insights. This approach not only optimizes customer operations but also builds stronger relationships. Executives must recognize the importance of such customer-focused initiatives and ensure that their organizations prioritize customer engagement.

Improving commercial efforts also involves refining sales processes. Executives must move beyond traditional sales techniques and adopt more sophisticated, data-driven approaches. Dow Chemical, for instance, employs advanced analytics to identify high-value customers and develop targeted sales strategies. By leveraging data insights, Dow can optimize its sales efforts and improve conversion rates.

General Electric (GE) has taken a similar approach by using its Predix platform to gather comprehensive data on customer interactions and equipment performance. This information enables GE to offer personalized solutions and anticipate customer needs more accurately. Executives must champion the integration of advanced analytics into sales processes to enhance effectiveness and drive revenue growth.

Innovation is critical for achieving Commercial Excellence. Executives must foster a culture that encourages creativity and collaboration across all levels of the organization. BASF, for example, collaborates closely with customers to co-develop new products and solutions. This customer-driven approach to innovation ensures that offerings align with market needs and anticipate future trends.

ExxonMobil has restructured its product portfolio to focus on high-growth areas such as renewable energy and digital solutions. By aligning its product mix with emerging market demands, ExxonMobil can better meet customer expectations and enhance its competitive position. Leaders must support continuous innovation to sustain growth and create value.

To successfully navigate this transition, executives must invest in their development and that of their teams. Comprehensive training programs are essential to equip leaders with the skills and knowledge needed to drive Commercial Excellence. Siemens, for instance, has implemented training initiatives that promote continuous improvement and customer focus. By fostering a learning culture, executives can ensure that their teams are well-prepared to meet new challenges.

ExxonMobil's approach to leadership development emphasizes the importance of both technical knowledge and customer engagement techniques. By providing tailored training, ExxonMobil ensures that its leaders can effectively navigate complex sales cycles and build lasting customer relationships.

The shift towards Commercial Excellence represents a new frontier for executives in technical industries. By embracing customer-centric approaches, refining sales processes, fostering innovation, and investing in leadership development, manufacturing companies can drive significant business improvements and achieve long-term success. The examples of Siemens, Honeywell, Dow Chemical, GE, BASF, and ExxonMobil illustrate how these changes can lead to enhanced customer satisfaction, stronger relationships, and increased profitability. Adopting a new mindset focused on Commercial Excellence is essential for executives seeking to unlock new value and maintain competitiveness.

Common Challenges Faced by Executives

The transition from operational to Commercial Excellence presents considerable challenges for leaders and executives within manufacturing companies. This shift requires a significant change in mindset, focusing on customer engagement, innovative practices, and advanced analytics. As executives embark on this journey, they must overcome various obstacles to ensure their companies achieve sustained growth and profitability.

One of the primary challenges is embracing a customer-centric approach. Traditionally, manufacturing companies have prioritized operational efficiency and product quality. However, achieving Commercial Excellence necessitates a deeper understanding of customer needs and preferences. Executives must shift their focus to customer satisfaction and loyalty, fostering a culture that prioritizes these values.

For example, Siemens has developed customer-centric platforms that offer real-time insights and personalized solutions. By focusing on customer engagement, Siemens enhances satisfaction and builds stronger relationships. Executives must recognize the importance of such initiatives and ensure their organizations prioritize customer needs.

Another significant challenge is adapting to the use of advanced analytics. Data-driven decision-making is essential for optimizing commercial strategies, yet many executives lack the necessary expertise. Companies like BASF and Dow Chemical use sophisticated analytics to refine product offerings and tailor services to market demands. BASF employs data-driven insights to prioritize high-margin products and adjust production schedules, maximizing revenue and profitability.

Similarly, Dow Chemical uses predictive analytics to anticipate market shifts and adapt its product mix in real-time. Executives must champion the integration of advanced analytics into their decision-making processes, ensuring their teams have the skills and tools needed to leverage these insights effectively.

Fostering a culture of innovation is critical for sustaining Commercial Excellence. Executives must encourage creativity and collaboration across all levels of the organization. General Electric (GE) has made significant strides by encouraging cross-functional collaboration and open communication. By breaking down silos, GE ensures all departments are aligned with the company's commercial goals and customer expectations.

ExxonMobil's focus on renewable energy and digital solutions demonstrates the importance of aligning product portfolios with market demands. Leaders must support continuous innovation to meet evolving customer needs and maintain a competitive edge.

Leadership development is vital for navigating the transition to Commercial Excellence. Executives must invest in their development and that of their teams. Comprehensive training programs are essential to equip leaders with the skills and knowledge needed to drive commercial success. Siemens, for instance, has implemented training initiatives that promote continuous improvement and customer focus. By fostering a learning culture, executives can ensure their teams are prepared to meet new challenges.

ExxonMobil emphasizes the importance of both technical knowledge and customer engagement techniques in its leadership development programs. Tailored training ensures leaders can effectively navigate complex sales cycles and build lasting customer relationships.

The shift towards Commercial Excellence presents considerable challenges for executives in manufacturing companies. By embracing customer-centric approaches, adapting to advanced analytics, fostering innovation, and investing in leadership development, these leaders can navigate the transition successfully. The examples of Siemens, BASF, Dow Chemical, GE, and ExxonMobil illustrate how overcoming these challenges can lead to enhanced customer satisfaction, stronger relationships, and increased profitability.

Developing a Commercial Mindset

As manufacturing companies prioritize Commercial Excellence, the need for a mindset shift among leaders and executives becomes paramount. Traditionally, these industries have emphasized technical prowess and operational efficiency. However, achieving Commercial Excellence necessitates a broader focus that includes customer engagement, market adaptation, and value creation. Executives must transition from a purely technical mindset to a commercial one to navigate this transformation successfully.

71

A critical aspect of this mindset shift is the emphasis on customer engagement. Leaders must prioritize understanding and meeting customer needs to build stronger relationships and drive satisfaction. For instance, Honeywell has successfully implemented its Forge platform, which provides real-time data and actionable insights to customers. This approach not only adds value but also fosters long-term loyalty.

Similarly, Siemens has developed customer-centric platforms that offer personalized solutions based on real-time insights. By focusing on customer engagement, Siemens enhances satisfaction and loyalty, key components of Commercial Excellence. Executives must champion such initiatives, ensuring their organizations are aligned with customer-centric values.

Transitioning to a commercial mindset also involves adapting to market changes and leveraging data analytics. Executives must move beyond traditional metrics and incorporate advanced analytics to understand market trends and customer behavior. Dow Chemical, for example, uses predictive analytics to monitor market shifts and adjust its product mix accordingly. This proactive approach allows Dow to stay ahead of competitors and meet evolving customer demands.

General Electric (GE) employs its Predix platform to gather comprehensive data on customer interactions and equipment performance. By analyzing this data, GE can offer personalized solutions and anticipate customer needs more accurately. Leaders must embrace these analytical tools to enhance decision-making and drive commercial success.

Innovation is another critical element in the transition from a technical to a commercial mindset. Executives must foster a culture that encourages creativity and collaboration. BASF, for instance, collaborates closely with customers to co-develop new products and solutions. This customer-driven approach ensures that offerings align with market needs and anticipate future trends.

ExxonMobil's focus on renewable energy and digital solutions illustrates the importance of aligning product portfolios with emerging market demands. By supporting continuous innovation, executives can ensure their companies remain competitive and responsive to customer needs.

To facilitate this mindset shift, investing in leadership development is essential. Comprehensive training programs equip leaders with the necessary skills and knowledge to drive Commercial Excellence. Siemens has implemented initiatives that promote continuous improvement and customer focus. By fostering a learning culture, Siemens ensures that its leaders are prepared to meet new challenges.

ExxonMobil emphasizes the importance of both technical knowledge and customer engagement techniques in its leadership development programs. Tailored training ensures that leaders can effectively navigate complex sales cycles and build lasting customer relationships.

The shift towards Commercial Excellence requires a significant mindset change among executives in manufacturing companies. By embracing customer engagement, adapting to market changes, fostering innovation, and investing in leadership development, leaders can navigate this transformation successfully.

The Importance of a Renewed Commercial Focus

Embracing commercial strategies is essential for achieving sustained growth and competitiveness. By focusing on customer engagement, leveraging advanced analytics, fostering innovation, and refining sales processes, executives can drive their companies toward commercial success.

One of the primary facets of adopting commercial strategies is placing a strong emphasis on customer engagement. Manufacturing companies must move beyond their traditional focus on product quality and operational efficiency to understand and meet the evolving needs of their customers. For instance, Honeywell's Forge platform exemplifies how customer-centric solutions can enhance value. By providing real-time data and insights, Honeywell helps customers optimize their operations, thereby fostering stronger relationships and long-term loyalty.

Similarly, Siemens has developed customer-centric platforms that deliver personalized solutions based on real-time insights. This approach ensures that Siemens stays closely aligned with customer needs, enhancing satisfaction and driving loyalty. Executives must prioritize such customer engagement initiatives to ensure their organizations remain competitive and relevant.

The integration of advanced analytics into commercial strategies is another critical component for success. Companies like BASF and Dow Chemical have demonstrated how data-driven insights can optimize product offerings and enhance decision-making. BASF, for example, uses sophisticated analytics to prioritize high-margin products, ensuring efficient resource allocation and maximized profitability.

Dow Chemical employs predictive analytics to monitor market trends and adjust its product mix in real-time. This proactive approach allows Dow to stay ahead of market shifts and meet customer demands effectively. Leaders must champion the use of advanced analytics to refine commercial strategies and drive business growth.

Innovation is a key driver of Commercial Excellence. Executives must cultivate a culture that encourages creativity and continuous improvement. BASF's collaborative approach to product development, which involves close customer engagement, ensures that its offerings align with market needs and anticipate future trends.

ExxonMobil's focus on renewable energy and digital solutions highlights the importance of aligning product portfolios with emerging market demands. By fostering innovation, executives can ensure their companies remain responsive to changing customer needs and maintain a competitive edge.

Optimizing sales processes is essential for commercial success. Companies must move beyond traditional sales techniques to adopt more sophisticated, data-driven approaches. General Electric (GE) uses its Predix platform to gather comprehensive data on customer interactions and equipment performance, enabling personalized solutions and accurate anticipation of customer needs.

Additionally, ExxonMobil has implemented comprehensive training programs to enhance the skills of its salesforce. By focusing on both technical knowledge and customer engagement techniques, ExxonMobil ensures that its sales teams are well-equipped to navigate complex sales cycles and close deals effectively. Executives must invest in refining sales processes to enhance efficiency and drive revenue growth.

Adopting commercial strategies is necessary for manufacturing companies aiming to achieve sustained growth and competitiveness. By embracing customer engagement, leveraging advanced analytics, fostering innovation, and refining sales processes, leaders can drive their companies toward Commercial Excellence.

Prioritizing Customer Focus

A successful pivot towards Commercial Excellence requires that leaders and executives within manufacturing companies adopt a new mindset that prioritizes understanding and meeting customer needs. This customer-centric approach is essential for driving growth, fostering loyalty, and maintaining a competitive edge in the market. By leveraging data analytics, enhancing customer engagement, and fostering innovation, companies can achieve Commercial Excellence and long-term success.

One of the fundamental changes needed is a deeper understanding of customer needs. Manufacturing companies have traditionally focused on product quality and operational efficiency. However, to achieve Commercial Excellence, executives must place the customer at the center of their strategies. This involves gathering and analyzing customer feedback to tailor products and services accordingly. For instance, Siemens has developed customer-centric platforms that provide real-time insights and personalized solutions. By focusing on the specific needs of their customers, Siemens enhances satisfaction and loyalty, which are necessary for long-term success.

Similarly, Honeywell's Forge platform exemplifies the shift towards customer-centricity. By offering real-time data and actionable insights, Forge helps customers optimize their operations. This not only adds significant value but also builds stronger relationships, encouraging repeat business. Executives must champion such initiatives to ensure their organizations remain aligned with customer expectations.

Data analytics plays a critical role in becoming more customer focused. Companies like BASF and Dow Chemical have demonstrated how data-driven insights can optimize product offerings and enhance decision-making. BASF employs sophisticated analytics to prioritize high-margin products and adjust production schedules, ensuring efficient resource allocation and maximized profitability. By understanding customer preferences and market trends, BASF can better meet customer demands and drive commercial success.

Dow Chemical uses predictive analytics to monitor market shifts and adapt its product mix in real-time. This proactive approach allows Dow to anticipate customer needs and stay ahead of competitors. Executives must integrate advanced analytics into their strategies to enhance customer focus and achieve business growth.

Improving customer engagement is essential for fostering loyalty and driving Commercial Excellence. Personalized interactions and tailored solutions help build stronger relationships with customers. ExxonMobil's Chemical Customer Portal provides personalized product recommendations, performance metrics, and technical support. This level of customization builds trust and ensures that customers feel valued, which is critical for long-term loyalty.

General Electric (GE) uses its Predix platform to gather comprehensive data on customer interactions and equipment performance. By analyzing this data, GE can offer personalized solutions and anticipate customer needs more accurately. Executives must prioritize personalized customer engagement to enhance satisfaction and loyalty.

Innovation is key to sustaining customer focus. Companies must continuously develop new products and solutions that meet evolving market needs. For example, BASF collaborates closely with customers to co-develop products, ensuring they align with specific requirements and preferences. This customer-driven approach to innovation helps address current market demands and anticipate future trends.

ExxonMobil's focus on renewable energy and digital solutions highlights the importance of aligning product portfolios with emerging market demands. By fostering innovation, executives can ensure their companies remain responsive to changing customer needs and maintain a competitive edge.

The emphasis on customer focus is a critical shift for manufacturing companies aiming to achieve Commercial Excellence. By understanding customer needs, leveraging data analytics, enhancing customer engagement, and fostering innovation, leaders can drive significant business improvements and achieve long-term success.

New Approaches and Skillsets

The transition from operational to Commercial Excellence in manufacturing demands a significant transformation in the approaches and skillsets of executives. As companies aim to enhance customer engagement, refine sales processes, and drive value creation, leaders must adopt new competencies that align with these commercial objectives. This shift is essential for fostering growth and maintaining a competitive edge in the industry.

A critical aspect of this transformation is the development of analytical proficiency. Executives need to leverage advanced data analytics to make informed decisions and optimize commercial strategies. For instance, BASF employs sophisticated data analytics to prioritize high-margin products, ensuring efficient resource allocation and maximized profitability. By understanding market trends and customer preferences, executives can better align their offerings with demand, driving commercial success.

Similarly, Dow Chemical utilizes predictive analytics to monitor market shifts and adjust its product mix in real-time. This proactive approach enables Dow to stay ahead of competitors and meet evolving customer needs. Executives must cultivate a deep understanding of data analytics to enhance their decision-making capabilities and support Commercial Excellence.

Improving customer engagement is fundamental to achieving Commercial Excellence. Leaders must develop skills in building and maintaining strong customer relationships. Siemens, for example, has developed customer-centric platforms that offer real-time insights and personalized solutions. By focusing on customer engagement, Siemens enhances satisfaction and loyalty, which are necessary for long-term success.

Honeywell's Forge platform exemplifies how real-time data and actionable insights can strengthen customer interactions. This approach not only adds significant value but also fosters long-term loyalty. Executives must prioritize customer engagement by developing the skills necessary to understand and meet customer needs effectively.

Innovation is key to sustaining Commercial Excellence. Executives must foster a culture that encourages creativity and continuous improvement. BASF's collaborative approach to product development, which involves close customer engagement, ensures that its offerings align with market needs and anticipate future trends. This customer-driven approach to innovation helps address current market demands and prepare for future opportunities.

ExxonMobil's focus on renewable energy and digital solutions highlights the importance of aligning product portfolios with emerging market demands. By supporting continuous innovation, executives can ensure their companies remain responsive to changing customer needs and maintain a competitive edge.

To successfully navigate this transition, executives must strengthen their leadership capabilities. Comprehensive training programs are essential to equip leaders with the skills and knowledge needed to drive commercial success. Siemens, for instance, has implemented initiatives that promote continuous improvement and customer focus. By fostering a learning culture, Siemens ensures that its leaders are prepared to meet new challenges.

ExxonMobil emphasizes the importance of both technical knowledge and customer engagement techniques in its leadership development programs. Tailored training ensures that leaders can effectively navigate complex sales cycles and build lasting customer relationships.

The transition to Commercial Excellence requires a significant transformation in the skillsets of executives within manufacturing companies. By embracing analytical proficiency, enhancing customer engagement skills, fostering a culture of innovation, and strengthening leadership capabilities, leaders can drive their companies towards sustained growth and success.

Strategic Reorientation

For manufacturing companies to achieve Commercial Excellence, a strategic reorientation of the entire organization is essential. This transformation requires leaders and executives to adopt a customer-centric mindset, integrating commercial practices into the core of their operations. By focusing on customer engagement, leveraging advanced analytics, fostering innovation, and enhancing leadership capabilities, companies can drive sustained growth and maintain a competitive edge.

A critical aspect of this strategic shift is placing the customer at the center of all business activities. Traditional manufacturing companies have prioritized operational efficiency and product quality. However, achieving Commercial Excellence necessitates a deeper understanding of customer needs and preferences. Siemens, for example, has developed customer-centric platforms that offer real-time insights and personalized solutions. By focusing on customer engagement, Siemens enhances satisfaction and loyalty, necessary components for long-term success.

Honeywell's Forge platform exemplifies how real-time data and actionable insights can strengthen customer interactions. By helping customers optimize their operations, Honeywell adds significant value and fosters stronger relationships. Leaders must champion such initiatives, ensuring that their organizations prioritize customer needs.

Data analytics play a pivotal role in supporting commercial and customer-centric practices. Companies like BASF and Dow Chemical have demonstrated how data-driven insights can optimize product offerings and enhance decision-making. BASF, for instance, uses sophisticated analytics to prioritize high-margin products and adjust production schedules accordingly. By understanding market trends and customer preferences, BASF can better align its offerings with demand, driving commercial success.

Similarly, Dow Chemical employs predictive analytics to monitor market shifts and adapt its product mix in real-time. This proactive approach allows Dow to stay ahead of competitors and meet evolving customer demands. Leaders must integrate advanced analytics into their strategies to enhance decision-making and support Commercial Excellence.

Innovation is key to maintaining a customer-centric approach. Executives must cultivate a culture that encourages creativity and continuous improvement. BASF's collaborative approach to product development, which involves close customer engagement, ensures that its offerings align with market needs and anticipate future trends. This customer-driven approach to innovation helps address current market demands and prepare for future opportunities.

ExxonMobil's focus on renewable energy and digital solutions highlights the importance of aligning product portfolios with emerging market demands. By supporting continuous innovation, leaders can ensure their companies remain responsive to changing customer needs and maintain a competitive edge.

To facilitate this strategic reorientation, executives must enhance their leadership capabilities. Comprehensive training programs are essential to equip leaders with the skills and knowledge needed to drive commercial success. Siemens has implemented initiatives that promote continuous improvement and customer focus. By fostering a learning culture, Siemens ensures that its leaders are prepared to meet new challenges.

ExxonMobil emphasizes the importance of both technical knowledge and customer engagement techniques in its leadership development programs. Tailored training ensures that leaders can effectively navigate complex sales cycles and build lasting customer relationships.

The shift towards Commercial Excellence requires a strategic reorientation of the entire organization, with a strong emphasis on customer-centric practices. By embracing customer engagement, leveraging advanced analytics, fostering innovation, and enhancing leadership capabilities, manufacturing companies can achieve sustained growth and maintain competitiveness.

Key Success Factors

Successful Commercial Excellence involves committed leadership, a company-wide behavioral transformation, and aligning scientific methods with customer engagement. These are very similar to the capabilities required in the pursuit of Operational Excellence; companies that have succeeded on their journey to Operational Excellence are likely to find that the organizational muscle that they built through that transformation can be leveraged to good effect when embarking on a program to achieve

Commercial Excellence.

The Importance of Strong and Committed Leadership

Achieving Commercial Excellence in manufacturing companies requires more than just strategic shifts and technological advancements; it necessitates strong, effective leadership. Leaders and executives play a pivotal role in driving the transition from Operational Excellence to Commercial Excellence, guiding their organizations through the complexities of market demands, customer engagement, and innovation.

Effective leaders provide visionary guidance, setting a clear direction for their organizations. This involves not only identifying new market opportunities but also articulating a compelling vision that aligns with the company's long-term goals. For example, General Electric (GE) has demonstrated strong leadership by pivoting its focus towards renewable energy and digital solutions. This strategic shift, driven by top leadership, has positioned GE to meet emerging market demands and maintain a competitive edge.

In addition, ExxonMobil's emphasis on sustainability and innovation reflects its leadership's forward-thinking approach. By investing in renewable energy sources and digital transformation, ExxonMobil's leaders are steering the company towards a more sustainable and profitable future. Leaders must cultivate the ability to foresee market trends and guide their organizations accordingly.

Leadership in Commercial Excellence also requires strategic decision-making capabilities. Executives must leverage data analytics to make informed decisions that enhance customer satisfaction and drive profitability. For instance, BASF employs sophisticated data analytics to prioritize high-margin products, ensuring efficient resource allocation and maximized revenue. This data-driven approach allows BASF's leaders to make strategic decisions that align with market demands.

Similarly, Dow Chemical uses predictive analytics to monitor market shifts and adapt its product mix in real-time. This proactive strategy enables Dow to stay ahead of competitors and meet evolving customer needs. Leaders must integrate advanced analytics into their decision-making processes to support commercial success and sustain growth.

Creating and maintaining a customer-centric culture is essential for achieving Commercial Excellence. Effective leaders prioritize customer needs and foster an organizational culture that values customer satisfaction. Siemens exemplifies this approach by developing customer-centric platforms that provide real-time insights and personalized solutions. By focusing on customer engagement, Siemens enhances satisfaction and loyalty, which are necessary for long-term success.

Honeywell's Forge platform is another example of leadership driving customer-centric initiatives. By offering real-time data and actionable insights, Honeywell helps customers optimize their operations, adding significant value and fostering stronger relationships. Leaders must champion customer-focused initiatives, ensuring that their organizations prioritize and meet customer needs.

To navigate the complexities of Commercial Excellence, leaders must continuously develop their capabilities. Comprehensive training programs are essential for equipping leaders with the skills and knowledge needed to drive commercial success. Siemens has implemented initiatives that promote continuous improvement and customer focus, fostering a learning culture that prepares leaders for new challenges.

ExxonMobil's emphasis on both technical knowledge and customer engagement techniques in its leadership development programs highlights the importance of well-rounded leadership. Tailored training ensures that leaders can effectively navigate complex sales cycles and build lasting customer relationships.

Strong leadership is the backbone of achieving Commercial Excellence in manufacturing companies. By providing visionary guidance, making strategic decisions, fostering a customer-centric culture, and enhancing their capabilities, leaders can drive their organizations towards sustained growth and competitiveness.

A Shift in Organizational Behavior

Achieving Commercial Excellence in manufacturing companies requires more than just strategic and technological advancements; it necessitates a profound behavioral transformation across the organization. This shift involves changing how employees think, interact, and approach their work, fostering a culture that prioritizes customer-centricity, continuous improvement, and innovation. Leaders and executives play a pivotal role in driving this transformation, ensuring that the entire organization aligns with the new commercial objectives.

A significant aspect of behavioral transformation is cultivating a customer-centric culture. Traditionally, manufacturing companies have focused on operational efficiency and product quality. However, to achieve Commercial Excellence, organizations must prioritize understanding and meeting customer needs. Siemens, for example, has developed customer-centric platforms that offer real-time insights and personalized solutions. By emphasizing customer engagement, Siemens enhances satisfaction and loyalty, critical components for long-term success.

Similarly, Honeywell's Forge platform exemplifies the shift towards customer-centricity. By providing real-time data and actionable insights, Honeywell helps customers optimize their operations, adding significant value and fostering stronger relationships. Leaders must champion initiatives that prioritize customer needs, ensuring that the organization consistently delivers exceptional customer experiences.

Continuous improvement is another cornerstone of behavioral transformation. Companies must foster a mindset that encourages employees to seek incremental improvements in all aspects of their work. For instance, BASF employs a collaborative approach to product development, involving close customer engagement to ensure offerings align with market needs and anticipate future trends. This customer-driven approach to innovation helps address current market demands and prepares for future opportunities.

General Electric (GE) has also embraced continuous improvement through its Lean Six Sigma programs, which focus on reducing waste and improving efficiency. By fostering a culture that values continuous improvement, GE ensures that all employees are committed to enhancing processes and delivering better value to customers.

Behavioral transformation requires fostering a culture of collaboration and innovation. Leaders must break down silos and encourage cross-functional teamwork to drive commercial success. For example, ExxonMobil has restructured its product portfolio to focus on high-growth areas such as renewable energy and digital solutions. By aligning its product mix with emerging market demands, ExxonMobil ensures that its teams work collaboratively to innovate and meet customer needs.

Dow Chemical utilizes predictive analytics to monitor market shifts and adapt its product mix in real-time. This proactive approach allows Dow to stay ahead of competitors and meet evolving customer demands. Encouraging collaboration and innovation ensures that organizations remain agile and responsive to market changes.

Effective leadership is critical for driving behavioral transformation. Executives must lead by example, demonstrating a commitment to customer-centricity and continuous improvement. Comprehensive training programs are essential for equipping leaders with the skills and knowledge needed to guide their teams through this transformation. Siemens, for instance, has implemented initiatives that promote continuous improvement and customer focus, fostering a learning culture that prepares leaders for new challenges.

Additionally, Honeywell emphasizes the importance of both technical knowledge and customer engagement techniques in its leadership development programs. Tailored training ensures that leaders can effectively navigate complex sales cycles and build lasting customer relationships.

Behavioral transformation is essential for manufacturing companies aiming to achieve Commercial Excellence. By cultivating a customer-centric culture, embracing continuous improvement, encouraging collaboration and innovation, and strengthening leadership, organizations can drive significant business improvements and achieve long-term success.

Aligning Scientific Methods

Aligning scientific methods with commercial objectives is essential for manufacturing companies aiming to achieve Commercial Excellence. This alignment ensures that technical innovations and process improvements directly contribute to business growth, customer satisfaction, and profitability. By integrating scientific rigor with commercial goals, companies can drive significant value and maintain a competitive edge.

A critical component of aligning scientific methods with commercial objectives is the integration of data analytics. Companies like BASF and Dow Chemical have effectively utilized advanced analytics to optimize product offerings and enhance decision-making. BASF, for instance, employs data-driven insights to prioritize high-margin products, ensuring efficient resource allocation and maximizing revenue. This alignment of scientific methods with commercial goals enables BASF to better meet market demands and drive business success.

Similarly, Dow Chemical uses predictive analytics to monitor market trends and adapt its product mix in real-time. By leveraging data analytics, Dow can stay ahead of competitors and meet evolving customer needs. Executives must embrace advanced analytics to support informed decision-making and drive Commercial Excellence.

Aligning scientific methods with commercial objectives also involves enhancing research and development (R&D) efforts. Companies must ensure that their R&D initiatives are closely tied to market needs and customer preferences. For example, ExxonMobil has restructured its product portfolio to focus on high-growth areas such as renewable energy and digital solutions. By aligning R&D efforts with commercial goals, ExxonMobil ensures that its innovations meet emerging market demands and drive profitability.

General Electric (GE) has also demonstrated the importance of aligning R&D with commercial objectives. GE's focus on renewable energy and digital transformation reflects its commitment to meeting customer needs and staying ahead of industry trends. By prioritizing R&D initiatives that align with commercial goals, companies can foster innovation and maintain a competitive edge.

Effective alignment of scientific methods with commercial objectives requires fostering collaboration between technical and commercial departments. Cross-functional teams can ensure that scientific innovations translate into commercially viable products and services. Siemens exemplifies this approach by encouraging collaboration between its R&D and marketing teams. By breaking down silos and promoting teamwork, Siemens ensures that scientific advancements align with customer needs and market opportunities.

Honeywell's Forge platform further illustrates the benefits of cross-functional collaboration. By integrating real-time data and actionable insights, Forge helps customers optimize their operations and adds significant value. This integration of technical and commercial efforts ensures that Honeywell's innovations drive customer satisfaction and business growth.

To align scientific methods successfully with commercial objectives, strong leadership is essential. Executives must guide their organizations through this alignment, ensuring that all departments work towards common goals. Siemens has implemented leadership development programs that emphasize the importance of aligning scientific and commercial efforts. By fostering a culture of continuous improvement and customer focus, Siemens prepares its leaders to navigate the complexities of this alignment.

BASF emphasizes the importance of leadership in driving commercial success. By equipping leaders with the skills and knowledge needed to integrate scientific methods with commercial objectives, BASF ensures that its innovations meet market needs and drive profitability.

Aligning scientific methods with commercial objectives is crucial for manufacturing companies aiming to achieve Commercial Excellence. By integrating data analytics, enhancing R&D efforts, fostering cross-functional collaboration, and strengthening leadership capabilities, companies can drive significant value and maintain a competitive edge.

Ensuring Customer Engagement

Enhancing customer engagement is an essential element for achieving Commercial Excellence within manufacturing companies. As organizations shift from a focus on operational efficiency to customer-centric practices, the importance of engaging with customers in meaningful ways cannot be overstated. Effective customer engagement drives satisfaction, fosters loyalty, and ultimately contributes to business growth and profitability.

A fundamental aspect of enhancing customer engagement is understanding and addressing customer needs. Manufacturing companies must go beyond their traditional focus on product quality to gain deeper insights into their customers' preferences and expectations. Siemens, for example, has developed customer-centric platforms that offer real-time insights and personalized solutions. By focusing on the specific needs of their customers, Siemens enhances satisfaction and builds stronger relationships.

Similarly, Honeywell's Forge platform exemplifies how providing real-time data and actionable insights can strengthen customer interactions. This approach not only adds significant value but also fosters long-term loyalty. Leaders must prioritize initiatives that help them understand and meet customer needs effectively.

Integrating advanced analytics into customer engagement practices is necessary for manufacturing companies aiming to achieve Commercial Excellence. Companies like BASF and Dow Chemical have successfully utilized data-driven insights to optimize their offerings and enhance decision-making. BASF employs sophisticated analytics to prioritize high-margin products and adjust production schedules accordingly. By understanding market trends and customer preferences, BASF can better align its offerings with demand, driving commercial success.

Dow Chemical uses predictive analytics to monitor market shifts and adapt its product mix in real-time. This proactive approach allows Dow to stay ahead of competitors and meet evolving customer needs. Executives must embrace advanced analytics to support informed decision-making and drive effective customer engagement strategies.

Personalized customer interactions are vital for fostering strong relationships and enhancing engagement. General Electric (GE) has demonstrated the effectiveness of personalized solutions through its Predix platform, which gathers comprehensive data on customer interactions and equipment performance. By analyzing this data, GE can offer tailored solutions that anticipate customer needs more accurately.

ExxonMobil's Chemical Customer Portal further illustrates the benefits of personalized interactions. By providing customized product recommendations, performance metrics, and technical support, ExxonMobil builds trust and ensures that customers feel valued. Personalized customer engagement is essential for driving satisfaction and loyalty.

Innovation is key to sustaining customer engagement. Companies must continuously develop new products and solutions that meet evolving market needs. BASF collaborates closely with customers to co-develop products, ensuring they align with specific requirements and preferences.

This customer-driven approach to innovation helps address current market demands and anticipate future opportunities.

Additionally, Siemens emphasizes the importance of continuous improvement in customer engagement. By fostering a culture of innovation and responsiveness, Siemens ensures that its offerings remain relevant and valuable to customers. Leaders must encourage ongoing improvement to maintain high levels of customer engagement.

Enhancing customer engagement is a necessary component of achieving Commercial Excellence in manufacturing companies. By understanding customer needs, leveraging advanced analytics, personalizing interactions, and fostering innovation, organizations can drive significant business improvements and achieve long-term success.

Leveraging Past Success in Operation Excellence

As organizations now pivot towards achieving Commercial Excellence, they can leverage the strategies and lessons learned from their Operational Excellence initiatives. By applying these proven approaches, companies can drive growth, improve customer engagement, and sustain long-term success.

Data analytics have been a cornerstone of Operational Excellence, enabling companies to optimize processes and reduce inefficiencies. This same analytical rigor can be applied to Commercial Excellence. For example, BASF employs sophisticated data analytics to prioritize high-margin products and adjust production schedules. By understanding market trends and customer preferences through data, BASF aligns its offerings with demand, driving commercial success.

Similarly, Dow Chemical utilizes predictive analytics to monitor market shifts and adapt its product mix in real-time. This proactive approach, initially developed for operational improvements, now helps Dow stay ahead of competitors and meet evolving customer needs. By integrating advanced analytics into their commercial strategies, companies can enhance decision-making and achieve better business outcomes.

The principles of continuous improvement that underpin Operational Excellence are equally applicable to Commercial Excellence. Companies must foster a culture that encourages employees to seek incremental improvements in all aspects of their work. General Electric (GE) has embraced this approach through its Lean Six Sigma programs, focusing on reducing waste and improving efficiency. This mindset of continuous improvement can be extended to commercial practices, ensuring that customer engagement, sales processes, and product offerings are constantly refined.

Honeywell's Forge platform, which provides real-time data and actionable insights, exemplifies the importance of continuous improvement in customer engagement. By leveraging data to optimize customer interactions, Honeywell enhances satisfaction and loyalty. Leaders must champion continuous improvement initiatives to ensure their organizations remain competitive and responsive to market changes.

Operational excellence often requires cross-functional collaboration to streamline processes and improve outcomes. This collaborative approach is also vital for achieving Commercial Excellence. Siemens, for instance, encourages collaboration between its R&D and marketing teams to ensure that scientific innovations translate into commercially viable products. By breaking down silos and promoting teamwork, Siemens aligns its technical capabilities with customer needs and market opportunities.

ExxonMobil's emphasis on collaboration is evident in its focus on renewable energy and digital solutions. By aligning product development with commercial goals, ExxonMobil ensures that its innovations meet emerging market demands. Encouraging cross-functional collaboration ensures that all departments work together to drive commercial success.

Effective leadership and employee engagement are critical for both operational and Commercial Excellence. Leaders must guide their organizations through the transition, ensuring that all employees are aligned with the new commercial objectives. Siemens has implemented leadership development programs that emphasize the importance of aligning scientific and commercial efforts. By fostering a culture of continuous improvement and customer focus, Siemens prepares its leaders to navigate the complexities of Commercial Excellence.

Additionally, BASF emphasizes the importance of leadership in driving business success. By equipping leaders with the skills and knowledge needed to integrate scientific methods with commercial objectives, BASF ensures that its innovations meet market needs and drive profitability.

The strategies and principles that have driven Operational Excellence in manufacturing companies provide a robust foundation for achieving Commercial Excellence. By leveraging data analytics, fostering a culture of continuous improvement, encouraging cross-functional collaboration, and strengthening leadership, organizations can drive significant business improvements and achieve long-term success.

The Benefits of an Integrated Strategy

Achieving Commercial Excellence in manufacturing companies requires a comprehensive and integrated strategy. This holistic approach must encompass customer engagement, data analytics, continuous improvement, cross-functional collaboration, and strong leadership. By weaving these elements into a unified strategy, organizations can drive growth, enhance customer satisfaction, and maintain a competitive edge.

Customer engagement is a cornerstone of Commercial Excellence. Manufacturing companies must shift from a product-centric focus to a customer-centric approach, understanding and addressing the specific needs and preferences of their customers. For example, Siemens has developed platforms that provide real-time insights and personalized solutions, enhancing customer satisfaction and loyalty. Similarly, Honeywell's Forge platform offers real-time data and actionable insights, helping customers optimize their operations and fostering long-term relationships.

By prioritizing customer engagement, companies can build stronger connections with their customers, driving repeat business and long-term loyalty. Leaders must champion initiatives that focus on understanding and meeting customer needs, ensuring that their organizations deliver exceptional customer experiences.

Integrating advanced data analytics is necessary for informed decision-making and optimizing commercial strategies. Companies like BASF and Dow Chemical have demonstrated the power of data-driven insights in refining product offerings and enhancing market responsiveness. BASF employs sophisticated analytics to prioritize high-margin products and align production schedules with market demand. Dow Chemical uses predictive analytics to monitor market shifts and adjust its product mix in real-time, staying ahead of competitors and meeting evolving customer needs.

By embedding data analytics into their commercial strategies, companies can make informed decisions that drive profitability and growth. Executives must embrace analytics to support effective decision-making and enhance overall business performance.

A culture of continuous improvement is essential for sustaining Commercial Excellence. Manufacturing companies must encourage employees to seek incremental improvements in all aspects of their work. General Electric (GE) exemplifies this approach through its Lean Six Sigma programs, which focus on reducing waste and improving efficiency. Honeywell's Forge platform further illustrates the importance of continuous improvement in customer engagement, using data to optimize interactions and enhance satisfaction.

Leaders must promote a mindset of continuous improvement across their organizations, ensuring that processes, products, and customer interactions are constantly refined and optimized.

Cross-functional collaboration is vital for aligning scientific innovations with commercial objectives. Companies must break down silos and promote teamwork between technical and commercial departments. Siemens encourages collaboration between its R&D and marketing teams, ensuring that scientific advancements translate into commercially viable products. ExxonMobil's focus on renewable energy and digital solutions highlights the importance of aligning product development with market demands.

By fostering collaboration, companies can ensure that all departments work together to drive commercial success and meet customer needs effectively.

Strong leadership is critical for guiding organizations through the transition to Commercial Excellence. Executives must lead by example, demonstrating a commitment to customer-centricity, continuous improvement, and collaboration. Siemens has implemented leadership development programs that emphasize these values, preparing leaders to navigate the complexities of Commercial Excellence. Similarly, BASF equips its leaders with the skills needed to integrate scientific methods with commercial objectives, driving innovation and profitability.

Effective leadership ensures that the entire organization is aligned with commercial goals, fostering a culture of excellence and continuous improvement.

Achieving Commercial Excellence in manufacturing companies requires a holistic strategy that integrates customer engagement, data analytics, continuous improvement, cross-functional collaboration, and strong leadership. By weaving these elements into a unified approach, organizations can drive significant business improvements, enhance customer satisfaction, and secure long-term success.

Continuous Improvement

Achieving Commercial Excellence in manufacturing companies requires an unwavering commitment to continuous improvement in commercial practices. This approach ensures that organizations remain agile, competitive, and responsive to evolving market demands. By embedding a culture of continuous improvement, companies can enhance customer satisfaction, drive growth, and secure long-term success.

For manufacturing companies, fostering a culture of continuous improvement means encouraging employees at all levels to seek incremental enhancements in their work processes and interactions with customers. This mindset is not confined to operational processes but extends to all commercial activities, including sales, marketing, and customer engagement. General Electric (GE) has demonstrated the effectiveness of this approach through its Lean Six Sigma programs, which focus on reducing waste and improving efficiency. By applying these principles to commercial practices, GE continuously refines its customer interactions and business processes to deliver better value.

Honeywell's Forge platform exemplifies the integration of continuous improvement in customer engagement. By leveraging real-time data and actionable insights, Honeywell enhances customer interactions, optimizing their operations and fostering stronger relationships. This commitment to ongoing enhancement ensures that customer needs are consistently met and exceeded.

Data analytics are key to driving continuous improvement in commercial practices. Companies must harness the power of data to gain insights into customer behavior, market trends, and operational performance. BASF, for instance, employs sophisticated analytics to prioritize high-margin products and adjust production schedules. This data-driven approach enables BASF to align its offerings with market demand, ensuring commercial success.

Dow Chemical uses predictive analytics to monitor market shifts and adapt its product mix in real-time. This proactive strategy allows Dow to stay ahead of competitors and meet evolving customer needs effectively. By embedding data analytics into their continuous improvement efforts, companies can make informed decisions that drive profitability and growth.

Continuous improvement in commercial practices also involves fostering cross-functional collaboration. Breaking down silos and promoting teamwork between different departments ensures that scientific innovations align with commercial goals. Siemens encourages collaboration between its R&D and marketing teams, ensuring that technical advancements translate into commercially viable products. This collaborative approach ensures that customer needs and market opportunities are effectively addressed.

ExxonMobil's focus on renewable energy and digital solutions highlights the importance of aligning product development with market demands. By encouraging cross-functional collaboration, ExxonMobil ensures that its innovations meet emerging market needs, driving commercial success.

Effective leadership is essential for embedding a culture of continuous improvement in commercial practices. Leaders must guide their organizations through this transformation, ensuring that all employees are aligned with the new commercial objectives. Siemens has implemented leadership development programs that emphasize the importance of continuous improvement and customer focus. By fostering a learning culture, Siemens prepares its leaders to navigate the complexities of Commercial Excellence.

BASF also emphasizes the role of leadership in driving business success. By equipping leaders with the skills and knowledge needed to integrate scientific methods with commercial objectives, BASF ensures that its innovations meet market needs and drive profitability.

Continuous improvement is the cornerstone of achieving Commercial Excellence in manufacturing companies. By embedding a culture of continuous improvement, leveraging data analytics, encouraging cross-functional collaboration, and strengthening leadership capabilities, organizations can drive significant business improvements and achieve long-term success.

Organizational Cohesion

Achieving Commercial Excellence requires cohesive efforts across the entire organization. This cohesion ensures that all departments are aligned with the company's commercial goals, fostering a unified approach to customer engagement, innovation, and market responsiveness. By integrating efforts across various functions, companies can drive significant business improvements and secure long-term success.

For an organization to achieve Commercial Excellence, it must first establish a unified vision and set of goals that resonate with every department. Leaders play a critical role in articulating this vision and ensuring that it is understood and embraced throughout the organization. General Electric (GE), for example, has successfully integrated its focus on renewable energy and digital transformation into its corporate strategy. This clear, unified direction allows GE to align its operational and commercial efforts, ensuring that all departments work towards common objectives.

Similarly, ExxonMobil's emphasis on sustainability and innovation reflects its commitment to a cohesive organizational strategy. By prioritizing renewable energy and digital solutions, ExxonMobil aligns its R&D, marketing, and sales teams around a shared vision, driving consistency and focus across its commercial activities.

Cross-functional collaboration is essential for fostering organizational cohesion. When departments work together seamlessly, they can leverage their collective expertise to develop and implement effective commercial initiatives. Siemens exemplifies this approach by encouraging collaboration between its R&D and marketing teams. This integration ensures that scientific advancements are translated into commercially viable products that meet market demands.

Dow Chemical has also demonstrated the benefits of cross-functional collaboration through its use of predictive analytics. By integrating insights from various departments, Dow can adapt its product mix in real-time to stay ahead of market trends. This collaborative approach allows Dow to respond swiftly to customer needs and maintain a competitive edge.

Effective communication is a cornerstone of organizational cohesion. Regular, transparent communication ensures that all employees are informed about the company's commercial goals and their roles in achieving them. Honeywell's Forge platform facilitates real-time communication and data sharing across departments, helping employees stay aligned with customer needs and operational objectives. This level of transparency fosters a culture of accountability and collaboration, essential for commercial success.

Additionally, BASF employs comprehensive communication strategies to keep its workforce informed and engaged. By regularly updating employees on market trends, customer feedback, and company performance, BASF ensures that everyone is working towards the same commercial goals. This consistent communication helps to break down silos and encourages a unified effort across the organization.

Strong leadership is critical for maintaining organizational cohesion. Leaders must inspire and motivate employees, ensuring that they are committed to the company's commercial objectives. Siemens has implemented leadership development programs that emphasize the importance of cohesive efforts and customer focus. By fostering a learning culture, Siemens prepares its leaders to guide their teams through the complexities of achieving Commercial Excellence.

Employee engagement is equally important. When employees feel valued and understand their contributions to the company's success, they are more likely to be committed and productive. ExxonMobil's leadership development initiatives highlight the importance of both technical expertise and customer engagement, ensuring that employees are equipped to drive commercial success.

Organizational cohesion is a fundamental requirement for achieving Commercial Excellence in manufacturing companies. By fostering a unified vision, encouraging cross-functional collaboration, maintaining consistent communication, and strengthening leadership, organizations can align their efforts towards common commercial goals.

Chapter 3

Catching a fever

> *« Rien ne réussit comme le succès »*
>
> — *Alexandre Dumas*

Initial Focus on Short-Term Value

Expanding sales volume with existing customers offers a strategic avenue for achieving rapid, short-term financial impact. By leveraging established relationships and understanding customer needs, companies can significantly boost their revenue without the substantial investments required to acquire new customers. This approach involves deepening engagements, optimizing cross-selling and up-selling opportunities, and enhancing customer loyalty.

One of the primary advantages of focusing on existing customers is the established trust and familiarity. Companies already have valuable insights into their customers' preferences and behaviors, which can be used to tailor offerings more effectively. For instance, General Electric (GE) has successfully leveraged its customer data through its Predix platform, providing personalized solutions that enhance customer satisfaction and encourage repeat business. By deepening these relationships, GE has managed to drive significant revenue growth from its existing customer base.

Similarly, Honeywell utilizes its Forge platform to offer real-time data and actionable insights that help customers optimize their operations. This not only adds value to the customer experience but also fosters long-term loyalty, leading to increased sales volume. By continuously engaging with their customers and addressing their evolving needs, Honeywell strengthens its market position and drives revenue growth.

Cross-selling and up-selling are powerful tools for increasing sales volume with existing customers. By identifying complementary products or higher-value alternatives that meet customer needs, companies can boost their revenue per customer. BASF, for example, employs sophisticated analytics to understand customer purchasing patterns and identify opportunities for cross-selling and up-selling. This data-driven approach ensures that BASF can offer relevant products and services, maximizing the value extracted from each customer relationship.

Dow Chemical has also demonstrated success in optimizing cross-selling and up-selling. By using predictive analytics to monitor market trends and customer behavior, Dow can tailor its offerings to meet specific customer needs. This proactive strategy not only enhances customer satisfaction but also drives substantial revenue growth by increasing the sales volume of higher-margin products.

Fostering customer loyalty is necessary for sustaining sales volume expansion. Loyal customers are more likely to make repeat purchases and recommend the company to others, creating a virtuous cycle of revenue growth. ExxonMobil has focused on enhancing customer loyalty through its Chemical Customer Portal, which provides personalized product recommendations, performance metrics, and technical support. This tailored approach builds trust and ensures that customers feel valued, leading to increased sales volume and long-term loyalty.

Siemens has developed customer-centric platforms that offer personalized solutions based on real-time insights. By prioritizing customer engagement and addressing specific needs, Siemens enhances customer loyalty and drives repeat business. This focus on building strong customer relationships ensures that Siemens can expand its sales volume effectively, leveraging existing customer bases to achieve substantial revenue growth.

Expanding sales volume with existing customers presents a highly effective strategy for driving rapid, short-term financial impact. By leveraging established relationships, optimizing cross-selling and up-selling opportunities, and enhancing customer loyalty, companies can significantly boost their revenue.

Pricing Improvements

Enhancing pricing strategies for current customers is a highly effective approach for achieving rapid, short-term financial impact. By refining how prices are set and adjusted, companies can significantly boost their top line. This approach involves leveraging data analytics, understanding customer value perception, and employing dynamic pricing models.

Data analytics is critical for developing effective pricing strategies. Companies can use data to understand customer behavior, market trends, and price sensitivity. For instance, BASF utilizes advanced analytics to identify the optimal price points for its products. By analyzing customer purchasing patterns and market conditions, BASF can set prices that maximize revenue while remaining competitive.

Similarly, Dow Chemical employs predictive analytics to anticipate market changes and adjust prices in real-time. This proactive approach enables Dow to stay ahead of competitors and capture additional value from its existing customer base. Leveraging data analytics allows companies to make informed pricing decisions that drive significant top-line growth.

A deep understanding of how customers perceive value is essential for enhancing pricing strategies. Companies must align their pricing with the perceived value of their products and services. Honeywell's Forge platform, for example, offers real-time data and actionable insights that help customers optimize their operations. By demonstrating the value of these insights, Honeywell can justify premium pricing for its services.

General Electric (GE) uses its Predix platform to provide personalized solutions based on customer data. By clearly communicating the value of these tailored solutions, GE can implement value-based pricing, ensuring that prices reflect the benefits customers receive. Understanding and communicating customer value perception enables companies to enhance their pricing strategies effectively.

Dynamic pricing models allow companies to adjust prices based on real-time market conditions and customer demand. This flexibility ensures that prices remain competitive while maximizing revenue. ExxonMobil has implemented dynamic pricing for its Chemical Customer Portal, adjusting prices based on factors such as market demand and production costs. This approach ensures that ExxonMobil captures the maximum value from each transaction.

Siemens has also adopted dynamic pricing strategies for its customer-centric platforms. By continuously monitoring market trends and customer needs, Siemens can adjust prices to reflect current conditions, ensuring optimal revenue generation. Employing dynamic pricing models enables companies to respond swiftly to market changes and capture additional value.

Effective pricing strategies require strong leadership and continuous training. Leaders must ensure that their teams understand the importance of pricing and are equipped with the skills needed to implement and manage pricing strategies. Siemens has invested in leadership development programs that emphasize the role of pricing in commercial success. By fostering a culture of continuous improvement and customer focus, Siemens prepares its leaders to navigate the complexities of pricing.

BASF also emphasizes leadership in driving pricing improvements. By providing leaders with the necessary tools and knowledge, BASF ensures that its pricing strategies align with market demands and customer expectations. Strong leadership and training are essential for maintaining effective pricing strategies that drive top-line growth.

Enhancing pricing strategies for current customers is a powerful approach for achieving rapid, short-term financial impact. By leveraging data analytics, understanding customer value perception, employing dynamic pricing models, and strengthening leadership, companies can significantly boost their top line.

Service Cost Optimization

Reducing service costs is a critical strategy for improving financial performance, offering a pathway to rapid, short-term financial impact. By streamlining service operations, leveraging technology, and enhancing efficiency, companies can significantly reduce costs and improve their bottom line.

Streamlining service operations involves identifying inefficiencies and implementing processes that enhance productivity. For instance, General Electric (GE) has employed Lean Six Sigma methodologies to reduce waste and improve service efficiency. By analyzing service workflows and eliminating non-value-added activities, GE has been able to cut costs significantly while maintaining high service standards.

Similarly, Siemens has optimized its service operations through continuous improvement initiatives. By fostering a culture of efficiency and accountability, Siemens ensures that its service teams consistently seek ways to improve processes and reduce costs. Streamlining operations not only reduces expenses but also enhances service quality, leading to increased customer satisfaction and loyalty.

Leveraging technology is a necessary component of service cost optimization. Companies can use advanced technologies to automate routine tasks, monitor performance, and manage resources more effectively. Honeywell's Forge platform, for example, uses real-time data and analytics to optimize service delivery. By providing actionable insights, Forge helps service teams address issues proactively, reducing downtime and minimizing costs.

ExxonMobil has also implemented technology-driven solutions to optimize service costs. By utilizing predictive maintenance tools, ExxonMobil can anticipate equipment failures and schedule maintenance activities more efficiently. This proactive approach reduces the need for emergency repairs, which are often more costly and disruptive. Technology not only streamlines service operations but also improves reliability and customer satisfaction.

Improving workforce productivity is another key element of service cost optimization. Companies must ensure that their service teams are well-trained, motivated, and equipped with the right tools to perform their tasks efficiently. BASF, for instance, invests in comprehensive training programs to enhance the skills and productivity of its service personnel. By equipping employees with the knowledge and tools they need, BASF ensures that service tasks are completed quickly and accurately, reducing costs and improving performance.

Dow Chemical emphasizes the importance of employee engagement in optimizing service costs. By fostering a supportive work environment and recognizing employee contributions, Dow motivates its service teams to perform at their best. Engaged employees are more likely to identify and implement cost-saving measures, contributing to overall financial improvement.

Effective leadership and strategic planning are essential for successful service cost optimization. Leaders must set clear cost-saving goals and provide the resources and support needed to achieve them. Siemens, for example, has implemented leadership development programs that focus on cost management and efficiency. By training leaders to prioritize cost-saving initiatives, Siemens ensures that service cost optimization is integrated into the company's strategic planning.

Honeywell also highlights the role of leadership in driving service cost optimization. By aligning leadership goals with cost-saving objectives, Honeywell ensures that its service teams are focused on efficiency and financial performance. Strong leadership provides the direction and motivation needed to achieve significant cost reductions.

Service cost optimization is a critical strategy for improving financial performance in the short term. By streamlining service operations, leveraging technology, enhancing workforce productivity, and providing strong leadership, companies can significantly reduce service costs and improve their bottom line.

Short-Term Financial Impact

Delivering some quick financial impact is critical for building momentum as companies start their journey towards Commercial Excellence. By focusing on expanding sales volume, improving pricing strategies with existing customers, and optimizing service costs, companies can

107

significantly enhance their revenue within a short timeframe. These initiatives, when executed effectively, provide a robust foundation for long-term financial health and competitive advantage.

Expanding sales volume with existing customers is a strategic move that leverages established relationships to drive revenue growth. General Electric (GE) exemplifies this approach through its Predix platform, which offers tailored solutions based on comprehensive customer data. By deepening customer engagements and addressing specific needs, GE not only increases sales volume but also enhances customer satisfaction and loyalty.

Similarly, Honeywell's Forge platform provides real-time data and actionable insights, enabling customers to optimize their operations. This added value encourages repeat business and fosters long-term loyalty, leading to a substantial increase in sales volume. Focusing on existing customers allows companies to maximize revenue without the substantial costs associated with acquiring new customers.

Enhancing pricing strategies for current customers can significantly boost the top line. Companies like BASF and Dow Chemical have successfully utilized data-driven insights to refine their pricing models. BASF employs advanced analytics to identify optimal price points, ensuring that prices reflect the true value of their products and services. By aligning pricing with market demand and customer value perception, BASF can maximize revenue while maintaining competitiveness.

Dow Chemical leverages predictive analytics to adjust prices in real-time based on market conditions. This proactive approach enables Dow to capture additional value and stay ahead of competitors. Effective pricing strategies require a deep understanding of customer behavior and market trends, allowing companies to set prices that drive profitability and growth.

Reducing service costs is critical for improving financial performance and achieving rapid revenue enhancement. Streamlining service operations and leveraging technology can lead to significant cost savings. Siemens, for example, has implemented continuous improvement initiatives to enhance service efficiency and reduce costs. By fostering a culture of accountability and efficiency, Siemens ensures that its service teams consistently seek ways to improve processes and deliver value.

ExxonMobil's use of predictive maintenance tools illustrates how technology can optimize service costs. By anticipating equipment failures and scheduling maintenance proactively, ExxonMobil reduces emergency repair costs and minimizes downtime. This approach not only lowers service costs but also improves reliability and customer satisfaction.

Integrating these strategic initiatives – expanding sales volume, improving pricing, and optimizing service costs – creates a comprehensive approach to rapidly enhance revenue. Effective leadership and strategic planning are essential for aligning these initiatives with the company's overall goals. Siemens has invested in leadership development programs that emphasize cost management, efficiency, and customer focus. This holistic approach ensures that all departments work together towards common objectives, driving substantial financial improvements.

Honeywell's alignment of leadership goals with cost-saving initiatives further underscores the importance of cohesive efforts. By integrating strategic initiatives across the organization, Honeywell enhances its ability to respond to market demands and achieve rapid revenue growth.

Customer Retention

Focusing initially on existing customers offers companies a path to rapid, short-term financial impact. By prioritizing customer retention, companies can enhance revenue, improve profitability, and achieve sustainable growth.

Capitalizing on established relationships with existing customers is necessary for achieving rapid financial gains. General Electric (GE) has demonstrated the effectiveness of this approach through its Predix platform, which provides personalized solutions based on extensive customer data.

By understanding and addressing specific customer needs, GE enhances satisfaction and loyalty, leading to increased repeat business and higher revenue.

Similarly, Honeywell's Forge platform offers real-time data and actionable insights that help customers optimize their operations. This value-added service strengthens customer relationships and encourages long-term loyalty, driving revenue growth. Focusing on existing customers allows companies to maximize the value of established relationships without the significant costs associated with acquiring new customers.

Customer retention is closely linked to customer satisfaction. Companies that prioritize delivering exceptional service and addressing customer needs effectively can significantly boost retention rates. Siemens, for example, has developed customer-centric platforms that provide real-time insights and personalized solutions. By focusing on customer engagement, Siemens ensures high levels of satisfaction and loyalty, which translates into repeat business and increased revenue.

ExxonMobil has also emphasized customer satisfaction through its Chemical Customer Portal, offering personalized product recommendations, performance metrics, and technical support. This tailored approach not only meets customer needs but also builds trust and loyalty, leading to higher retention rates and enhanced financial performance.

Loyalty programs are an effective tool for retaining existing customers and driving revenue growth. BASF has successfully implemented loyalty programs that reward customers for repeat purchases and long-term relationships. These programs create a sense of value and appreciation, encouraging customers to continue their business with BASF. By incentivizing repeat purchases, loyalty programs contribute to a stable and predictable revenue stream.

Dow Chemical has also utilized loyalty programs to enhance customer retention. By offering exclusive benefits and rewards to long-term customers, Dow fosters a strong sense of loyalty and commitment. This approach not only retains existing customers but also attracts new ones through positive word-of-mouth and referrals.

Continuous improvement in customer service is essential for maintaining high retention rates. Companies must consistently seek ways to enhance the customer experience and address evolving needs. General Electric (GE) employs Lean Six Sigma methodologies to streamline service operations and reduce inefficiencies. By continuously improving service delivery, GE ensures that customers remain satisfied and loyal, driving repeat business and revenue growth.

Honeywell's commitment to continuous improvement is evident in its Forge platform, which leverages real-time data to optimize customer interactions. By proactively addressing issues and enhancing service quality, Honeywell maintains high levels of customer satisfaction and retention.

Focusing on existing customers is key to achieving rapid, short-term financial improvements. By leveraging established relationships, enhancing customer satisfaction, implementing loyalty programs, and fostering continuous improvement, companies can drive substantial revenue growth and profitability.

An Integrated Approach to Short-Term Impact

By combining sales expansion, pricing enhancement, and cost optimization, organizations can create a comprehensive strategy that drives substantial revenue growth and improves profitability.

Expanding sales volume with existing customers is a necessary component of a holistic growth strategy. Companies can leverage established relationships to drive revenue growth by understanding and addressing specific customer needs. General Electric (GE) has successfully implemented this approach through its Predix platform, offering tailored solutions based on extensive customer data. This personalized approach

111

enhances customer satisfaction and encourages repeat business, leading to increased sales volume and higher revenue. Similarly, Honeywell's Forge platform provides real-time data and actionable insights that help customers optimize their operations. By delivering added value, Honeywell strengthens customer relationships and fosters long-term loyalty, driving revenue growth from existing customers. Focusing on expanding sales volume allows companies to maximize the value of their customer base without incurring significant acquisition costs.

Improving pricing strategies is another critical element of a holistic growth approach. Companies can significantly boost their top line by refining how prices are set and adjusted. BASF, for example, uses advanced analytics to identify optimal price points, ensuring that prices reflect the true value of their products and services. By aligning pricing with market demand and customer value perception, BASF can maximize revenue while maintaining competitiveness.

Dow Chemical employs predictive analytics to adjust prices in real-time based on market conditions. This proactive strategy enables Dow to capture additional value and stay ahead of competitors. Effective pricing strategies require a deep understanding of customer behavior and market trends, allowing companies to set prices that drive profitability and growth.

Reducing service costs is essential for improving financial performance and achieving rapid revenue enhancement. Streamlining service operations and leveraging technology can lead to significant cost savings. Siemens, for example, has implemented continuous improvement initiatives to enhance service efficiency and reduce costs. By fostering a culture of accountability and efficiency, Siemens ensures that its service teams consistently seek ways to improve processes and deliver value.

ExxonMobil's use of predictive maintenance tools illustrates how technology can optimize service costs. By anticipating equipment failures and scheduling maintenance proactively, ExxonMobil reduces emergency repair costs and minimizes downtime. This approach not only lowers service costs but also improves reliability and customer satisfaction.

A comprehensive approach to growth involves integrating sales expansion, pricing enhancement, and cost optimization. Effective leadership and strategic planning are essential for aligning these initiatives with the company's overall goals. Siemens has invested in leadership development programs that emphasize cost management, efficiency, and customer focus. This holistic approach ensures that all departments work together towards common objectives, driving substantial financial improvements.

Honeywell's alignment of leadership goals with cost-saving initiatives further underscores the importance of cohesive efforts. By integrating strategic initiatives across the organization, Honeywell enhances its ability to respond to market demands and achieve rapid revenue growth.

Combining sales expansion, pricing enhancement, and cost optimization forms a powerful integrated framework for achieving rapid, short-term financial impact.

Maximizing Impact from Limited Resources

Focusing an organization's limited sales resources on customers that have the greatest upside potential translates to faster and more profitable sales growth without a commensurate investment in expanding the salesforce

Focus on High-Potential Customers

Maximizing financial impact in the manufacturing sector requires a strategic approach that concentrates sales efforts on customers with the greatest potential for growth. By identifying and prioritizing these high-potential customers, companies can drive significant revenue increases and improve overall profitability.

The first step in concentrating sales efforts on high-potential customers is identifying which customers offer the most growth opportunities. This requires a thorough analysis of customer data, including purchasing patterns, revenue potential, and market positioning. General Electric (GE)

113

has effectively utilized its Predix platform to gather and analyze customer data, allowing it to identify key accounts that are likely to deliver substantial revenue growth. By focusing on these high-potential customers, GE ensures that its sales efforts are both targeted and efficient.

Similarly, BASF employs advanced analytics to segment its customer base and identify those with the highest growth potential. By leveraging data-driven insights, BASF can tailor its sales strategies to meet the specific needs of these customers, driving significant revenue increases.

Once high-potential customers have been identified, it is critical to prioritize engagement with these accounts. Honeywell's Forge platform offers a prime example of how to effectively engage with high-potential customers. By providing real-time data and actionable insights, Honeywell enhances its customers' operational efficiency and adds significant value to the relationship. This proactive engagement fosters long-term loyalty, and drives repeat business, maximizing revenue from high-potential accounts. ExxonMobil has also demonstrated the importance of prioritizing customer engagement. Through its Chemical Customer Portal, ExxonMobil offers personalized product recommendations, performance metrics, and technical support, ensuring that high-potential customers receive tailored solutions that meet their specific needs. This focused engagement strategy not only strengthens customer relationships but also drives substantial revenue growth.

Tailoring solutions to the unique needs of high-potential customers is essential for maximizing financial impact. Dow Chemical uses predictive analytics to monitor market trends and customer behavior, enabling it to develop customized solutions that address specific customer requirements. By aligning its product offerings with the needs of high-potential customers, Dow can drive significant revenue growth and improve customer satisfaction. Siemens has also embraced this approach, developing customer-centric platforms that provide personalized solutions based on real-time insights. By understanding and addressing the unique needs of high-potential customers, Siemens enhances customer loyalty and drives substantial revenue increases.

Continuous measurement and optimization of sales efforts are critical for maintaining focus on high-potential customers. Companies must regularly assess the performance of their sales strategies and make necessary adjustments to ensure they remain effective. BASF, for example, employs comprehensive performance metrics to monitor the success of its customer engagement initiatives. By continuously refining its approach, BASF ensures that it maximizes revenue from high-potential accounts. Similarly, Honeywell uses real-time data analytics to measure the effectiveness of its engagement strategies. By continuously optimizing its approach, Honeywell ensures that it delivers maximum value to high-potential customers, driving sustained revenue growth.

Focusing on high-potential customers is a strategic approach that can drive significant revenue growth and improve overall profitability. By identifying and prioritizing these customers, engaging with them proactively, tailoring solutions to their needs, and continuously measuring and optimizing performance, manufacturing companies can achieve rapid, short-term financial impact.

Efficient Resource Allocation

In the quest for Commercial Excellence, effective allocation of sales time and energy is important for maximizing financial impact. By prioritizing efforts on high-potential customers, companies can drive substantial revenue growth and enhance profitability.

Effective time and energy allocation begins with identifying high-potential customers. These are clients who present the greatest opportunities for growth and profitability. General Electric (GE) exemplifies this approach through its Predix platform, which collects and analyzes customer data to identify key accounts. By focusing on these high-potential customers, GE ensures that its sales teams spend their time on the most promising

115

opportunities, maximizing revenue growth. Similarly, Honeywell leverages its Forge platform to gather real-time data and insights about customer operations. This information helps Honeywell identify which customers are likely to benefit most from their services, allowing them to prioritize engagement with these high-potential clients. By concentrating efforts on the right customers, Honeywell can drive significant financial impact.

Once high-potential customers have been identified, it is essential to tailor sales efforts to meet their specific needs. BASF employs advanced analytics to understand customer purchasing patterns and preferences. This allows BASF to customize its sales approach, ensuring that each interaction is relevant and valuable to the customer. By focusing on personalized engagement, BASF enhances customer satisfaction and loyalty, leading to increased sales and revenue.

Dow Chemical uses predictive analytics to monitor market trends and customer behavior, enabling them to develop tailored solutions for high-potential customers. This proactive approach ensures that Dow's sales teams are always prepared to address the unique needs of their clients, driving both customer satisfaction and financial performance.

Optimizing the productivity of sales teams is another critical aspect of effective time and energy allocation. Siemens has implemented continuous improvement initiatives that streamline sales processes and eliminate inefficiencies. By providing sales teams with the tools and training they need to be more productive, Siemens ensures that they can focus their efforts on high-potential customers and deliver maximum value.

ExxonMobil's use of predictive maintenance tools also highlights the importance of optimizing productivity. By anticipating customer needs and addressing potential issues before they arise, ExxonMobil's sales teams can maintain high levels of efficiency and effectiveness. This proactive approach not only reduces costs but also enhances customer satisfaction, driving repeat business and revenue growth.

Continuous measurement and adjustment of sales efforts are essential for maintaining focus on high-potential customers. Honeywell uses real-time data analytics to track the performance of its sales strategies and make necessary adjustments. By continuously refining their approach, Honeywell ensures that sales teams remain focused on the most promising opportunities, maximizing financial impact.

BASF also employs comprehensive performance metrics to monitor the success of its sales initiatives. By regularly assessing and optimizing their sales efforts, BASF can ensure that resources are allocated effectively and that high-potential customers receive the attention they deserve.

Prioritizing sales time and energy on high-potential customers is essential for maximizing financial impact. By identifying key accounts, tailoring sales efforts, optimizing team productivity, and continuously measuring performance, companies can drive substantial revenue growth and enhance profitability.

Accelerating Growth without Increasing the Salesforce

Focusing on customers with the greatest potential can lead to accelerated sales growth without the need to expand the salesforce. This approach, grounded in strategic customer selection and targeted engagement, allows companies to drive substantial revenue increases efficiently.

The cornerstone of this approach is identifying customers who offer the most significant growth opportunities. General Electric (GE) leverages its Predix platform to analyze customer data, pinpointing those with the highest potential. By focusing on these key accounts, GE ensures that its sales efforts are directed towards the most promising opportunities, leading to rapid sales growth. Similarly, Honeywell's Forge platform gathers real-time insights about customer operations, helping identify those who stand to benefit the most from their services. This targeted focus ensures that sales teams spend their time and energy on high-value customers, driving swift revenue increases.

Once high-potential customers are identified, tailoring engagement

117

strategies to meet their specific needs is critical. BASF uses advanced analytics to understand customer preferences and purchasing behaviors. This enables BASF to customize its sales approaches, ensuring each interaction is relevant and valuable. Personalized engagement not only enhances customer satisfaction but also accelerates sales growth.

Dow Chemical employs predictive analytics to monitor market trends and customer behaviors. By aligning their product offerings with the specific needs of high-potential customers, Dow ensures effective engagement, leading to faster sales growth without increasing the salesforce.

Optimizing the productivity of existing sales teams is essential for achieving rapid growth. Siemens has implemented continuous improvement initiatives that streamline sales processes and eliminate inefficiencies. This focus on productivity ensures that sales teams can concentrate on high-potential customers and deliver maximum value, driving accelerated sales growth.

ExxonMobil's use of predictive maintenance tools highlights the importance of optimizing productivity. By proactively addressing customer needs and potential issues, ExxonMobil's sales teams maintain high efficiency and effectiveness, contributing to faster sales growth.

Building and maintaining strong customer relationships is fundamental to fostering loyalty and driving repeat business. Siemens develops customer-centric platforms that provide personalized solutions based on real-time insights. This approach strengthens customer relationships, ensuring high-potential customers remain loyal and contribute to ongoing sales growth.

ExxonMobil's Chemical Customer Portal offers personalized product recommendations and technical support, enhancing customer satisfaction and loyalty. By focusing on high-potential customers and fostering strong relationships, ExxonMobil drives repeat business, leading to sustained sales growth.

Continuous measurement and adjustment of sales strategies are critical for maintaining focus on high-potential customers. Honeywell uses real-time data analytics to track the performance of its engagement strategies, making necessary adjustments to ensure effectiveness. This continuous refinement process ensures that sales teams remain focused on the most promising opportunities, driving accelerated sales growth.

BASF employs comprehensive performance metrics to monitor the success of its sales initiatives. By regularly assessing and optimizing their approaches, BASF ensures that resources are allocated effectively, leading to faster sales growth without the need to expand the salesforce.

Focusing on high-potential customers is a powerful strategy for achieving rapid sales growth without expanding the salesforce. By identifying key accounts, tailoring engagement strategies, optimizing sales productivity, and continuously measuring performance, companies can drive substantial revenue increases efficiently.

Strategic Customer Selection

By identifying and targeting customers with the highest upside potential, companies can drive significant revenue growth and enhance overall profitability. This approach involves leveraging data analytics, refining customer engagement strategies, and continuously monitoring performance.

The foundation of strategic customer selection lies in leveraging data analytics to identify high-potential customers. Companies like General Electric (GE) utilize platforms such as Predix to gather and analyze customer data, pinpointing those accounts that promise substantial growth opportunities. By focusing on these high-potential customers, GE ensures its sales teams concentrate their efforts where they can yield the highest returns. Similarly, BASF employs advanced analytics to segment its customer base, identifying those with the greatest potential for growth. Through this data-driven approach, BASF tailors its sales strategies to meet the specific needs of these high-value customers, driving significant revenue increases.

Once high-potential customers have been identified, it is necessary to refine engagement strategies to cater to their unique needs. Honeywell's Forge platform is an exemplary tool that provides real-time insights into customer operations, allowing for highly personalized engagement. By delivering tailored solutions, Honeywell not only enhances customer satisfaction but also fosters long-term loyalty, leading to increased sales and revenue.

Dow Chemical utilizes predictive analytics to anticipate market trends and customer behaviors, enabling them to offer customized solutions to high-potential customers. This proactive approach ensures that Dow's engagement strategies are always aligned with the specific requirements of their most valuable clients, driving both customer satisfaction and financial performance.

Optimizing the productivity of sales teams is another critical aspect of strategic customer selection. Siemens has implemented continuous improvement initiatives that streamline sales processes and eliminate inefficiencies. By providing their sales teams with the necessary tools and training, Siemens ensures that they can focus on high-potential customers and deliver maximum value, driving accelerated sales growth.

ExxonMobil's use of predictive maintenance tools also highlights the importance of optimizing productivity. By proactively addressing customer needs and potential issues, ExxonMobil's sales teams maintain high efficiency and effectiveness, contributing to faster sales growth and enhanced profitability.

Continuous monitoring and adjustment of sales strategies are essential for maintaining focus on high-potential customers. Honeywell employs real-time data analytics to track the performance of its engagement strategies, making necessary adjustments to ensure ongoing effectiveness. This continuous refinement process ensures that sales teams remain focused on the most promising opportunities, driving sustained revenue growth.

BASF also uses comprehensive performance metrics to monitor the success of its sales initiatives. By regularly assessing and optimizing their strategies, BASF ensures that resources are allocated effectively, leading to faster sales growth and improved financial performance.

Strategic customer selection is a powerful approach for maximizing financial impact. By leveraging data analytics, refining engagement strategies, optimizing sales team productivity, and continuously monitoring performance, companies can drive substantial revenue growth and enhance profitability.

Setting an Optimized Sales Strategy

An optimized sales strategy that focuses on customers with the greatest potential can drive substantial financial impact. By strategically allocating resources and efforts towards high-value customers, companies can achieve significant revenue growth and improved profitability.

The foundation of an optimized sales strategy lies in identifying customers with the highest growth potential. Companies like General Electric (GE) leverage platforms such as Predix to collect and analyze customer data, enabling them to pinpoint accounts that promise substantial returns. By concentrating on these high-potential customers, GE ensures that its sales teams focus their efforts where they can achieve the highest impact.

Similarly, BASF uses advanced analytics to segment its customer base and identify those with the greatest potential for growth. Through this data-driven approach, BASF tailors its sales tactics to meet the specific needs of these high-value customers, driving significant revenue increases and fostering long-term loyalty.

Once high-potential customers are identified, it is necessary to tailor engagement strategies to address their unique needs. Honeywell's Forge platform provides a prime example of how real-time insights into customer operations can enable personalized engagement. By offering tailored solutions that directly address customer challenges, Honeywell not only enhances satisfaction but also fosters loyalty and repeat business, driving sustained revenue growth.

Dow Chemical employs predictive analytics to monitor market trends and customer behavior, allowing them to customize their offerings to meet specific customer requirements. This proactive engagement ensures that Dow remains aligned with the evolving needs of its high-potential customers, leading to enhanced customer satisfaction and financial performance.

Optimizing sales team efficiency is another critical component of an effective sales strategy. Siemens has implemented continuous improvement initiatives to streamline sales processes and eliminate inefficiencies. By providing their sales teams with the necessary tools and training, Siemens ensures they can focus on high-potential customers and deliver maximum value, driving accelerated sales growth.

ExxonMobil's use of predictive maintenance tools also highlights the importance of optimizing productivity. By proactively addressing customer needs and potential issues, ExxonMobil's sales teams maintain high efficiency and effectiveness, contributing to faster sales growth and enhanced profitability.

Continuous monitoring and adjustment of sales efforts are essential for maintaining focus on high-potential customers. Honeywell employs real-time data analytics to track the performance of its engagement strategies, making necessary adjustments to ensure ongoing effectiveness. This continuous refinement process ensures that sales teams remain focused on the most promising opportunities, driving sustained revenue growth.

BASF uses comprehensive performance metrics to monitor the success of its sales initiatives. By regularly assessing and optimizing their strategies, BASF ensures that resources are allocated effectively, leading to faster sales growth and improved financial performance.

Implementing an optimized sales strategy that focuses on high-potential customers is essential for achieving substantial financial impact. By strategically identifying key accounts, tailoring engagement approaches, enhancing sales team efficiency, and continuously monitoring performance, companies can drive significant revenue growth and improve overall profitability.

The Paramount Importance of Quick Wins

Achieving early successes (or Quick Wins), communicating their impact within the organization, and recognizing the individuals and teams who contributed to each success will help generate motivation, focus, and momentum that will all be critical as the organization's efforts expand to embrace more challenging, medium-term initiatives.

By delivering early, tangible results, companies can generate enthusiasm and commitment among employees and stakeholders. For instance, when Honeywell launched its Forge platform, the initial success stories from early adopters provided compelling evidence of the platform's value. These early victories not only validated the initiative but also inspired other customers to embrace the new technology, accelerating overall adoption and revenue growth. Similarly, General Electric (GE) achieved early success with its Predix platform by focusing on key customers who were able to realize immediate benefits. These initial successes helped GE build credibility and momentum, encouraging broader acceptance and investment in the platform across various industries.

Early successes play a very important role in securing stakeholder buy-in for a transformation program. Demonstrating quick, positive results can help convince skeptical stakeholders of the program's viability and potential benefits. When Siemens introduced its customer-centric platforms, the company highlighted Quick Wins achieved through personalized solutions based on real-time insights. These early successes showcased the platform's effectiveness, garnering support from both internal and external

ExxonMobil's Chemical Customer Portal also leveraged early successes to gain stakeholder buy-in. By providing personalized product recommendations and technical support, the portal quickly demonstrated its value, leading to increased usage and support from customers and internal teams alike.

Quick Wins are vital for demonstrating the potential of a Commercial Excellence transformation program. By achieving and communicating early successes, companies can illustrate the broader impact of their initiatives. BASF, for example, used advanced analytics to identify high-potential customers and deliver tailored solutions. The early success stories from these targeted engagements demonstrated the effectiveness of BASF's data-driven approach, encouraging wider adoption and further investment in analytics capabilities. Dow Chemical similarly showcased the potential of its predictive analytics tools by achieving early successes in monitoring market trends and customer behavior. These initial victories provided concrete examples of how predictive analytics could drive revenue growth and customer satisfaction, reinforcing the value of Dow's investment in advanced technologies.

Effectively communicating early successes is as important as achieving them. Companies must ensure that these Quick Wins are shared widely within the organization and with external stakeholders. Honeywell, for instance, actively promoted the success stories of its Forge platform through case studies and customer testimonials. This strategic communication helped build a narrative of success, reinforcing the platform's value and driving further engagement. Siemens also emphasizes the importance of sharing success stories. By regularly communicating the impact of its customer-centric platforms, Siemens ensures that employees and stakeholders remain informed and motivated, fostering a culture of continuous improvement and innovation.

Achieving and communicating early successes, or Quick Wins, is critical to the overall success of a Commercial Excellence transformation program. These initial victories build momentum, secure stakeholder buy-in, and demonstrate the potential of the transformation efforts.

Celebrating the Impact of Initial Success

Achieving initial victories, known as "Quick Wins," is important, but conveying these successes within the organization amplifies their impact.

Communicating the impact of early successes is necessary for building and sustaining momentum in a transformation program. When General Electric (GE) launched its Predix platform, the company made a concerted effort to highlight early achievements to its internal teams and stakeholders. These initial victories were shared through internal newsletters, team meetings, and corporate announcements, creating a ripple effect of enthusiasm and commitment across the organization. Similarly, Siemens emphasized the importance of communication when it introduced its customer-centric platforms. By regularly updating employees and stakeholders on the platform's successes through detailed reports and case studies, Siemens maintained a high level of engagement and motivation throughout the transformation process.

Gaining stakeholder buy-in is essential for the long-term success of any transformation initiative. Early successes provide tangible proof of the program's potential, but effectively communicating these successes is what secures the support of stakeholders. Honeywell's approach with its Forge platform involved showcasing success stories through various communication channels, including internal presentations and external publications. This strategy ensured that stakeholders at all levels understood the value of the platform and were invested in its continued success. ExxonMobil also demonstrated the importance of communication in securing stakeholder buy-in. When rolling out its Chemical Customer Portal, the company used detailed case studies and success metrics to highlight the portal's benefits. These communications were shared through internal portals, town hall meetings, and executive briefings, ensuring that everyone from frontline employees to top executives was aligned and supportive of the initiative.

Early successes not only validate the transformation efforts but also demonstrate the broader potential of the program. Effectively communicating these successes helps to illustrate the full scope of what the program can achieve. BASF, for example, utilized advanced analytics to identify high-potential customers and deliver tailored solutions. By sharing these early success stories through internal reports and presentations, BASF was able to showcase the broader impact of its data-driven approach, encouraging wider adoption and further investment in analytics capabilities. Dow Chemical took a similar approach with its predictive analytics tools. By communicating early successes in monitoring market trends and customer behavior, Dow provided concrete examples of the tools' effectiveness. These stories were shared through company-wide emails, webinars, and strategic meetings, reinforcing the value of the analytics tools and encouraging continued use and support.

Selecting the right communication channels and methods is vital for ensuring the impact of early successes is widely recognized. Honeywell, for example, used a mix of digital and face-to-face communication channels, including email newsletters, intranet updates, and interactive webinars. This multifaceted approach ensured that the success stories reached a broad audience and were understood by all relevant stakeholders.

Siemens also employed a variety of communication methods to share its success stories. By using internal social media platforms, video testimonials, and detailed case studies, Siemens ensured that the successes were communicated effectively and resonated with different audiences within the organization.

Effective communication of early successes is critical to the overall success of a Commercial Excellence transformation program. By highlighting and sharing Quick Wins, companies can build momentum, secure stakeholder buy-in, and demonstrate the broader potential of their initiatives.

Recognizing Key Contributors

Achieving and communicating early success stories, or "Quick Wins," is vital in a Commercial Excellence transformation program. However, recognizing the individuals and teams who contribute to these successes is equally important. This recognition not only fosters a culture of appreciation and motivation but also drives continued engagement and commitment to the transformation process.

Recognition of contributors plays a pivotal role in fostering a culture of appreciation within an organization. When employees feel valued and acknowledged for their efforts, they are more likely to remain engaged and motivated. General Electric (GE) exemplifies this approach by celebrating the achievements of its teams through internal awards and recognition programs. For instance, GE's internal recognition events highlight the efforts of teams that have driven significant advancements in the Predix platform, fostering a sense of pride and accomplishment. Similarly, Siemens has implemented programs to recognize and reward employees who contribute to its customer-centric initiatives. By publicly acknowledging the efforts of these individuals and teams, Siemens not only boosts morale but also encourages others to strive for similar achievements. This culture of appreciation is essential for maintaining high levels of engagement and commitment throughout the transformation journey.

Recognizing contributors is also necessary for driving continued engagement in a transformation program. When employees see that their hard work is acknowledged and rewarded, they are more likely to stay committed to the program's goals. Honeywell's Forge platform success can be attributed in part to its robust recognition programs. By celebrating the achievements of teams that have successfully implemented the platform, Honeywell ensures that employees remain enthusiastic and dedicated to its continued success.

ExxonMobil has also demonstrated the importance of recognition in maintaining engagement. The company's Chemical Customer Portal project included recognition initiatives that highlighted the contributions of key team members. By publicly celebrating these successes, ExxonMobil

127

fostered a sense of ownership and accountability among its employees, driving sustained engagement and effort.

Recognition of contributors not only motivates individuals but also encourages the dissemination of best practices across the organization. When employees are recognized for their successful efforts, their methods and approaches can be shared and adopted by others. BASF, for example, has established a platform where recognized teams can share their strategies and insights. This approach ensures that successful practices are replicated across the organization, driving overall improvement and success. Dow Chemical employs a similar tactic by hosting internal forums where recognized teams present their successful projects. These forums provide an opportunity for knowledge sharing and collaboration, ensuring that effective practices are communicated and adopted throughout the company. This dissemination of best practices is crucial for achieving and sustaining Commercial Excellence.

Effective recognition creates a positive feedback loop that reinforces desired behaviors and outcomes. Siemens, for instance, regularly updates its internal communication channels with stories of employee achievements. This continuous recognition not only motivates current employees but also sets a standard for new hires, establishing a culture of excellence from the outset.

Honeywell's regular communication of success stories through newsletters and meetings ensures that employees at all levels are aware of and inspired by their peers' accomplishments. This positive feedback loop reinforces the importance of dedication and innovation, driving continuous improvement and success.

Recognizing the individuals and teams who contribute to early successes is critical for the overall success of a Commercial Excellence transformation program. By fostering a culture of appreciation, driving continued engagement, encouraging the dissemination of best practices, and creating a positive feedback loop, companies can ensure sustained commitment and motivation.

Generating Self-Sustaining Motivation

Early successes play a pivotal role in any transformation initiative. They provide tangible proof that the program is on the right track, instilling confidence and enthusiasm among employees. General Electric (GE) exemplified this approach through its Predix platform, where initial successes were highlighted and celebrated within the organization. These Quick Wins helped to build momentum, making employees more eager to participate and contribute to the ongoing success of the program.

Similarly, Siemens achieved early victories with its customer-centric platforms by focusing on delivering immediate benefits to key customers. These initial successes were widely communicated within the company, demonstrating the platform's value and encouraging broader engagement.

Celebrating Quick Wins is essential for maintaining high levels of motivation and engagement. Honeywell's Forge platform success can be attributed in part to the company's commitment to celebrating early achievements. By acknowledging and celebrating these wins through internal communications, awards, and recognition events, Honeywell ensured that employees felt valued and motivated to continue their efforts. ExxonMobil's Chemical Customer Portal also leveraged the celebration of early successes to drive engagement. By sharing stories of successful implementations and customer satisfaction, ExxonMobil created a sense of pride and accomplishment among its employees, fostering a positive and motivated work environment.

Recognition of key contributors is a powerful motivator. When employees see their efforts acknowledged, they are more likely to stay committed and continue striving for excellence. BASF, for example, has implemented recognition programs that highlight the contributions of individuals and teams to the company's early successes. By publicly acknowledging these efforts, BASF boosts morale and encourages a culture of appreciation and

129

high performance. Dow Chemical also understands the importance of recognition. The company regularly highlights the achievements of its employees through internal newsletters and recognition events. This approach not only rewards those who contribute to the company's success but also sets a standard for others to follow, driving continuous improvement and engagement.

Achieving early successes and celebrating them effectively helps to enhance focus on organizational goals. When employees see the tangible benefits of their efforts, they are more likely to align their work with the company's objectives. Honeywell's continuous communication of success stories through various channels ensures that employees remain aware of the program's goals and their role in achieving them. Siemens employs a similar strategy by regularly updating its employees on the progress and impact of its customer-centric initiatives. This ongoing communication keeps employees focused on the end goals and motivated to contribute to the company's success.

Building Momentum for More Ambitious Goals

Early successes, or "Quick Wins," serve as proof points that a transformation program is on the right track. They provide tangible evidence that the efforts are yielding positive results, which is essential for gaining buy-in from employees and stakeholders. General Electric (GE) exemplifies this approach through its successful implementation of the Predix platform. By highlighting initial successes and sharing them widely within the organization, GE was able to build momentum and encourage broader participation in the program. Similarly, Honeywell's Forge platform achieved early victories by focusing on delivering immediate benefits to key customers. These successes were communicated effectively within the company, generating excitement and commitment among employees. This early momentum was critical as Honeywell expanded its efforts to more complex, medium-term initiatives.

Effectively communicating early success stories is vital for maintaining and building momentum. When employees and stakeholders are informed about the positive impact of initial efforts, they are more likely to stay engaged and supportive. Siemens, for example, regularly shares detailed case studies and success metrics related to its customer-centric platforms. By showcasing these early achievements, Siemens not only reinforces the value of the program but also inspires others to contribute to its success.

ExxonMobil's Chemical Customer Portal also highlights the importance of communication. By disseminating stories of successful implementations and customer satisfaction through internal channels, ExxonMobil ensured that its employees remained motivated and focused on achieving the program's goals. This continuous communication helped sustain momentum as the company moved on to more challenging projects.

Early successes help build confidence and demonstrate the company's capability to achieve its goals. BASF, for instance, leveraged advanced analytics to identify high-potential customers and deliver tailored solutions. The early wins from these targeted efforts were communicated effectively, showcasing the company's ability to harness data-driven insights for substantial gains. This not only boosted confidence within the organization but also laid the groundwork for tackling more ambitious initiatives. Dow Chemical employed a similar approach by using predictive analytics to anticipate market trends and customer behaviors. The early successes from these initiatives were shared widely, reinforcing the company's ability to leverage advanced technologies for competitive advantage. This foundation of confidence and capability was crucial as Dow expanded its efforts to more complex, medium-term projects.

Building momentum through early successes is essential for preparing a company to take on more challenging, medium-term initiatives. As employees and stakeholders see the tangible benefits of the initial efforts, they become more willing to invest time and resources in the program's continued success. Siemens' continuous improvement initiatives, for example, ensured that the company was well-prepared to tackle more complex projects by building on the momentum generated from early wins. Similarly, Honeywell's strategic communication of success stories helped create a culture of continuous improvement and innovation. By maintaining a focus on early successes and effectively communicating their impact, Honeywell ensured that its employees remained motivated and ready to take on more ambitious initiatives.

Building momentum through early successes is a critical step for any Commercial Excellence transformation program. By achieving and communicating these initial wins, companies can foster enthusiasm, build confidence, and prepare for more challenging, medium-term initiatives.

Chapter 4

If speaking is silver, listening is gold

"For though we love both the truth and our friends, piety requires us to honor the truth first"

— *Aristotle*

Understanding Customer Priorities

Across the manufacturing sector, underestimating the resources and investment necessary to truly grasp customer needs and behaviors remains the most common failure mode.

Manufacturing companies often operate under the misconception that understanding customers is a straightforward task. However, this process involves extensive data collection, sophisticated analytics, and continuous engagement. For instance, General Electric (GE) has made substantial investments in its Predix platform, which collects and analyzes vast amounts of data to understand customer needs better. GE's commitment to leveraging advanced analytics underscores the complexity and resource-intensive nature of customer understanding. Similarly, BASF has invested heavily in advanced analytics to segment its customer base accurately. By dedicating significant resources to understanding customer preferences and behaviors, BASF can tailor its offerings to meet specific needs, driving customer satisfaction and loyalty. This level of investment highlights the effort and financial commitment required to gain meaningful insights into customer behavior.

The financial investment needed to understand customers extends beyond mere data collection. It encompasses the development and maintenance of technological infrastructure, the implementation of advanced analytics tools, and the training of personnel. Honeywell's Forge platform serves as a prime example. The platform's success is attributed to Honeywell's substantial investment in real-time data analytics and customer insights. This investment has enabled Honeywell to provide personalized solutions that enhance customer satisfaction and loyalty.

Dow Chemical also exemplifies the significant financial commitment required. By investing in predictive analytics tools to monitor market trends and customer behaviors, Dow can anticipate customer needs and adjust its strategies accordingly. This proactive approach, fueled by considerable financial investment, ensures that Dow remains responsive to customer demands and maintains a competitive edge.

Underestimating the resources and investment required to understand customers can lead to several adverse outcomes. When companies fail to allocate sufficient resources, they often rely on superficial data and assumptions, resulting in misguided strategies and missed opportunities. Siemens, for instance, has demonstrated the pitfalls of underinvestment through its continuous improvement initiatives. By recognizing the importance of adequate investment in customer insights, Siemens has avoided the common pitfalls and driven significant business improvements.

ExxonMobil's experience with its Chemical Customer Portal further illustrates the consequences of underinvestment. Initially, the portal faced challenges due to insufficient resources allocated to understanding customer needs. However, ExxonMobil's subsequent investment in detailed customer insights and personalized support transformed the portal into a valuable tool that significantly enhanced customer satisfaction and engagement.

To avoid the pitfalls of underestimating customer understanding, manufacturing companies must adopt a strategic approach that prioritizes adequate resource allocation. This includes investing in advanced analytics, building robust technological infrastructure, and continuously engaging with customers to gather meaningful insights. Honeywell's success with its Forge platform, driven by significant financial investment, underscores the importance of a strategic, resource-intensive approach to customer understanding. Similarly, BASF's commitment to advanced analytics and customer segmentation demonstrates how strategic investment can lead to enhanced customer satisfaction and loyalty. By recognizing the true complexity and resource requirements of understanding customers, manufacturing companies can develop strategies that drive long-term success and competitive advantage.

Underestimating Investment Requirements

Understanding customer preferences and priorities is a complex, effort-intensive process that demands meaningful financial investment. Numerous case studies from the public domain highlight companies that failed to allocate the necessary resources, leading to disappointing or unfavorable business outcomes.

One prominent example is the case of Blockbuster. In the early 2000s, Blockbuster failed to recognize the growing customer preference for online streaming and convenient home delivery services. Despite having the resources to pivot, the company did not invest adequately in understanding these emerging preferences. Netflix, in contrast, invested heavily in understanding customer desires for convenience and flexibility, leading to its eventual dominance in the market. Blockbuster's failure to adapt resulted in its decline and eventual bankruptcy in 2010.

Another illustrative case is Kodak. Kodak's reluctance to invest in understanding the shift towards digital photography significantly hampered its ability to compete. Despite inventing the first digital camera, Kodak did not allocate sufficient resources to develop this technology further or understand the changing customer preferences. This oversight allowed competitors like Canon and Sony to capture the market, leading to Kodak filing for bankruptcy in 2012.

In the automotive industry, the case of General Motors (GM) in the early 2000s serves as a cautionary tale. GM failed to recognize the growing customer demand for fuel-efficient vehicles, continuing to focus on producing large SUVs and trucks. This misreading of market signals, coupled with insufficient investment in understanding customer priorities, led to a significant loss of market share to companies like Toyota and Honda, which had invested in fuel-efficient technologies. The culmination of these missteps was GM's bankruptcy filing in 2009, highlighting the dire consequences of not aligning product offerings with customer preferences.

Another critical lesson comes from the retail sector with J.C. Penney. Under the leadership of CEO Ron Johnson, the company implemented drastic changes to its pricing and store layout strategies without thoroughly understanding customer preferences. The lack of continuous engagement and insufficient investment in customer research led to a significant drop in sales and a loss of customer loyalty. This case underscores the importance of continuous customer engagement and the risks of making sweeping changes without adequate research and understanding.

Conversely, companies that have successfully invested in understanding their customers provide valuable lessons. For instance, Apple's success can be attributed to its relentless focus on customer experience and preferences. Apple invests heavily in customer research, continuously refining its products based on customer feedback. This investment in understanding customer needs has resulted in highly successful product lines and strong brand loyalty.

Amazon is another example of a company that excels in understanding customer preferences. Through significant investments in data analytics and customer feedback mechanisms, Amazon continuously adapts its services to meet evolving customer needs. This customer-centric approach has been a cornerstone of its sustained growth and market leadership.

The case studies of Blockbuster, Kodak, General Motors, and J.C. Penney illustrate the critical importance of investing time and resources into understanding customer preferences and priorities. Failing to do so can lead to significant business setbacks or even bankruptcy. On the other hand, companies like Apple and Amazon demonstrate that meaningful investment in customer understanding can drive innovation, customer loyalty, and long-term success.

Understanding Customers can Revolutionize Offerings

When companies approach the task of understanding customer priorities with the right mindset and effectively utilize the information gathered, they can transform both product design and service quality. This transformation not only enhances customer satisfaction but also fundamentally improves operational efficiency and business performance.

Understanding customer priorities begins with strategic data collection. Companies must invest in robust data-gathering mechanisms to capture relevant customer insights. General Electric (GE) exemplifies this approach through its Predix platform, which aggregates data from various sources to provide a comprehensive view of customer needs and behaviors. By investing in advanced analytics, GE can tailor its products and services to meet specific customer demands, leading to enhanced customer satisfaction and loyalty. Similarly, Amazon's use of data analytics to understand customer preferences has revolutionized its operations. By continuously collecting and analyzing customer data, Amazon can personalize recommendations, optimize inventory management, and streamline supply chain processes. This customer-centric approach has been instrumental in Amazon's success, driving both revenue growth and operational efficiency.

Effective use of customer insights can lead to significant improvements in product design. Apple is a prime example of a company that has revolutionized its product offerings based on a deep understanding of customer priorities. By investing in extensive market research and user experience studies, Apple designs products that meet and exceed customer expectations. The iterative design process, fueled by continuous feedback, ensures that each product release resonates with its target audience. Tesla also demonstrates the impact of understanding customer priorities on product design. By focusing on customer demands for sustainable and high-performance vehicles, Tesla has been able to innovate rapidly and dominate the electric vehicle market. The company's commitment to incorporating customer feedback into its design process has resulted in products that not only meet but often exceed market expectations.

Service quality is another area that can be dramatically enhanced through a better understanding of customer priorities. For instance, Ritz-Carlton has built its brand on exceptional customer service by deeply understanding the needs and preferences of its guests. By training its staff to anticipate and respond to customer needs, Ritz-Carlton ensures a personalized and memorable experience for each guest, fostering strong customer loyalty.

In the tech industry, Salesforce leverages customer insights to enhance its service offerings. By analyzing customer data, Salesforce identifies pain points and areas for improvement, allowing the company to provide more responsive and effective support. This focus on customer service quality has been a key factor in Salesforce's growth and customer retention.

Understanding customer priorities can also lead to significant operational improvements. Toyota's implementation of the Toyota Production System (TPS) is a notable example. By incorporating customer feedback into its manufacturing processes, Toyota continuously improves product quality and production efficiency. This customer-centric approach has enabled Toyota to reduce waste, lower costs, and deliver high-quality vehicles that meet customer expectations. Procter & Gamble (P&G) also leverages customer insights to drive operational improvements. By understanding customer preferences, P&G optimizes its product formulations and supply chain processes, ensuring that it can deliver high-quality products efficiently. This focus on Operational Excellence, guided by customer insights, has been pivotal in maintaining P&G's market leadership.

Revolutionizing Operations

When companies approach the task of understanding customer priorities with the right mindset and effectively utilize the information gathered, they can transform both product design and service quality. This transformation not only enhances customer satisfaction but also fundamentally improves operational efficiency and business performance.

Understanding customer priorities begins with strategic data collection. Companies must invest in robust data-gathering mechanisms to capture relevant customer insights. General Electric (GE) exemplifies this approach through its Predix platform, which aggregates data from various sources to provide a comprehensive view of customer needs and behaviors. By

139

investing in advanced analytics, GE can tailor its products and services to meet specific customer demands, leading to enhanced customer satisfaction and loyalty. Similarly, Amazon's use of data analytics to understand customer preferences has revolutionized its operations. By continuously collecting and analyzing customer data, Amazon can personalize recommendations, optimize inventory management, and streamline supply chain processes. This customer-centric approach has been instrumental in Amazon's success, driving both revenue growth and operational efficiency.

Effective use of customer insights can lead to significant improvements in product design. Apple is a prime example of a company that has revolutionized its product offerings based on a deep understanding of customer priorities. By investing in extensive market research and user experience studies, Apple designs products that meet and exceed customer expectations. The iterative design process, fueled by continuous feedback, ensures that each product release resonates with its target audience. Tesla also demonstrates the impact of understanding customer priorities on product design. By focusing on customer demands for sustainable and high-performance vehicles, Tesla has been able to innovate rapidly and dominate the electric vehicle market. The company's commitment to incorporating customer feedback into its design process has resulted in products that not only meet but often exceed market expectations.

Service quality is another area that can be dramatically enhanced through a better understanding of customer priorities. For instance, Ritz-Carlton has built its brand on exceptional customer service by deeply understanding the needs and preferences of its guests. By training its staff to anticipate and respond to customer needs, Ritz-Carlton ensures a personalized and memorable experience for each guest, fostering strong customer loyalty.

In the tech industry, Salesforce leverages customer insights to enhance its service offerings. By analyzing customer data, Salesforce identifies pain points and areas for improvement, allowing the company to provide more responsive and effective support. This focus on customer service quality has been a key factor in Salesforce's growth and customer retention.

Understanding customer priorities can also lead to significant operational improvements. Toyota's implementation of the Toyota Production System (TPS) is a notable example. By incorporating customer feedback into its manufacturing processes, Toyota continuously improves product quality and production efficiency. This customer-centric approach has enabled Toyota to reduce waste, lower costs, and deliver high-quality vehicles that meet customer expectations. Procter & Gamble (P&G) also leverages customer insights to drive operational improvements. By understanding customer preferences, P&G optimizes its product formulations and supply chain processes, ensuring that it can deliver high-quality products efficiently. This focus on Operational Excellence, guided by customer insights, has been pivotal in maintaining P&G's market leadership.

The Impact of Enhanced Product and Service Offerings

Understanding customer needs is an effort-intensive process that requires substantial financial investment. However, when companies improve both the product and service components of their customer offerings, they can achieve a higher level of Operational Excellence.

Investing in understanding customer preferences allows companies to tailor their products to meet specific needs, resulting in higher customer satisfaction and operational efficiency. Apple's continuous innovation in product design, driven by extensive customer research, exemplifies this approach. By listening to customer feedback and anticipating their needs, Apple consistently delivers products that resonate with its audience, such as the iterative improvements seen in the iPhone. This customer-focused innovation has helped Apple maintain a competitive edge and achieve Operational Excellence. Similarly, Tesla's focus on customer needs has led to significant advancements in electric vehicle technology. Tesla's vehicles are designed with features that directly address customer desires for sustainability, performance, and cutting-edge technology. This approach not only enhances customer satisfaction but also streamlines Tesla's production processes, contributing to operational efficiency.

Service quality is a critical component of customer offerings that can significantly impact Operational Excellence. Ritz-Carlton's commitment to exceptional customer service is a prime example. By investing in staff training and creating a culture that prioritizes customer satisfaction, Ritz-Carlton ensures a consistent and high-quality service experience. This focus on service excellence leads to increased customer loyalty and streamlined operations, as satisfied customers are more likely to return and recommend the brand to others. Salesforce also demonstrates the importance of service quality. The company continually analyzes customer feedback to improve its support services, ensuring that clients receive prompt and effective assistance. This dedication to service excellence not only enhances customer satisfaction but also improves operational efficiency by reducing the time and resources needed to address customer issues.

Combining product and service enhancements can lead to synergistic benefits, driving Operational Excellence. For example, Amazon's approach to integrating product offerings with superior service has set a high standard in the retail industry. By leveraging customer data, Amazon tailors its product recommendations and optimizes its inventory management, ensuring that customers find what they need quickly and easily. Additionally, Amazon's investment in efficient delivery services, such as Amazon Prime, enhances the overall customer experience. This integration of product and service improvements has streamlined Amazon's operations, reduced costs, and boosted customer loyalty.

Procter & Gamble (P&G) provides another example of this integrated approach. By using customer insights to improve product formulations and enhance service delivery, P&G ensures that its offerings meet customer expectations. This customer-centric focus leads to operational efficiencies, such as optimized supply chain management and reduced waste, contributing to overall Operational Excellence.

Chapter 5

The eyes have it

« Le seul véritable voyage...ce ne serait pas d'aller vers de nouveaux paysages, mais d'avoir d'autres yeux »

— *Marcel Proust*

Digital Insights: CRM, analytics, and beyond

Many leading companies have implemented detailed programs to identify their most profitable customers by analyzing purchasing patterns, customer behavior, and profitability metrics. These programs use advanced analytics to segment customers based on their potential value and tailor sales strategies accordingly.

1. Machine Learning Algorithms

These include classification and clustering techniques like K-means, decision trees, and neural networks. They help in identifying patterns and grouping customers based on similar behaviors and characteristics. Generative AI can augment traditional Machine Learning (ML) by generating synthetic data to fill gaps, improve model training, and enhance clustering techniques. It can also create more complex models that capture nuanced customer behaviors. Example: Generative Adversarial Networks (GANs) can generate realistic customer behavior scenarios, enriching the data available for training segmentation models.

2. Predictive Analytics

Utilizing regression models, time series analysis, and forecasting methods, predictive analytics allows companies to anticipate future customer behaviors and trends, enabling proactive strategy development. Generative AI can improve predictive models by simulating various future scenarios based on current trends and historical data. It helps in stress-testing models and understanding potential future customer behaviors. Example: Using AI to generate potential market conditions and customer responses to new product launches, aiding in more robust predictions.

3. Big Data Analytics

Leveraging large datasets from multiple sources, big data analytics tools such as Apache Hadoop and Spark enable comprehensive analysis of customer interactions and transactions to uncover deep insights. Generative AI can synthesize large volumes of data, identify hidden patterns, and generate insights that are not immediately apparent from raw data alone.

Example: AI models can generate customer segments based on complex interactions across multiple data sources, providing a more holistic view.

4. Customer Lifetime Value (CLV) Analysis

Tools that calculate the projected revenue from a customer over their entire relationship with the company help prioritize high-value customers. These tools often integrate with CRM systems to provide actionable insights. Generative AI can predict changes in customer value over time by simulating various customer journey scenarios and identifying key drivers of long-term value. Example: AI-generated models can forecast how changes in customer engagement strategies might impact CLV, allowing companies to optimize their approaches proactively.

5. Behavioral Analytics

Focusing on understanding customer actions and preferences through tools like heat-maps, session replays, and journey mapping, behavioral analytics helps in creating highly personalized marketing and sales strategies. Generative AI can create detailed simulations of customer behaviors, helping to test and refine behavioral models. It can also generate personalized content and interactions based on individual customer profiles. Example: AI-driven simulations can model customer responses to different website layouts or marketing messages, providing insights into optimal engagement strategies.

These five categories of analytical tools and approaches are pivotal for manufacturing companies aiming to optimize their customer segmentation efforts and drive targeted, profitable growth. However, the potential of Generative AI to produce deep, actionable insights is already emerging and promises to reach far beyond the limits of the five traditional analytical approaches listed above. This emerging sixth approach involves techniques such as generating detailed customer personas, synthetic data sets for testing, and predictive scenarios that help companies anticipate and shape customer behavior.

6. Generative Customer Insights (GCI)

Persona Generation in Manufacturing Companies

Understanding Existing Customers

- **Data Collection:** Manufacturing companies, such as those in oil and gas or oil refining, often have access to extensive data from various sources, including purchase histories, customer feedback, service interactions, and market research. Generative AI can utilize this data to create detailed customer personas.

- **Profile Creation:** AI analyzes the collected data to identify patterns and characteristics of different customer segments. These personas may include information such as purchasing preferences, typical spending patterns, common behaviors, and specific needs.

- **Insight Extraction:** With these personas, companies can better understand the motivations and pain points of their customers. For instance, an AI-generated persona might reveal that a segment of industrial customers prioritizes sustainability and is willing to pay a premium for environmentally friendly products.

- **Strategy Tailoring:** Companies can use these insights to tailor their marketing, sales, and service strategies. For example, if the persona highlights a preference for digital interactions, the company might invest more in online customer portals and digital marketing efforts.

Identifying Potential Customers

- **Minimal Input Data Utilization:** Even with limited initial data, Generative AI can extrapolate likely characteristics of potential customers by comparing them to existing personas and market trends.

- **Market Expansion:** AI-generated personas can help identify new customer segments that the company might not have previously considered. For instance, an oil refining company might discover a potential market in emerging industries that require specialized lubricants.

- **Targeted Outreach:** By understanding the potential preferences and behaviors of these new customer segments, companies can design targeted marketing campaigns. For instance, they could develop educational content that addresses the specific concerns and interests of these potential customers, increasing the likelihood of engagement and conversion.

Enhancing Customer Experience

- **Personalized Interactions:** Detailed personas allow companies to personalize their interactions with customers. For example, an oil and gas company might use AI to identify a segment of customers who prefer proactive communication about service disruptions or maintenance schedules.

- **Product Development:** Understanding customer personas helps in developing new products or modifying existing ones to better meet customer needs. For instance, an oil refining company might identify a demand for lower-emission fuels and invest in R&D accordingly.

- **Feedback Loop:** By continually updating personas with new data and feedback, companies can keep their strategies aligned with evolving customer preferences. This ongoing process ensures that customer service remains relevant and effective.

Spending Pattern Analysis

- **Revenue Optimization:** AI-generated personas can reveal detailed spending patterns, helping companies identify which products or services generate the most revenue from specific customer segments.

- **Price Sensitivity:** Understanding the spending behaviors of different personas allows companies to adjust pricing strategies. For instance, they might identify that a certain segment is less price-sensitive and more value-focused, enabling higher pricing for premium services or products.

- **Cross-Selling and Up-Selling:** Detailed personas can highlight opportunities for cross-selling and up-selling. For example, an AI persona might show that customers who purchase industrial lubricants are also likely to need maintenance services, leading to bundled offerings.

As an example, let's take the case of an oil and gas company that has targeted an improvement in its customer engagement and service offerings.

Process

- **Data Integration:** The company integrates various data sources, including purchase histories, feedback forms, service logs, and market research.

- **Persona Generation:** Using Generative AI, the company creates detailed personas of their customers, such as industrial clients, small business owners, and large corporate buyers.

- **Insight Utilization:** The personas reveal that industrial clients prioritize efficiency and are willing to invest in high-performance, low-maintenance products.

- **Strategy Development:** The company tailors its product development and marketing strategies to emphasize these features, creating targeted campaigns that address specific client needs.

- **Feedback Incorporation:** The company continually updates the personas with new data, ensuring that their strategies remain aligned with customer expectations and market trends.

By leveraging Generative AI for persona generation, manufacturing companies can gain a deeper understanding of their customers, allowing them to optimize their strategies, enhance customer satisfaction, and ultimately drive growth and profitability.

Understanding Market Conditions

- **Simulation of Economic Scenarios:** Manufacturing companies, such as those in oil and gas or oil refining, can use AI to simulate various economic conditions, such as fluctuations in oil prices, changes in regulatory environments, or shifts in global supply chains. These simulations help companies anticipate how different scenarios might impact their operations and customer behaviors.

- **Market Trends Analysis:** AI can analyze historical data and predict future trends, allowing companies to understand potential market developments. For example, an oil refining company can simulate scenarios involving increased demand for renewable energy sources to see how it might affect customer preferences for traditional fuels.

Customer Reaction Simulation

- **Behavioral Modeling:** AI can create models that predict how customers might react to changes in pricing, product offerings, or market conditions. For instance, if an oil company plans to introduce a new type of fuel, AI can simulate customer adoption rates based on past behaviors and preferences.

- **Preference Changes:** By simulating various scenarios, companies can predict shifts in customer preferences. For example, AI can model how customers might respond to an increase in fuel prices due to new environmental regulations, helping the company plan accordingly.

Strategic Planning:

- **Optimizing Product Mix:** AI simulations can help companies determine the optimal product mix under different market conditions. For instance, an oil refining company can use AI to simulate the profitability of various fuel types under scenarios of changing crude oil prices or environmental regulations.

- **Pricing Strategies:** By simulating customer reactions to different pricing strategies, companies can identify the most effective pricing models. For example, AI can help an oil company determine the impact of tiered pricing on customer segments and overall revenue.

149

Spending Pattern Analysis

- **Forecasting Customer Expenditure:** AI simulations can predict how different market conditions might affect customer spending patterns. For instance, an oil company can model how industrial customers' fuel consumption might change in response to economic growth or recession scenarios.

- **Identifying Spending Trends:** AI can identify trends in customer spending, such as increased investment in energy-efficient technologies. This information helps companies tailor their offerings to meet emerging customer needs.

Risk Management

- **Mitigating Risks:** AI simulations help companies anticipate potential risks and develop strategies to mitigate them. For example, an oil refining company can simulate the impact of a major supply chain disruption and develop contingency plans to ensure continued service to customers.

- **Scenario Planning:** By exploring a range of potential scenarios, companies can prepare for various outcomes. This proactive approach ensures that companies are better equipped to handle uncertainties in the market.

Let's now assume that the same oil and gas company aims to understand the potential impact of a shift towards electric vehicles (EVs) on its fuel business.

Process:

- **Data Integration:** The company integrates historical data on fuel consumption, customer demographics, and trends in the automotive industry.

- **Simulation Setup:** Using AI, the company simulates various scenarios, such as rapid adoption of EVs, moderate growth, and slow adoption rates.

- **Behavioral Modeling:** AI models how different customer segments might respond to each scenario, including changes in fuel consumption and preferences for alternative energy sources.

- **Strategic Insights:** The simulations reveal that rapid EV adoption could significantly reduce demand for gasoline but increase demand for EV-related services and infrastructure.

- **Strategic Planning:** The company uses these insights to diversify its product offerings, investing in EV charging infrastructure and developing new revenue streams.

Enhancing Customer Experience:

- **Personalized Marketing:** AI simulations can predict which customers are most likely to respond to specific marketing campaigns or new product launches. This enables companies to tailor their marketing efforts to maximize impact.

- **Service Customization:** Understanding potential customer reactions helps companies customize their services to meet evolving needs. For example, an oil company might offer personalized energy solutions to industrial clients based on simulated demand patterns.

By leveraging scenario simulation, manufacturing companies can gain a comprehensive understanding of how various market conditions and strategic changes might impact customer preferences, behaviors, and spending patterns. This proactive approach allows companies to develop robust strategies, mitigate risks, and optimize their operations to better serve existing and potential customers, ultimately driving growth and profitability.

Furthermore, by focusing on high-value customers, companies can optimize their resources and efforts, resulting in more effective marketing and sales campaigns. These targeted initiatives often include personalized offers, long-term discounts, and enhanced customer service, which increase customer satisfaction and retention. As a result, these companies experience substantial profit increases and a stronger competitive position in the market.

Optimizing Resources by Focusing on High-Value Customers

Focusing on high-value customers enables companies to allocate their resources and efforts more efficiently. High-value customers typically generate most of a company's revenue, so targeting this segment allows businesses to maximize their return on investment. By identifying and segmenting these customers through advanced analytics and customer relationship management (CRM) systems, companies can tailor their marketing and sales strategies to meet the specific needs and preferences of this lucrative group. This focused approach ensures that marketing budgets are spent on initiatives with the highest potential for return, rather than being diluted across a broader, less profitable customer base.

High-value customers often provide more valuable insights into market trends and product development needs. By engaging closely with these customers, companies can gather detailed feedback that can inform product innovation and improvement. This feedback loop not only helps in enhancing existing products but also in developing new offerings that are more likely to succeed in the market. Additionally, companies can streamline their sales efforts by focusing on high-value customers, as these customers are often more receptive to cross-selling and up-selling opportunities. Sales teams can be trained to recognize and capitalize on these opportunities, further increasing revenue without a proportional increase in effort.

By prioritizing these high-value customers, companies can also achieve greater efficiency in their customer service operations. High-value customers typically expect and warrant a higher level of service, and by focusing resources on this group, companies can ensure that their customer service teams are well-equipped to meet these expectations. This not only enhances customer satisfaction but also builds loyalty, as customers feel valued and understood. In turn, this loyalty translates into repeat business and referrals, creating a virtuous cycle of growth and profitability.

Personalized Offers and Long-Term Discounts

One of the most effective ways to engage high-value customers is through personalized offers and long-term discounts. Personalized marketing involves tailoring promotions and product recommendations based on individual customer data, such as purchase history, browsing behavior, and demographic information. This level of personalization makes customers feel recognized and valued, increasing their likelihood of making a purchase. Advanced data analytics and Machine Learning (ML) algorithms play a very important role in identifying the right offers for the right customers, ensuring that marketing efforts are both relevant and impactful.

Long-term discounts, such as loyalty programs and subscription models, provide high-value customers with ongoing incentives to remain loyal to the brand. These discounts can be structured in various ways, such as cumulative discounts based on total spending, exclusive access to new products, or personalized rewards that resonate with the customer's interests. By offering these benefits, companies not only increase the lifetime value of their customers but also create a sense of exclusivity and appreciation. High-value customers who feel rewarded for their loyalty are less likely to switch to competitors, even if they are offered similar products at a slightly lower price.

Enhanced customer service is another critical component of this strategy. High-value customers often have higher expectations and require more personalized attention. By investing in customer service training and technology, companies can provide a superior experience that addresses these needs. This might include dedicated account managers, faster response times, and proactive communication about new products and services. Enhanced customer service not only improves satisfaction but also builds deeper relationships with customers, fostering long-term loyalty. These relationships are essential for gathering ongoing feedback and ensuring that the company continues to meet the evolving needs of its most valuable customers.

Profit Increases and Competitive Position

The combination of optimized resource allocation, personalized offers, long-term discounts, and enhanced customer service leads to significant profit increases and a stronger competitive position in the market. When companies focus on high-value customers, they maximize their revenue potential by ensuring that their best customers are satisfied and loyal. This customer-centric approach leads to higher customer retention rates, reducing the costs associated with acquiring new customers. Retained customers are also more likely to engage in word-of-mouth marketing, referring friends and colleagues to the company, which further enhances revenue without additional marketing expenses.

Additionally, the insights gained from high-value customers help companies stay ahead of market trends and competitors. By understanding the preferences and behaviors of their most valuable customers, companies can innovate more effectively and tailor their product offerings to meet market demands. This agility allows them to respond quickly to changes in the market and capitalize on new opportunities, giving them a competitive edge. High-value customers also tend to be more forgiving and loyal, providing companies with a stable revenue base even during economic downturns.

In the long run, focusing on high-value customers builds a strong brand reputation. Companies known for excellent customer service, personalized experiences, and loyalty rewards are more likely to attract and retain top-tier customers. This reputation not only attracts new high-value customers but also discourages existing ones from switching to competitors. Furthermore, the increased revenue and profitability from high-value customers enable companies to invest in further growth initiatives, such as expanding product lines, entering new markets, or enhancing technology infrastructure. These investments create a cycle of continuous improvement and competitive strength, ensuring sustained success in the market.

Chapter 6

Good ol' supply and demand

"Virtue is the golden mean between two vices, the one of excess and the other of deficiency"

— *Aristotle*

Optimizing the Supply Side of Commercial Excellence

Optimizing product and customer mix is a critical element in any effort to boost revenue and profitability. One the supply side, companies must understand which of their products have the capacity to earn the highest total margins and make sure that their manufacturing and investment plans support the production of these most profitable products.

For companies aiming to enhance their revenue and profitability, optimizing the product and customer mix is crucial. This process involves identifying which products can generate the highest total margins and ensuring that manufacturing and investment plans support the production of these most profitable products. By focusing on this optimization, companies can achieve significant financial gains and streamline their operations.

The first step in optimizing the product mix is identifying which products have the potential to earn the highest margins. Companies need to invest in robust data analytics to evaluate their product lines comprehensively. General Electric (GE), for instance, utilizes its Predix platform to analyze product performance and customer demand. This data-driven approach allows GE to focus on high-margin products, ensuring that their manufacturing resources are allocated efficiently.

Similarly, Procter & Gamble (P&G) employs advanced analytics to monitor and assess the profitability of its diverse product range. By continuously analyzing sales data and market trends, P&G can identify which products offer the best margins. This enables the company to make informed decisions about production priorities and investment, thereby maximizing profitability.

Once high-margin products have been identified, it is essential to align manufacturing and investment plans to support their production. Tesla provides a compelling example of this approach. By focusing on the production of its high-margin electric vehicles, Tesla has been able to optimize its manufacturing processes and allocate investment toward expanding production capacity. This strategic focus has allowed Tesla to maintain strong profit margins while meeting growing customer demand.

Apple also exemplifies the importance of aligning production and investment with high-margin products. By prioritizing the development and production of its flagship products, such as the iPhone and MacBook, Apple ensures that its resources are directed toward the most profitable segments of its business. This alignment not only boosts revenue but also enhances operational efficiency.

In addition to focusing on high-margin products, companies must also optimize their customer mix. This involves identifying and targeting customers who are likely to contribute the most to revenue and profitability. Amazon, for example, uses sophisticated customer segmentation techniques to identify high-value customers. By offering personalized recommendations and tailored marketing campaigns, Amazon can maximize the lifetime value of its customers, thereby boosting overall profitability. Similarly, Salesforce leverages customer relationship management (CRM) systems to segment its customer base and identify high-potential clients. By focusing sales efforts on these clients, Salesforce can enhance revenue growth without the need for extensive expansion of its salesforce. This targeted approach ensures that resources are utilized efficiently, driving profitability.

Optimizing the product and customer mix is a fundamental step for companies aiming to boost revenue and profitability. By identifying high-margin products and aligning manufacturing and investment plans accordingly, companies can achieve significant financial gains. Additionally, targeting high-value customers ensures that resources are used efficiently, driving overall profitability.

Understanding Product Margins

Identifying which products can earn the highest total margins is a critical business imperative for companies seeking to optimize their manufacturing and investment plans. By focusing on high-margin products, businesses can drive profitability and ensure sustained growth.

Product margin analysis is essential for making informed business decisions. Companies need to understand which products generate the highest profits to allocate resources efficiently and maximize returns. For instance, Apple has consistently focused on high-margin products such as the iPhone and MacBook. By prioritizing these flagship products, Apple ensures that its resources are directed towards areas with the highest potential for profitability, thereby maintaining its market leadership and financial success.

Tesla provides another example of the importance of product margin analysis. Tesla's strategic focus on high-margin electric vehicles, particularly the Model S and Model X, has allowed the company to optimize its production processes and scale operations effectively. This emphasis on profitable products has driven Tesla's revenue growth and established its dominance in the electric vehicle market.

To identify high-margin products, companies must invest in robust data analytics and financial modeling. This involves analyzing sales data, production costs, and market demand to determine which products offer the best return on investment. General Electric (GE) leverages its Predix platform to analyze product performance and customer demand. This data-driven approach enables GE to focus on high-margin products and allocate resources accordingly, which enhances overall profitability. Similarly, Procter & Gamble (P&G) employs advanced analytics to monitor and assess the profitability of its diverse product portfolio. By continuously analyzing sales data and market trends, P&G can identify which products offer the highest margins. This enables the company to make informed decisions about production priorities and investment, maximizing profitability and ensuring efficient resource allocation.

Once high-margin products have been identified, it is important to align manufacturing and investment plans to support their production. This alignment ensures that resources are used efficiently and that the company can meet market demand effectively. For example, Apple's manufacturing strategy prioritizes the production of its high-margin products, ensuring that these items are readily available to consumers and that production costs are kept in check. Tesla's alignment of manufacturing and investment plans with its high-margin products is evident in its expansion of production facilities. By investing in Gigafactories and advanced manufacturing technologies, Tesla can produce high-margin vehicles at scale, reducing unit costs and increasing profitability.

Understanding which products can earn the highest total margins is a fundamental aspect of business strategy. Companies must invest in robust data analytics and financial modeling to identify high-margin products and align their manufacturing and investment plans accordingly.

Manufacturing Plans

To achieve Commercial Excellence, companies must focus on products that offer the highest total margins. Ensuring that manufacturing plans support the production of these high-margin products is therefore essential for driving profitability and maintaining a competitive edge.

The first step in ensuring that manufacturing plans support high-margin products is to identify which products generate the most profit. This requires a thorough analysis of production costs, sales data, and market demand. Apple, for instance, has excelled in this area by focusing on its high-margin products such as the iPhone and MacBook. By consistently analyzing market trends and consumer preferences, Apple ensures that its resources are directed towards the most profitable segments of its product lineup. Similarly, Tesla has identified its high-margin electric vehicles, such as the Model S and Model X, as key drivers of profitability. Tesla's focus on these high-margin products has enabled the company to optimize its manufacturing processes and scale production effectively, leading to sustained revenue growth and market leadership.

Once high-margin products have been identified, it is important to align manufacturing plans to support their production. This involves optimizing production processes, investing in advanced manufacturing technologies, and ensuring that supply chains are capable of meeting demand efficiently. General Electric (GE) provides a notable example of this approach. Through its Predix platform, GE analyzes product performance and customer demand to prioritize the production of high-margin products. This data-driven strategy ensures that manufacturing resources are allocated efficiently, enhancing overall profitability. Procter & Gamble (P&G) also demonstrates the importance of aligning manufacturing plans with high-margin products. By continuously monitoring and assessing the profitability of its diverse product portfolio, P&G can make informed decisions about production priorities. This alignment of manufacturing resources with high-margin products ensures that P&G maximizes profitability while maintaining operational efficiency.

Investing in advanced manufacturing technologies is a key component of supporting the production of high-margin products. Tesla's investment in Gigafactories and cutting-edge manufacturing technologies is a prime example. These investments enable Tesla to produce high-margin vehicles at scale, reducing unit costs and increasing profitability. By aligning its manufacturing plans with high-margin products, Tesla can meet growing market demand while maintaining strong profit margins.

Apple's investment in automation and advanced manufacturing processes further illustrates the benefits of this approach. By leveraging technology to streamline production, Apple ensures that its high-margin products are produced efficiently and at a high quality. This not only boosts profitability but also enhances customer satisfaction by ensuring product availability and reliability.

Ensuring that manufacturing plans support the production of high-margin products is essential for driving profitability and maintaining a competitive edge. Companies must invest in robust data analytics to identify high-margin products and align their manufacturing strategies accordingly.

Investment Plans

Optimizing the supply side of Commercial Excellence requires that companies align their investment plans with the goal of producing high-margin products. This strategic alignment involves directing resources towards the development and production of products that offer the highest returns, thereby optimizing overall business performance.

The first step in aligning investment plans with high-margin product goals is identifying which products generate the highest margins. This requires a thorough analysis of production costs, sales data, and market demand. Companies must invest in robust data analytics tools to gain insights into their product portfolio. For instance, Apple continually analyzes market trends and consumer preferences to prioritize high-margin products like the iPhone and MacBook. By focusing on these flagship products, Apple ensures that its investment plans support the most profitable segments of its business.

Tesla also exemplifies this approach. The company focuses on high-margin electric vehicles, such as the Model S and Model X. By identifying these products as key drivers of profitability, Tesla directs significant investment towards expanding production capacity and enhancing product features, ensuring sustained revenue growth and market leadership.

Once high-margin products have been identified, companies must align their investment plans to support their production. This involves allocating resources for research and development, production facilities, and marketing efforts. General Electric (GE) provides a notable example of this approach. Through its Predix platform, GE analyzes product performance and customer demand, allowing the company to prioritize investments in high-margin products. This data-driven strategy ensures that financial resources are used efficiently, enhancing overall profitability.

Procter & Gamble (P&G) also demonstrates the importance of aligning investments with high-margin products. By continuously monitoring the profitability of its diverse product range, P&G makes informed decisions about where to allocate resources. This strategic alignment of investments ensures that P&G maximizes returns on high-margin products while maintaining operational efficiency.

To support the production of high-margin products, companies must invest in advanced manufacturing technologies and innovation. Tesla's investment in Gigafactories and cutting-edge production technologies is a prime example. These investments enable Tesla to produce high-margin vehicles at scale, reducing unit costs and increasing profitability. By aligning its investment plans with high-margin product goals, Tesla can meet growing market demand while maintaining strong profit margins.

Apple's investment in automation and advanced manufacturing processes further illustrates this approach. By leveraging technology to streamline production, Apple ensures that its high-margin products are produced efficiently and at a high quality. This investment not only boosts profitability but also enhances customer satisfaction by ensuring product availability and reliability.

Aligning investment plans with the goal of producing high-margin products is essential for driving profitability and maintaining a competitive edge. Companies must invest in robust data analytics to identify high-margin products and allocate resources accordingly.

Supply-Side Focus

Understanding which products have the potential to earn the highest margins and ensuring that manufacturing and investment plans support these products is crucial.

The first step in optimizing product mix is identifying which products generate the highest margins. This requires thorough analysis of production costs, sales data, and market demand. Companies must invest in robust data analytics tools to gain insights into their product portfolio. Apple exemplifies this approach by continuously analyzing market trends and consumer preferences to prioritize high-margin products like the iPhone and MacBook. By focusing on these flagship products, Apple ensures that its resources are directed towards the most profitable segments of its business. Similarly, Tesla focuses on high-margin electric vehicles such as the Model S and Model X. By identifying these products as key drivers of profitability, Tesla directs significant investment towards expanding production capacity and enhancing product features, ensuring sustained revenue growth and market leadership.

Once high-margin products have been identified, companies must align their manufacturing plans to support their production. This involves optimizing production processes, investing in advanced manufacturing technologies, and ensuring that supply chains are capable of meeting demand efficiently. General Electric (GE) provides a notable example of this approach. Through its Predix platform, GE analyzes product performance and customer demand, allowing the company to prioritize the production of high-margin products. This data-driven strategy ensures that manufacturing resources are allocated efficiently, enhancing overall profitability. Procter & Gamble (P&G) also demonstrates the importance of aligning manufacturing plans with high-margin products. By continuously monitoring and assessing the profitability of its diverse product range, P&G can make informed decisions about production priorities. This alignment of manufacturing resources with high-margin products ensures that P&G maximizes profitability while maintaining operational efficiency.

Investing in advanced manufacturing technologies is a key component of supporting the production of high-margin products. Tesla's investment in Gigafactories and cutting-edge manufacturing technologies is a prime example. These investments enable Tesla to produce high-margin vehicles at scale, reducing unit costs and increasing profitability. By aligning its manufacturing plans with high-margin products, Tesla can meet growing market demand while maintaining strong profit margins.

Apple's investment in automation and advanced manufacturing processes further illustrates the benefits of this approach. By leveraging technology to streamline production, Apple ensures that its high-margin products are produced efficiently and at high quality. This not only boosts profitability but also enhances customer satisfaction by ensuring product availability and reliability.

Attention to the supply side is critical for optimizing product mix. Companies must invest in robust data analytics to identify high-margin products and align their manufacturing strategies accordingly.

Production Capacity

High-margin products significantly impact a company's profitability and overall financial health. Identifying these products requires a thorough analysis of production costs, sales data, and market demand. Apple, for example, continuously evaluates its product portfolio to prioritize high-margin items like the iPhone and MacBook. By focusing on these flagship products, Apple ensures that its resources are directed towards segments that yield the highest returns, thereby maintaining its market leadership and robust financial performance. Similarly, Tesla's emphasis on high-margin electric vehicles, such as the Model S and Model X, demonstrates the importance of understanding product margins. Tesla's strategic focus on these vehicles has allowed it to optimize production processes and allocate investments effectively, leading to sustained revenue growth and market dominance.

A data-driven approach to product margin analysis is essential for making informed business decisions. General Electric (GE) utilizes its Predix platform to analyze product performance and customer demand, enabling the company to identify and prioritize high-margin products. This data-driven strategy ensures that manufacturing resources are used efficiently, enhancing overall profitability. Procter & Gamble (P&G) also exemplifies the importance of data-driven product margin analysis. By continuously monitoring and assessing the profitability of its diverse product range, P&G can make informed decisions about production priorities. This approach allows P&G to maximize returns on high-margin products while maintaining operational efficiency.

Once high-margin products are identified, companies must align their manufacturing and investment plans to support their production. This involves optimizing production processes, investing in advanced manufacturing technologies, and ensuring that supply chains are capable of meeting demand efficiently. Tesla's investment in Gigafactories and cutting-edge manufacturing technologies is a prime example. These investments enable Tesla to produce high-margin vehicles at scale, reducing unit costs and increasing profitability.

Apple's investment in automation and advanced manufacturing processes further illustrates the benefits of aligning manufacturing and investment plans with high-margin products. By leveraging technology to streamline production, Apple ensures that its high-margin products are produced efficiently and at high quality. This investment not only boosts profitability but also enhances customer satisfaction by ensuring product availability and reliability.

Understanding which products have the capacity to generate high margins is vital for driving profitability and maintaining a competitive edge. Companies must invest in robust data analytics to identify high-margin products and align their manufacturing and investment strategies accordingly.

Boosting Revenues and Profits

The first step in optimizing the product mix is to identify which products offer the highest profit margins. Companies must invest in comprehensive data analysis to evaluate production costs, sales performance, and market demand. Apple serves as a prime example of this approach. By focusing on high-margin products like the iPhone and MacBook, Apple ensures that its manufacturing and investment plans are aligned with the most profitable segments of its product lineup. This strategic focus has enabled Apple to maintain robust financial health and market leadership.

Tesla also illustrates the significance of identifying high-margin products.

The company's emphasis on electric vehicles such as the Model S and Model X has allowed Tesla to optimize its production processes and allocate resources effectively. This focus on profitable products has driven Tesla's revenue growth and cemented its position in the automotive industry.

Targeting the Right Customers

In addition to optimizing the product mix, companies must also identify and target customer segments that are most likely to contribute to revenue growth and profitability. Amazon exemplifies this approach by using sophisticated data analytics to segment its customer base. By offering personalized recommendations and tailored marketing campaigns, Amazon maximizes the lifetime value of its customers, thereby enhancing overall profitability.

Similarly, Salesforce leverages advanced customer relationship management (CRM) systems to segment its clientele and identify high-potential customers. This targeted approach enables Salesforce to concentrate its sales efforts on customers with the greatest potential for growth, resulting in increased revenue without a proportional increase in costs.

Once high-margin products and key customer segments are identified, companies must align their manufacturing and investment plans accordingly. This involves optimizing production processes, investing in advanced manufacturing technologies, and ensuring that supply chains can meet demand efficiently. General Electric (GE) provides a notable example of this alignment. Through its Predix platform, GE analyzes product performance and customer demand, allowing the company to prioritize high-margin products. This data-driven strategy ensures that manufacturing resources are allocated efficiently, enhancing overall profitability. Procter & Gamble (P&G) also demonstrates the importance of aligning manufacturing and investment plans with high-margin products. By continuously monitoring the profitability of its diverse product range, P&G

makes informed decisions about where to allocate resources. This strategic alignment ensures that P&G maximizes returns on high-margin products while maintaining operational efficiency.

Optimizing the product and customer mix is critical for enhancing revenue and profitability. Companies must invest in robust data analytics to identify high-margin products and key customer segments, and then align their manufacturing and investment plans accordingly.

Strategic Alignment around High-Margin Products

The foundation of aligning manufacturing and investment strategies with high-margin products begins with identifying which products offer the highest profit margins. This requires thorough analysis of production costs, sales performance, and market demand. Apple serves as an exemplary case. By consistently focusing on high-margin products like the iPhone and MacBook, Apple ensures its resources are directed towards the most profitable segments of its product lineup. This strategic focus has enabled Apple to maintain robust financial health and market leadership. Similarly, Tesla illustrates the importance of identifying high-margin products. The company's emphasis on electric vehicles such as the Model S and Model X has allowed Tesla to optimize production processes and allocate investments effectively. This focus on profitable products has driven Tesla's revenue growth and cemented its position in the automotive industry.

Once high-margin products are identified, companies must align their manufacturing plans to support their production. This involves optimizing production processes, investing in advanced manufacturing technologies, and ensuring that supply chains are capable of meeting demand efficiently. General Electric (GE) exemplifies this approach. Through its Predix platform, GE analyzes product performance and customer demand, allowing the company to prioritize the production of high-margin products. This data-driven strategy ensures that manufacturing resources are allocated efficiently, enhancing overall profitability. Procter & Gamble

(P&G) also demonstrates the importance of aligning manufacturing plans with high-margin products. By continuously monitoring and assessing the profitability of its diverse product range, P&G can make informed decisions about production priorities. This alignment of manufacturing resources with high-margin products ensures that P&G maximizes profitability while maintaining operational efficiency.

Supporting the production of high-margin products requires strategic investment in advanced manufacturing technologies. Tesla's investment in Gigafactories and cutting-edge manufacturing technologies is a prime example. These investments enable Tesla to produce high-margin vehicles at scale, reducing unit costs and increasing profitability. By aligning its manufacturing plans with high-margin products, Tesla can meet growing market demand while maintaining strong profit margins.

Apple's investment in automation and advanced manufacturing processes further illustrates the benefits of this approach. By leveraging technology to streamline production, Apple ensures that its high-margin products are produced efficiently and at high quality. This not only boosts profitability but also enhances customer satisfaction by ensuring product availability and reliability.

Aligning manufacturing and investment strategies with high-margin products is essential for driving profitability and maintaining a competitive edge. Companies must invest in robust data analytics to identify high-margin products and allocate resources accordingly.

Optimizing the Demand Side of Commercial Excellence

On the demand side, companies must understand which customers would be willing to buy more of these higher margin products (including cross-selling opportunities), and which of those customers may be willing to pay the highest prices. Optimizing the product mix on the supply side and the customer mix on the demand side are the foundational principles of Commercial Excellence.

Demand-Side Understanding

For companies aiming to maximize profitability, understanding which customers are likely to purchase more high-margin products is critical. This knowledge enables businesses to tailor their marketing and sales efforts effectively, ensuring that resources are directed towards the most lucrative opportunities.

Identifying customers who are likely to buy high-margin products is critical for driving revenue and profitability. This requires a thorough analysis of customer data, including purchasing history, spending patterns, and demographic information. Companies must invest in advanced analytics tools to gain insights into customer behavior. For instance, Amazon leverages its vast data analytics capabilities to segment customers and identify those with the highest potential for purchasing high-margin products. By offering personalized recommendations and targeted marketing campaigns, Amazon maximizes customer lifetime value and enhances overall profitability.

Salesforce also exemplifies the importance of identifying high-margin customers. Using its sophisticated customer relationship management (CRM) systems, Salesforce segments its clientele and pinpoints high-potential customers. This targeted approach enables Salesforce to concentrate its sales efforts on customers with the greatest potential for growth, resulting in increased revenue without a proportional increase in costs.

A data-driven approach to customer analysis is essential for identifying high-margin customers. Companies must invest in robust data analytics tools to evaluate customer behavior and preferences. General Electric (GE) provides a notable example of this approach. Through its Predix platform, GE analyzes customer data to identify high-potential customers. This data-driven strategy ensures that marketing and sales resources are allocated efficiently, enhancing overall profitability. Procter & Gamble (P&G) also demonstrates the importance of data-driven customer analysis. By continuously monitoring customer behavior and preferences, P&G can make informed decisions about which customers to target with high-margin products. This strategic alignment of marketing and sales efforts with high-potential customers ensures that P&G maximizes returns on its investments.

Once high-potential customers are identified, companies must align their marketing and sales efforts to target these customers effectively. This involves creating personalized marketing campaigns, offering tailored promotions, and providing exceptional customer service. Apple, for example, uses targeted marketing campaigns to promote its high-margin products like the iPhone and MacBook to high-potential customers. By focusing on these customers, Apple ensures that its marketing and sales efforts are directed towards the most profitable opportunities.

Tesla also illustrates the benefits of aligning marketing and sales efforts with high-potential customers. By offering personalized marketing campaigns and tailored promotions, Tesla successfully targets customers who are most likely to purchase high-margin electric vehicles. This targeted approach has driven significant revenue growth and cemented Tesla's position in the automotive industry.

Identifying customers who are likely to purchase more high-margin products is essential for driving revenue and profitability. Companies must invest in robust data analytics to understand customer behavior and preferences, and to align their marketing and sales efforts accordingly.

Cross-Selling Opportunities

Cross-selling involves offering additional products or services to existing customers, enhancing their overall value and increasing company revenue. Identifying customers who are likely to respond positively to cross-selling initiatives requires a deep understanding of their preferences, purchasing behavior, and potential needs. Amazon is a prime example of a company that excels in cross-selling. By analyzing customer data, Amazon offers personalized recommendations, encouraging customers to purchase complementary products. This strategy has significantly boosted Amazon's sales and customer satisfaction.

Similarly, Salesforce leverages its CRM platform to identify cross-selling opportunities. By tracking customer interactions and preferences, Salesforce can recommend additional services that meet their clients' evolving needs. This targeted approach not only increases sales but also strengthens customer relationships, fostering long-term loyalty.

To effectively recognize cross-selling opportunities, companies must invest in robust data analytics tools. These tools help analyze customer data, identify patterns, and predict future behavior. For instance, Procter & Gamble (P&G) utilizes advanced analytics to understand customer buying habits and preferences. By identifying complementary products, P&G can create targeted marketing campaigns that encourage customers to purchase additional items. This data-driven strategy ensures that cross-selling efforts are focused on the most receptive customer segments, maximizing return on investment.

General Electric (GE) also demonstrates the importance of data-driven cross-selling. Using its Predix platform, GE analyzes customer data to identify potential cross-selling opportunities. This approach allows GE to offer tailored solutions that address specific customer needs, increasing the likelihood of additional sales. By leveraging data analytics, GE enhances its ability to cross-sell effectively, driving revenue growth and improving customer satisfaction.

Once cross-selling opportunities are identified, companies must align their marketing and sales efforts to capitalize on these insights. This involves creating personalized marketing campaigns, offering tailored promotions, and providing exceptional customer service. Apple, for example, uses targeted marketing campaigns to promote accessories and complementary products to iPhone and MacBook users. By focusing on cross-selling, Apple ensures that its marketing and sales efforts drive additional revenue from existing customers.

Tesla also illustrates the benefits of tailored cross-selling efforts. By offering services such as software upgrades, maintenance packages, and home charging solutions, Tesla successfully encourages its customers to purchase additional products. This targeted approach has driven significant revenue growth and strengthened Tesla's customer relationships.

Recognizing cross-selling opportunities with high-potential customers is essential for driving revenue and profitability. Companies must invest in robust data analytics to understand customer behavior and preferences, and to align their marketing and sales efforts accordingly.

Optimizing Product Mix

Understanding which products have the potential to generate the highest margins allows businesses to align their manufacturing and investment strategies effectively.

Identifying high-margin products is the first step in optimizing the product mix. This requires a comprehensive analysis of production costs, sales performance, and market demand. Apple exemplifies this approach by consistently focusing on high-margin products such as the iPhone and MacBook. By prioritizing these products, Apple ensures that its manufacturing resources are directed toward the most profitable segments, maintaining its financial health and market leadership.

Similarly, Tesla's emphasis on electric vehicles like the Model S and Model X illustrates the significance of focusing on high-margin products. By streamlining production processes and strategically allocating investments, Tesla has driven significant revenue growth and established a strong market position.

Once high-margin products are identified, aligning manufacturing plans to support their production is essential. This involves optimizing production processes, investing in advanced manufacturing technologies, and ensuring supply chain efficiency. General Electric (GE) provides a notable example of this strategy. Using its Predix platform, GE analyzes product performance and customer demand to prioritize high-margin products. This data-driven approach ensures efficient allocation of manufacturing resources, enhancing overall profitability. Procter & Gamble (P&G) also demonstrates the importance of aligning manufacturing plans with high-margin products. By continuously monitoring the profitability of its diverse product range, P&G makes informed decisions about production priorities. This alignment maximizes returns on high-margin products while maintaining operational efficiency.

Supporting the production of high-margin products requires strategic investment in advanced manufacturing technologies. Tesla's investment in Gigafactories and cutting-edge manufacturing processes is a prime example. These investments enable Tesla to produce high-margin vehicles at scale, reducing unit costs and increasing profitability. By aligning its manufacturing plans with high-margin products, Tesla meets growing market demand while maintaining strong profit margins.

Apple's investment in automation and advanced manufacturing processes further illustrates the benefits of this approach. By leveraging technology to streamline production, Apple ensures efficient and high-quality production of its high-margin products. This not only boosts profitability but also enhances customer satisfaction by ensuring product availability and reliability.

Optimizing the product mix on the supply side is foundational to business success. Companies must invest in robust data analytics to identify high-margin products and align their manufacturing and investment strategies accordingly.

Optimizing Customer Mix

Understanding which customers are willing to buy more or pay higher prices is essential for maximizing revenue and profitability.

The first step in optimizing the customer mix is to identify high-potential customers who are likely to purchase more products or pay premium prices.

This requires comprehensive data analysis, including purchase history, spending patterns, and demographic information. Amazon, for instance, leverages sophisticated data analytics to segment its customers and identify those with the highest potential for increased spending. By offering personalized recommendations and targeted marketing campaigns, Amazon maximizes the lifetime value of its customers and enhances overall profitability.

Salesforce also exemplifies the importance of identifying high-potential customers. Using its advanced CRM systems, Salesforce segments its clientele to pinpoint customers with significant growth potential. This targeted approach allows Salesforce to focus its sales efforts on the most promising customers, resulting in increased revenue without a proportional increase in costs.

Once high-potential customers are identified, companies must tailor their marketing and sales efforts to engage these customers effectively. This involves creating personalized marketing campaigns, offering tailored promotions, and providing exceptional customer service. Apple, for example, uses targeted marketing campaigns to promote high-margin products like the iPhone and MacBook to high-potential customers. By focusing on these customers, Apple ensures that its marketing and sales efforts drive additional revenue from the most lucrative segments. Similarly, Tesla's approach to targeting high-potential customers involves offering personalized marketing campaigns and tailored promotions for its high-margin electric vehicles. By focusing on customers who are likely to pay premium prices for advanced features, Tesla has driven significant revenue growth and strengthened its market position.

A data-driven approach to customer analysis is essential for identifying high-potential customers. Companies must invest in robust data analytics tools to evaluate customer behavior and preferences. General Electric (GE) provides a notable example of this strategy. Through its Predix platform, GE analyzes customer data to identify high-potential customers. This data-driven approach ensures that marketing and sales resources are allocated efficiently, enhancing overall profitability.

Procter & Gamble (P&G) also demonstrates the importance of data-driven customer analysis. By continuously monitoring customer behavior and preferences, P&G can make informed decisions about which customers to target with high-margin products. This strategic alignment of marketing and sales efforts with high-potential customers ensures that P&G maximizes returns on its investments.

Optimizing the customer mix on the demand side is foundational to business success. Companies must invest in robust data analytics to understand customer behavior and preferences and align their marketing and sales efforts accordingly.

A Balanced Approach to Commercial Excellence Principles

Understanding which products have the highest profit margins and which customers are willing to purchase more or pay higher prices is essential for optimizing overall business performance. This dual focus is a fundamental principle of Commercial Excellence and is necessary for achieving sustained growth and profitability.

On the supply side, identifying high-margin products is the first step toward optimizing the product mix. This involves a thorough analysis of production costs, sales performance, and market demand. For example, Apple has consistently prioritized high-margin products such as the iPhone and MacBook. By focusing on these products, Apple ensures that its manufacturing resources are directed towards the most profitable segments, maintaining robust financial health and market leadership. Similarly, Tesla's emphasis on high-margin electric vehicles like the Model S and Model X demonstrates the importance of understanding product profitability. By investing in advanced manufacturing technologies and streamlining production processes, Tesla has managed to reduce unit costs while increasing profitability, thereby securing a strong market position.

Once high-margin products are identified, it is essential to align manufacturing and investment plans to support their production. This requires optimizing production processes, investing in advanced technologies, and ensuring efficient supply chains. General Electric (GE) exemplifies this approach with its Predix platform, which analyzes product performance and customer demand to prioritize high-margin products. This data-driven strategy ensures efficient allocation of manufacturing resources, enhancing overall profitability. Procter & Gamble (P&G) also highlights the significance of aligning manufacturing plans with high-margin products. By continuously monitoring the profitability of its diverse product range, P&G makes informed decisions about production priorities. This alignment maximizes returns on high-margin products while maintaining operational efficiency.

On the demand side, companies must identify customers who are likely to purchase more products or pay higher prices. This requires comprehensive data analysis, including purchase history, spending patterns, and demographic information. Amazon leverages sophisticated data analytics to segment its customers and identify those with the highest potential for increased spending. Personalized recommendations and targeted marketing campaigns maximize customer lifetime value and enhance overall profitability.

Salesforce exemplifies the importance of identifying high-potential customers through advanced CRM systems. By segmenting its clientele and pinpointing customers with significant growth potential, Salesforce can focus its sales efforts on the most promising customers, resulting in increased revenue without a proportional increase in costs.

A balanced approach to Commercial Excellence integrates insights from both supply and demand sides. Companies must invest in robust data analytics tools to evaluate product profitability and customer behavior. This dual focus ensures that manufacturing and investment plans are aligned with high-margin products while marketing and sales efforts target high-potential customers.

Apple and Tesla illustrate the benefits of integrating supply and demand insights. Apple's strategic focus on high-margin products and targeted marketing campaigns ensures sustained financial performance. Tesla's investment in advanced manufacturing technologies and personalized marketing efforts drives significant revenue growth and strengthens its market position.

Adopting a balanced approach that addresses both supply and demand sides is fundamental to Commercial Excellence. Companies must prioritize the identification of high-margin products and high-potential customers to optimize resource allocation and achieve sustained growth.

Mix Optimization is a Foundational Best Practice

Optimizing both the product and customer mixes lays a solid foundation for the entire Commercial Excellence program. This balanced approach ensures that businesses not only produce the most profitable goods but also target the right customer segments, driving sustainable growth and profitability.

On the supply side, identifying high-margin products is crucial. This involves analyzing production costs, market demand, and sales performance. Companies like Apple have mastered this approach. By focusing on high-margin products such as the iPhone and MacBook, Apple ensures that its manufacturing resources are allocated efficiently, maximizing profitability. This focus on high-margin items allows Apple to maintain a strong market position and robust financial health. Similarly, Tesla's strategy of prioritizing its high-margin electric vehicles, like the Model S and Model X, illustrates the importance of understanding product profitability. By investing in advanced manufacturing technologies and streamlining production processes, Tesla can reduce unit costs and boost profit margins. This focus has propelled Tesla to the forefront of the electric vehicle market.

Once high-margin products are identified, it is essential to align manufacturing and investment plans to support their production. General Electric (GE) provides an excellent example of this approach. Through its Predix platform, GE analyzes product performance and customer demand, allowing it to prioritize high-margin products. This data-driven strategy ensures efficient resource allocation, enhancing overall profitability. Procter & Gamble (P&G) also demonstrates the importance of aligning manufacturing plans with high-margin products. By continuously monitoring product profitability, P&G makes informed decisions about production priorities, maximizing returns on high-margin items while maintaining operational efficiency.

On the demand side, identifying high-potential customers is equally important. This requires a thorough analysis of customer data, including purchase history, spending patterns, and demographic information. Amazon excels in this area, leveraging sophisticated data analytics to segment its customers and identify those with the highest potential for increased spending. By offering personalized recommendations and targeted marketing campaigns, Amazon maximizes customer lifetime value and enhances overall profitability.

Salesforce exemplifies the significance of identifying high-potential customers through its advanced CRM systems. By segmenting its clientele and pinpointing customers with significant growth potential, Salesforce can focus its sales efforts on the most promising customers, resulting in increased revenue without a proportional increase in costs.

A balanced approach to Commercial Excellence integrates insights from both supply and demand sides. This dual focus ensures that manufacturing and investment plans align with high-margin products while marketing and sales efforts target high-potential customers. The success stories of Apple, Tesla, GE, P&G, Amazon, and Salesforce highlight the transformative impact of this approach.

Optimizing both product and customer mixes is foundational to

Commercial Excellence. Companies must invest in robust data analytics to understand product profitability and customer behavior, aligning their strategies accordingly.

Challenges to Optimizing and Balancing Supply and Demand

Many companies struggle to optimize product and customer mix because:

- **Variability:** Production capacities and costs are dynamic, and the cost impacts of switching can be difficult to calculate accurately

- **Unpredictability:** Customer behaviors can change suddenly, and customers' decision-making processes and rationales are often deliberately opaque

For these reasons, Commercial Excellence requires companies to aim at a moving target with an incomplete set of information.

Making these decisions requires substantial organizational courage and strong alignment with an organization's leadership. These critical elements are often scarce commodities, and finding enough of both can be a challenge. However, companies usually find that they have a strong incentive to move forward, even based on imperfect information, because the only alternative is strategic paralysis.

Struggle with Mix Optimization

Companies often encounter significant challenges in optimizing their product and customer mix. Imperfect intelligence and the complexity of making accurate financial estimations exacerbate these difficulties. Despite best efforts, many organizations struggle to align their product offerings and target customers effectively.

One of the primary challenges in optimizing the product and customer mix is the complexity involved in financial estimations. Predicting the profitability of products and identifying high-potential customers requires sophisticated data analytics and accurate forecasting. However, even with advanced tools, companies can falter.

179

For instance, General Motors (GM) faced difficulties in the late 2000s when trying to optimize its product lineup. The company struggled to forecast market demand accurately and misjudged the profitability of several models. This misalignment contributed to significant financial losses and necessitated a major restructuring effort, including the discontinuation of underperforming brands like Pontiac and Saturn. Similarly, Nokia's fall from grace in the smartphone market highlights the pitfalls of misjudging product and customer priorities. Nokia underestimated the growing importance of smartphones and failed to align its product development with market trends. Despite its strong position in the mobile phone industry, Nokia's inability to optimize its product mix in response to changing customer preferences led to a dramatic decline in market share.

Another significant barrier to optimizing the product and customer mix is imperfect intelligence. Companies often rely on incomplete or outdated data, leading to suboptimal decisions. This is particularly challenging in rapidly changing industries where customer preferences and market conditions evolve quickly.

Blockbuster's downfall serves as a cautionary tale of how imperfect intelligence can hinder optimization efforts. The company failed to recognize the shift towards digital streaming and online rentals, focusing instead on its traditional brick-and-mortar rental model. Blockbuster's reliance on outdated intelligence prevented it from adapting to new customer behaviors, ultimately leading to its demise.

In the retail sector, Sears struggled with similar issues. Despite having access to extensive customer data, Sears was unable to effectively leverage this information to optimize its product offerings and customer targeting. The company's inability to adapt to the competitive marketplace and evolving consumer preferences contributed to its prolonged decline and eventual bankruptcy.

To overcome these challenges, companies must invest in advanced analytics and data-driven decision-making processes. Accurate financial estimations and comprehensive customer insights are necessary for optimizing the product and customer mix.

Amazon exemplifies the effective use of advanced analytics. By leveraging sophisticated algorithms and vast amounts of customer data, Amazon continually refines its product offerings and personalizes its marketing efforts. This data-driven approach enables Amazon to stay ahead of market trends and maintain a competitive edge.

Tesla also demonstrates the importance of advanced analytics in optimizing the product mix. The company's investment in data analytics allows it to predict market demand accurately and prioritize the production of high-margin vehicles. This strategic focus has been instrumental in Tesla's rapid growth and profitability.

Optimizing the product and customer mix is a complex but essential aspect of achieving Commercial Excellence. Companies must navigate the challenges of imperfect intelligence and complex financial estimations to align their offerings with market demand effectively.

Complex Production Dynamics

Companies often face the daunting task of optimizing their product and customer mix amidst constantly changing production capacities and related costs. This ongoing fluctuation presents a significant analytical challenge, requiring businesses to make complex trade-offs to maximize profitability and efficiency. Despite the availability of advanced data analytics, many organizations struggle to achieve the optimal balance, highlighting the need for robust analytical tools and strategic foresight.

One of the primary challenges in optimizing production capacities is the inherent variability in manufacturing processes. Production lines must adapt to changes in demand, supply chain disruptions, and technological advancements. For instance, General Motors (GM) frequently adjusts its production schedules to align with shifting market demands and supply chain fluctuations. This requires GM to continually assess the cost implications of these adjustments, ensuring that production remains economically viable.

Tesla also exemplifies the complexity of managing production capacities. The company's gigafactories must balance the production of high-demand models like the Model 3 and Model Y with the introduction of new models such as the Cybertruck. This balancing act involves continuous analysis of production costs, capacity constraints, and market demand to ensure optimal resource allocation.

Financial estimations play a very important role in making informed production decisions. Companies must accurately forecast costs associated with raw materials, labor, and overheads to determine the profitability of different product lines. However, these estimations are fraught with uncertainties. Fluctuating prices of raw materials, changes in labor costs, and evolving regulatory requirements add layers of complexity to the financial forecasting process.

A notable example is Boeing, which faced significant challenges with its 737 MAX production. The grounding of the aircraft led to unexpected costs and forced Boeing to reevaluate its production strategy. The company had to consider the financial trade-offs between continuing production, which incurred storage and maintenance costs, and halting production, which could disrupt supply chains and affect long-term profitability. Similarly, Apple's decision-making process involves intricate financial estimations. The tech giant must constantly evaluate the cost implications of producing high-end models like the iPhone 13 Pro while managing the production of more affordable models to capture different market segments. This requires a detailed understanding of production costs and market dynamics to ensure that investment in manufacturing aligns with profitability goals.

To navigate these complexities, companies increasingly rely on advanced analytical tools and techniques. Predictive analytics, Machine Learning

(ML), and simulation models are instrumental in providing insights into production capacities and cost structures. These tools enable businesses to anticipate potential disruptions, model different scenarios, and make data-driven decisions.

For example, Procter & Gamble (P&G) employs advanced analytics to optimize its production processes. By integrating real-time data from various sources, P&G can dynamically adjust production schedules, manage costs, and respond swiftly to market changes. This analytical approach enhances the company's ability to maintain a competitive edge and ensure operational efficiency.

Optimizing production capacities and managing related costs is a complex analytical challenge that requires a strategic and data-driven approach. Companies must continuously assess and adjust their production strategies.

Unpredictable Customer Behavior

Companies often find themselves grappling with sudden and unforeseen shifts in consumer preferences that pose a significant challenge to optimizing both product and customer mixes. This volatility makes it difficult for businesses to forecast demand accurately and align their strategies accordingly, often leading to suboptimal decisions and missed opportunities.

One of the primary hurdles that companies face is the inherent unpredictability of customer behavior. Consumer preferences can change overnight, influenced by a myriad of factors such as technological advancements, economic shifts, and cultural trends. For instance, the sudden rise in demand for remote work solutions during the COVID-19 pandemic caught many businesses off guard. Companies like Zoom and Microsoft Teams saw exponential growth, while others struggled to adapt to the rapid change in market dynamics.

Similarly, the fashion industry is notorious for its rapidly changing trends. Fast fashion brands like Zara and H&M must constantly monitor and respond to the latest consumer preferences to remain relevant. The unpredictability of what consumers will find appealing next season requires these companies to be agile and responsive, making it challenging to optimize their product lines and inventory levels.

The unpredictability of customer behavior is further complicated by the imperfect intelligence that companies often rely on. Data collected from past sales, customer surveys, and market research can provide valuable insights, but it is not always accurate or complete. This imperfect intelligence can lead to misguided decisions and strategic misalignments.

For example, Blockbuster's failure to recognize the shift towards digital streaming is a classic case of relying on outdated intelligence. Despite having access to extensive data on rental patterns and customer preferences, Blockbuster underestimated the impact of emerging technologies and changing consumer behaviors. This misjudgment ultimately led to its downfall, as it failed to compete with the likes of Netflix, which had a better grasp of the evolving market.

Making accurate financial estimations in the face of unpredictable customer behavior is another significant challenge. Companies must consider various factors, including production costs, marketing expenses, and potential revenue streams. However, the fluid nature of customer preferences makes these estimations highly complex and prone to error.

Apple, for instance, must continuously forecast the demand for its new products, balancing production costs with anticipated sales. The company's ability to gauge consumer interest in its latest iPhone models is critical to its financial success. Misjudging this interest could result in either excess inventory or lost sales opportunities, highlighting the delicate balance required in financial planning.

To mitigate the impact of unpredictable customer behaviors, companies are increasingly turning to advanced analytics and Machine Learning (ML) techniques. These tools enable businesses to analyze vast amounts of data in real-time, identify emerging trends, and make more informed decisions.

Amazon is a prime example of a company leveraging advanced analytics to stay ahead of consumer trends. By analyzing purchasing patterns, search queries, and customer reviews, Amazon can predict shifts in consumer preferences and adjust its product offerings accordingly. This proactive approach allows Amazon to optimize its product mix and enhance customer satisfaction, even in the face of unpredictable behaviors.

The unpredictability of customer behaviors presents a significant challenge for companies striving for Commercial Excellence. Imperfect intelligence and the complexity of financial estimations exacerbate this issue, making it difficult for businesses to optimize their product and customer mixes. However, by leveraging advanced analytics and remaining agile, companies can better navigate these uncertainties and align their strategies with evolving consumer preferences.

Opaque Customer Decision-Making

Companies attempts to optimize their customer and product mix can be frustrated by the fact that customers usually make their buying decisions behind closed doors, and often using their own proprietary decision-making framework. Often, their decisions are based on factors that are not immediately apparent to suppliers, leaving little room for anticipation and adjustment in production planning.

In addition, customers frequently make purchasing choices based on a blend of personal preferences, external influences, and situational factors. The factors behind their decisions can be complex, making it difficult for companies to discern the underlying motivations. For example, a customer's decision to switch from one brand to another might be influenced by factors such as perceived quality, social influence, or even a single negative experience, none of which are readily visible to the supplier.

The fashion industry provides a clear illustration of this phenomenon. Retailers like Zara and H&M must constantly adapt to ever-changing consumer tastes, which are influenced by a multitude of factors ranging from seasonal trends to cultural shifts. The opacity of these buying decisions requires these companies to remain highly agile and responsive to subtle changes in consumer behavior.

The lack of clear insights into customer decision-making processes results in imperfect intelligence, which complicates financial estimations and strategic planning. When companies cannot accurately predict demand, they risk either overproducing or underproducing their products, both of which have significant financial implications.

A notable example of this challenge is seen in the automotive industry. Companies like Ford and General Motors must predict consumer preferences for different models and features. The sudden shift in consumer preference towards electric vehicles (EVs) caught many traditional automakers off guard, leading to significant adjustments in production plans and investment strategies. The opacity of consumer decisions in this context meant that these companies had to quickly realign their production capabilities to meet the unexpected demand for EVs.

Making accurate financial estimations becomes particularly challenging when customer behavior is unpredictable and opaque. Companies must consider a variety of cost factors, including production, marketing, and distribution, while also trying to anticipate changes in consumer demand.

Apple's experience with its product launches highlights this complexity. The tech giant must estimate the demand for new iPhone models months in advance. Any misjudgment can easily lead either to an oversupply, resulting in excess inventory costs, or to an undersupply, leading to missed sales opportunities. The opaque nature of consumer buying decisions adds an additional layer of difficulty to these estimations.

To navigate the uncertainties of opaque customer decisions, companies are increasingly turning to advanced analytics. These tools can help uncover hidden patterns and provide deeper insights into consumer behavior. Machine Learning (ML) algorithms, for example, can analyze large datasets to identify subtle trends that might not be immediately apparent.

Amazon is a prime example of leveraging advanced analytics to understand customer behavior. By analyzing purchasing patterns and browsing histories, Amazon can make highly personalized product recommendations, thereby increasing the likelihood of purchase. This data-driven approach allows Amazon to better anticipate customer needs and adjust its product offerings accordingly.

The opacity of customer buying decisions presents a formidable challenge for companies striving for Commercial Excellence. The difficulty in understanding and anticipating these decisions can lead to imperfect intelligence and complex financial estimations. However, by investing in advanced analytical tools and fostering a culture of adaptability, companies can better navigate these uncertainties and optimize their product and customer mix.

Tolerance of Imperfect Information

Optimizing customer and product mixes can be a challenging task for many companies. The complexity of analysis, unpredictability of customer behavior, and the absence of reliable data and tools often leave businesses making important decisions based on incomplete information.

The optimization of customer and product mixes involves sophisticated analytical processes. These analyses must consider various factors such as market trends, customer behaviors, production capacities, and financial projections. The complexity of these variables makes it difficult to generate accurate and comprehensive insights. For instance, in the automotive industry, companies like Ford and Tesla must continuously evaluate consumer preferences for electric versus traditional vehicles, adjusting their production strategies accordingly. The analytical complexity in predicting such shifts can lead to suboptimal decisions if not managed effectively.

Even when companies have access to data, it may not always be reliable or comprehensive. Incomplete or outdated information can lead to erroneous conclusions. This is particularly evident in rapidly changing markets where real-time data is critical. Retail giants like Walmart and Amazon invest heavily in real-time data analytics to stay ahead of market trends. However, smaller retailers without access to such advanced tools may struggle to keep pace, making decisions based on incomplete datasets.

Given these constraints, companies are often forced to make decisions with an incomplete set of information. This reality underscores the importance of agility and flexibility in strategic planning. Businesses must develop robust frameworks that allow for quick adjustments as new data becomes available. For example, during the COVID-19 pandemic, many companies had to pivot rapidly to address sudden changes in consumer demand and supply chain disruptions. Those with flexible and adaptive strategies were better positioned to navigate the uncertainties.

To mitigate the risks associated with incomplete information, companies are increasingly turning to advanced technologies such as Artificial Intelligence (AI) and Machine Learning (ML). These tools can analyze vast amounts of data, identify patterns, and provide predictive insights that help bridge the information gap. For instance, Procter & Gamble uses AI-driven analytics to forecast demand and optimize its product mix. By leveraging these technologies, companies can enhance their decision-making processes even when data is imperfect.

The challenge of optimizing customer and product mixes in the face of incomplete information is a significant one. Analytical complexity, customer confidentiality, and the absence of reliable data and tools complicate this process. However, by embracing agility, leveraging advanced technologies, and adopting flexible strategies, companies can navigate these challenges effectively. Understanding and adapting to these constraints is critical for achieving Commercial Excellence and sustaining long-term success.

The Organizational Courage to Act

The process of optimizing customer and product mix is often fraught with challenges, primarily due to the necessary reliance on imperfect or incomplete information. Making such high-stakes decisions demands a combination of organizational courage and strong leadership alignment to manage the inherent risks effectively.

Businesses often operate in environments where complete and accurate data is a luxury. Market dynamics, changing consumer preferences, and competitive pressures contribute to the complexity of making well-informed decisions. For example, the consumer electronics industry frequently faces rapid technological advancements and shifting customer preferences. Companies like Samsung and Apple must continually adapt their product offerings based on forecasts that may not always capture the full picture. These decisions are necessary yet made under the cloud of uncertainty, emphasizing the need for strong leadership to guide the process.

Organizational courage involves the willingness to make bold decisions despite the risks associated with imperfect information. This courage is essential for driving innovation and staying competitive. A prime example is Tesla's decision to invest heavily in electric vehicles (EVs) long before the market fully embraced the technology. Despite facing skepticism and the lack of immediate demand, Tesla's leadership, under Elon Musk, demonstrated remarkable courage by committing to a vision of a sustainable future. This bold move paid off as Tesla now leads the EV market, highlighting how courageous decision-making can yield significant rewards.

Strong leadership alignment ensures that all levels of management understand and support the decisions made, even when based on incomplete data. This alignment fosters a unified approach to risk management and strategic execution. For instance, during the transition to cloud computing, Microsoft had to realign its leadership and strategy under Satya Nadella's guidance. Nadella's emphasis on a cloud-first approach required the entire organization to shift its focus and resources, despite uncertainties about market acceptance. The alignment of leadership at

Microsoft facilitated this transformation, resulting in the company becoming a dominant player in the cloud services sector.

Understanding and assuming risks associated with decisions made under uncertainty is critical. Companies must establish robust risk management frameworks that allow for flexibility and adaptation. A structured approach to risk assessment can help identify potential pitfalls and devise contingency plans. For example, Procter & Gamble (P&G) employs rigorous risk management practices to navigate market uncertainties. By continuously monitoring market trends and consumer behaviors, P&G can adjust its product mix and marketing strategies proactively, reducing the impact of unforeseen changes.

Although perfect information may be unattainable, leveraging advanced analytical tools can significantly enhance decision-making capabilities. Machine Learning (ML) and predictive analytics enable companies to generate insights from vast datasets, uncovering patterns that might not be immediately apparent. Amazon's use of data analytics to optimize its product recommendations and inventory management exemplifies this approach. By harnessing the power of data, Amazon can make more informed decisions, even in the face of incomplete information.

Making critical decisions about customer and product mix optimization in the presence of imperfect information is a complex yet essential endeavor. It requires organizational courage and strong leadership alignment to understand and manage the associated risks. Companies must foster a culture of bold decision-making, supported by robust risk management practices and advanced analytical tools. By doing so, they can navigate the uncertainties and achieve sustainable growth and profitability.

Avoiding Strategic Paralysis

The process of optimizing product and customer mixes is inherently complex and is often further complicated by the absence of perfect or complete information. The temptation to delay decision-making until perfect data is available can be strong. However, this approach, often referred to as *strategic paralysis*, can lead to significantly less favorable outcomes than making informed decisions based on the best available information.

Strategic paralysis occurs when companies, overwhelmed by the uncertainty and potential risks associated with incomplete data, choose to avoid making any decisions. This inaction can stymie growth, stifle innovation, and lead to missed opportunities. For instance, Kodak's reluctance to fully embrace digital photography, despite early indications of its potential, allowed competitors like Canon and Sony to dominate the market. Kodak's strategic hesitation, largely due to uncertainty and fear of cannibalizing its existing product lines, ultimately led to its decline.

In contrast, companies that embrace the challenge of making decisions with imperfect information often fare better. These businesses understand that waiting for perfect data can result in missed opportunities and lost competitive advantage. A dynamic approach that balances risk with informed action can drive innovation and growth, even in uncertain conditions.

Making decisions based on imperfect information requires a blend of analytical rigor and organizational courage. Companies must develop robust frameworks that allow for the integration of incomplete data into their decision-making processes. This approach involves setting clear objectives, identifying key assumptions, and continuously monitoring outcomes to make necessary adjustments.

Consider Amazon's early days. The company made strategic decisions about its product offerings and market expansion based on limited and often imperfect data. Despite this, Amazon's willingness to act decisively allowed it to quickly adapt and capitalize on emerging trends. This proactive approach facilitated Amazon's growth into a global e-commerce giant, demonstrating the power of good faith optimization.

Leveraging advanced analytics and Machine Learning (ML) can enhance a company's ability to make informed decisions with incomplete data. These technologies can identify patterns and provide predictive insights, enabling businesses to make more accurate forecasts and strategic choices. For example, Procter & Gamble uses data analytics to optimize its product mix and supply chain operations, allowing it to respond swiftly to market changes and consumer demands.

However, the human element remains crucial. Strong leadership is essential for fostering a culture that embraces informed risk-taking. Leaders must communicate the rationale behind decisions, align teams around shared goals, and encourage a mindset that views uncertainty as an opportunity rather than a barrier.

Waiting for perfect data to arrive, upon which a company can construct a perfect optimization calculation is often not a viable option. However, the failure to make timely decisions can substantially hinder commercial and operational health, leading to disastrous outcomes. Rather than allowing this situation to arise, companies must develop the organizational courage to make decisions based on the best available information, leveraging advanced analytics and strong leadership to navigate the inevitable uncertainties.

Chapter 7

The habit of duty without pain

"La diligencia es la madre de la buena fortuna"

— *Miguel de Cervantes (Don Quixote)*

Selective Prioritization

In manufacturing companies, salespeople often excel in building relationships and closing deals but sometimes shirk the less glamorous aspects of their roles. This issue stems from the fact that salespeople frequently hold valuable personal relationships with key decision-makers within their clients' organizations, leading their employers to overlook their reluctance to engage in the more tedious aspects of the job. Although this practice may yield short-term gains, it can hinder long-term success and organizational growth.

Sales teams that embrace the entirety of their responsibilities typically outperform those that do not. A well-rounded approach to sales involves not only maintaining customer relationships and closing deals but also engaging in administrative tasks, following up on leads, and providing thorough post-sales support. These activities, although less exciting, are essential for sustaining customer satisfaction and loyalty. For instance, a salesperson who diligently follows up on a customer's concerns or feedback can identify potential issues early, preventing dissatisfaction and fostering a stronger relationship.

Companies like Cisco have demonstrated the benefits of encouraging their sales teams to adopt a comprehensive approach. By emphasizing the importance of all aspects of the sales process, Cisco has seen significant improvements in customer satisfaction and overall sales performance. Their salespeople are trained to understand the technical aspects of their products, enabling them to provide more informed and effective support to their clients

However, changing the behavior of sales teams requires a cultural shift within the organization. Management must set clear expectations and provide the necessary support and training to ensure that salespeople understand and accept their full range of responsibilities. This can involve implementing performance metrics that reward not only sales figures but also the completion of administrative tasks and customer support activities.

For example, companies could introduce a balanced scorecard approach that evaluates sales performance based on multiple criteria, including customer feedback and follow-up rates.

Furthermore, employers must address the underlying reasons why salespeople avoid certain tasks. This can be achieved through regular training sessions and workshops designed to improve skills in areas such as time management, organization, and customer service. By equipping sales teams with the tools and knowledge they need to excel in all aspects of their roles, companies can foster a more balanced and effective sales force.

Additionally, organizations must create an environment that encourages accountability. This involves setting clear, achievable goals and regularly reviewing performance against these targets. By holding salespeople accountable for their actions and providing constructive feedback, employers can ensure that all aspects of the sales process are given the attention they deserve.

Although it may seem tempting for manufacturing companies to tolerate selective engagement from their sales teams due to their valuable client relationships, this approach is ultimately detrimental to long-term success. By promoting a culture that values all aspects of the sales role, providing comprehensive training, and fostering accountability, companies can ensure that their sales teams are well-rounded and effective. This holistic approach not only improves customer satisfaction and loyalty but also drives sustained organizational growth and success.

The Client Relationship Conundrum

Sales roles are often marked by a dichotomy between relationship-building activities and administrative tasks. It is well-documented that many salespeople gravitate toward the former, enjoying the engagement and rapport-building with clients while shying away from the latter. This tendency, though understandable, can have significant implications for a company's overall performance and efficiency.

Relationship-building is inherently gratifying for many sales professionals. Engaging with clients, understanding their needs, and providing solutions creates a sense of achievement and personal connection that is both motivating and fulfilling. However, the administrative side of sales, which includes data entry, report generation, and handling complex customer issues such as price negotiations, often takes a back seat. These tasks, although less enjoyable, are critical for maintaining accurate records, ensuring customer satisfaction, and optimizing sales processes.

One reason for this imbalance is the nature of sales incentives. Salespeople are typically rewarded based on their sales figures and client acquisitions, rather than their proficiency in administrative duties. This focus on immediate results can lead to the neglect of essential tasks that support long-term success. For instance, failing to properly document customer interactions can lead to misunderstandings and missed opportunities, ultimately affecting the company's bottom line.

In addition, avoiding difficult conversations such as price negotiations can undermine the sales process. These conversations are necessary for setting clear expectations and building trust. When salespeople evade these discussions, it can lead to unrealistic customer expectations and potential conflicts down the line. It's important to remember that customers value transparency and honesty; addressing issues head-on can strengthen relationships more effectively than avoiding them.

Leading companies recognize this challenge and implement measures to ensure that their sales teams embrace all aspects of their roles. Training programs that emphasize the importance of administrative tasks and difficult conversations are crucial. Additionally, integrating technology, such as customer relationship management (CRM) systems, can streamline administrative tasks, making them less burdensome for sales staff. CRM systems not only improve efficiency but also provide valuable insights that can enhance customer interactions.

Performance metrics should also be adjusted to reflect the importance of these tasks. By rewarding salespeople for maintaining accurate records and successfully navigating challenging conversations, companies can encourage a more balanced approach. This holistic view of sales performance not only enhances individual productivity but also contributes to the company's overall success.

Aligning Role Priorities with Company Priorities

Leading companies understand the importance of instilling organizational discipline within their sales teams. This discipline involves setting clear expectations that each salesperson's primary responsibility is to the immediate financial wellbeing of their employer. By prioritizing tasks based on their relative importance to the company's success, these companies ensure a balanced and effective approach to sales management.

Sales professionals often excel at building relationships and closing deals, but they may neglect the less enjoyable aspects of their roles, such as administrative duties and challenging customer conversations. Leading companies address this by fostering a culture of discipline that emphasizes the importance of these tasks. For example, Salesforce, a leader in customer relationship management software, encourages its sales teams to maintain meticulous records and engage in thorough follow-ups with clients. This practice ensures that no detail is overlooked, leading to better customer satisfaction and higher retention rates.

One key strategy is to integrate task prioritization into the sales process. This involves identifying tasks that have the greatest impact on the company's financial health and ensuring that these are completed first. Administrative duties, while often seen as mundane, are essential for maintaining accurate records and providing a solid foundation for future sales efforts. By emphasizing their importance, companies can ensure that sales teams do not overlook these critical tasks.

Another important aspect is the handling of difficult customer conversations, such as price negotiations. Leading companies equip their sales teams with the training and tools necessary to navigate these challenging discussions effectively. For instance, Microsoft provides its sales representatives with extensive negotiation training, enabling them to handle objections and secure favorable terms without compromising on value. This not only enhances the company's profitability but also builds trust and credibility with customers.

Performance metrics should also reflect the comprehensive nature of sales responsibilities. By incorporating administrative efficiency and successful negotiation outcomes into performance evaluations, companies can encourage a more balanced approach. This holistic view of performance ensures that sales teams are rewarded not just for closing deals, but also for maintaining the organizational health that supports sustained success.

Technology can also play a helpful role in supporting these efforts. Customer Relationship Management (CRM) systems, like those offered by HubSpot, streamline administrative tasks and provide valuable insights into customer behavior. These systems allow sales teams to manage their time more effectively, ensuring that all critical tasks are completed promptly.

Common Sales Team Failure Modes

Less successful companies often fall into the trap of allowing their sales teams to prioritize personal relationships with customers over critical sales objectives. Although maintaining close personal relationships is undeniably important, it should not come at the expense of essential tasks such as price negotiations, sharing customer updates, or inputting key data into customer relationship management (CRM) systems. This neglect can significantly hinder a company's overall performance and long-term success.

One major consequence of this approach is the lack of accurate and up-to-date information in CRM systems. These systems are vital for managing customer relationships, forecasting sales, and making informed business decisions. When salespeople fail to input key data, it creates information gaps that can lead to missed opportunities and inefficient resource allocation. For example, a study by Salesforce revealed that companies using CRM systems to their full potential can increase sales by up to 29%. However, this potential is only realized when the data is accurate and comprehensive.

Neglecting price negotiations can also have a direct impact on profitability. Salespeople who shy away from tough conversations about pricing may secure deals, but often at the expense of the company's margins. Effective price negotiations are necessary for maintaining profitability and ensuring that the value of the product or service is not undermined. Companies like Microsoft and Apple, known for their rigorous sales training programs, equip their sales teams with the skills needed to handle these negotiations effectively, thereby protecting their margins and enhancing profitability.

Another critical area often neglected is the sharing of customer updates. Regular updates about customer needs, preferences, and feedback are essential for refining product offerings and improving customer satisfaction. When sales teams fail to communicate this information, it creates a disconnect between the company's strategy and the actual needs of the market. This disconnect can lead to missed opportunities for innovation and a failure to meet customer expectations. For instance, IBM has a strong emphasis on customer feedback loops, ensuring that sales teams consistently relay valuable insights back to the company, which drives continuous improvement.

As a rule, less successful companies that allow their salespeople to neglect essential tasks in favor of maintaining relationships ultimately compromise their own long-term success.

Developing a Culture of Discipline is Key

Building a disciplined sales team is paramount for companies striving for Commercial Excellence. When sales teams neglect essential tasks such as data entry, price negotiations, and customer updates, it creates significant gaps in information and undermines a company's strategic initiatives. To counteract this, leading companies have recognized the wisdom in Mark Twain's advice: "Do something every day that you don't want to do." Embracing this mindset can transform a sales team's performance and foster a culture of accountability and success.

The failure to instill discipline within sales teams can quickly erode efforts to build a culture of Commercial Excellence. Without accurate and comprehensive data, analytics systems are deprived of the information necessary to drive informed decision-making. For instance, when salespeople neglect to update CRM systems with critical customer information, it leads to inaccurate forecasts, missed opportunities, and inefficient resource allocation. A Salesforce study highlights that companies effectively utilizing CRM systems can see sales increase by up to 29%, a potential realized only when data is complete and current.

Neglecting price negotiations is another area where a lack of discipline can severely impact a company's profitability. Salespeople who avoid tough pricing conversations may secure deals, but often at the expense of the company's margins. This avoidance can set a precedent, leading to a culture where underpricing becomes the norm. In contrast, companies like Microsoft and Apple invest heavily in training their sales teams to handle price negotiations effectively, ensuring that each deal contributes positively to the bottom line.

The reluctance to share customer updates can also create a significant disconnect between a company's strategy and market needs. Regularly updating the organization about customer preferences and feedback is necessary for refining products and services. For example, IBM has developed robust feedback loops where sales teams consistently relay valuable insights, driving continuous improvement. Without this flow of information, companies risk becoming out of touch with their customers, resulting in a failure to innovate and meet market expectations.

Leading companies understand that success in sales requires more than just relationship-building. It demands a comprehensive approach where all responsibilities, enjoyable or not, are given due importance. By cultivating a disciplined environment where salespeople are expected to perform a full range of tasks, these companies ensure alignment between their sales efforts and broader business goals. This approach not only drives immediate sales success but also supports long-term strategic initiatives.

Implementing a culture of discipline starts with leadership. Executives and sales managers must set clear expectations and provide the necessary support and training to help their teams succeed. Regular performance reviews and feedback sessions can help identify areas for improvement and ensure that all sales activities are aligned with the company's strategic objectives. Furthermore, recognizing and rewarding those who consistently meet their responsibilities reinforces the importance of a disciplined approach.

For example, General Electric (GE) has long been recognized for its rigorous sales training and performance management systems. GE's sales teams are trained to excel in all aspects of their roles, from customer relationship management to detailed data entry. This comprehensive training ensures that salespeople are well-equipped to handle every part of their job, fostering a culture of excellence and accountability.

Companies' failure to build discipline within sales teams can undermine a company's efforts to achieve Commercial Excellence. By adopting Mark Twain's advice to "Do something every day that you don't want to do; this is the golden rule for acquiring the habit of doing your duty without pain", sales teams can develop the habits necessary to fulfill all their responsibilities effectively. Leading companies that can instill this discipline within their sales teams routinely outperform those that allow critical tasks to be neglected. This comprehensive approach not only drives immediate sales success but also supports the long-term strategic goals essential for sustainable growth.

Chapter 8

The distributor tightrope walk

"Treat your men as you would your own beloved sons...If you are overly severe, they will become unmanageable; if you are overly indulgent, they will become spoiled"

— *Sun Tzu*

The Distributor Chimera

Distributors, or channel partners, occupy a unique position within the business ecosystem of manufacturing companies. They serve a dual role that is often challenging to balance: as customers who purchase products and as an extension of the manufacturer's salesforce, responsible for pushing those products into the market. This duality can be likened to the mythological chimera, a creature with multiple forms and functions. Striking the right balance between being demanding of distributors in their sales capacity and ensuring their satisfaction as customers is a nuanced task that many manufacturing companies struggle to master.

The primary challenge lies in the conflicting nature of these roles. As customers, distributors expect excellent service, competitive pricing, and product support from manufacturers. They need to feel valued and supported to remain loyal and motivated to promote the manufacturer's products. On the other hand, as part of the salesforce, they are expected to meet sales targets, provide market feedback, and align closely with the manufacturer's strategic goals. These expectations require a different set of interactions and pressures, often leading to friction if not managed correctly.

To navigate this complexity, manufacturing companies must develop a sophisticated approach that recognizes and addresses the dual nature of their relationship with distributors. One effective method is through establishing clear communication channels that facilitate regular feedback and ensure that both parties' expectations are met. For instance, holding regular joint planning sessions can help align goals and create a shared vision for market penetration and sales growth. This approach fosters a sense of partnership and mutual commitment to success.

Training and support are also necessary elements in maintaining a balanced relationship. Manufacturers should invest in comprehensive training programs that equip distributors with the knowledge and tools they need to sell effectively. This includes product training, sales techniques, and insights into market trends. By empowering distributors with the necessary skills and information, manufacturers can enhance their sales capabilities while also demonstrating their commitment to their success as customers.

Additionally, manufacturers need to implement robust performance management systems that fairly evaluate the contributions of distributors in both capacities. These systems should include metrics that reflect their sales achievements and their level of engagement and satisfaction as customers. For example, incorporating metrics such as Net Promoter Score (NPS) can provide valuable insights into the distributors' satisfaction and loyalty, while sales performance metrics can help track their effectiveness in driving market growth.

Building strong, collaborative relationships with distributors also requires manufacturers to be adaptable and responsive to their needs. This means being open to feedback, addressing concerns promptly, and continuously seeking ways to improve the partnership. For example, providing flexible pricing models or customized marketing support can enhance the value proposition for distributors and strengthen their commitment to the brand.

Real-world examples illustrate the importance of this balanced approach. For instance, Cisco has successfully managed its distributor relationships by creating a comprehensive partner program that offers extensive training, certification, and support. This program not only equips distributors with the necessary tools to succeed but also fosters a sense of loyalty and partnership, leading to sustained growth and market presence.

Treating distributors as both customers and an extension of the salesforce is a complex but essential task for manufacturing companies. By developing clear communication channels, providing robust training and support, implementing fair performance management systems, and being responsive to distributors' needs, manufacturers can strike the right balance. This approach not only drives sales growth but also ensures long-term, mutually beneficial relationships with their channel partners.

Setting Realistic Distributor Expectations

The relationship between manufacturers and their distributors is often pivotal to companies' success. Distributors occupy a unique position, serving both as customers who purchase products and as an extension of the manufacturer's salesforce, driving those products into the market. Despite this dual role, many manufacturing companies default to treating distributors primarily as customers, often shying away from setting realistic expectations for the commercial relationship. This tendency can hinder the effectiveness of the partnership and limit the potential for mutual success.

It can be said that "a happy distributor is a productive one", and it is often critical to ensure distributor's overall satisfaction. However, solely focusing on this aspect can lead to an imbalanced relationship where the manufacturer avoids necessary but difficult conversations about performance expectations. Treating distributors exclusively as customers may result in manufacturers failing to leverage the full potential of the distributor network, ultimately impacting overall sales performance.

The key to a successful distributor-manufacturer relationship lies in balancing the roles of customer and salesforce extension. Manufacturers need to adopt a nuanced approach that acknowledges the distributor's dual role and sets clear, realistic expectations for both aspects of the partnership. This involves open communication, regular performance reviews, and a collaborative approach to problem-solving.

Establishing transparent and realistic expectations is fundamental. Manufacturers should communicate performance targets, market strategies, and sales goals clearly to their distributors. These expectations should be mutually agreed upon, ensuring that both parties are aligned and committed to achieving the set objectives. For instance, quarterly business reviews can be an effective way to assess performance, address challenges, and recalibrate strategies as needed.

Furthermore, manufacturers should provide distributors with the necessary tools and support to meet these expectations. This includes comprehensive training programs, access to marketing resources, and real-time sales data. By equipping distributors with the right resources, manufacturers not only enhance their ability to sell but also demonstrate their commitment to the distributor's success. For example, Microsoft's Partner Network offers extensive training, certification programs, and marketing resources, which help partners thrive and contribute to Microsoft's overall market success.

It is also essential to foster a collaborative relationship where distributors feel valued and heard. Regular feedback loops, where distributors can share insights and suggestions, can significantly enhance the partnership. This two-way communication ensures that distributors are not just executing manufacturer directives but are actively involved in shaping strategies that work for their specific markets. For instance, Cisco's Partner Program emphasizes collaboration and feedback, allowing partners to contribute to strategic planning and product development.

Manufacturers should also be prepared to have candid discussions about performance issues when necessary. Avoiding these conversations can lead to unresolved problems that hinder market growth. By addressing performance gaps constructively and providing targeted support to overcome these challenges, manufacturers can help distributors improve and achieve their sales targets.

Balancing the roles of customer and salesforce extension is a delicate and critical task. By setting clear expectations, providing robust support, fostering collaboration, and maintaining open communication, manufacturers can build strong, productive relationships with their distributors. This balanced approach not only enhances distributor satisfaction and loyalty but also drives market growth and commercial success.

Although it is important to keep distributors happy, manufacturers must not shy away from setting realistic expectations and treating distributors as a vital part of their salesforce. By doing so, they can maximize the potential of their distributor network, ensuring a mutually beneficial and commercially successful partnership.

Maintaining a Deep Bench

To maximize the effectiveness of their distributor networks, leading companies establish structured workflows and processes for managing their distributors. This approach treats distributors not merely as passive customers but as an integral, evolving part of the salesforce whose performance must be actively managed and optimized over time.

Leading companies implement a performance management system that continuously evaluates and supports distributors. Distributors meeting or exceeding expectations receive ongoing support, training, and resources to help them sustain and enhance their performance. Regular performance reviews and open lines of communication are essential to identify areas for improvement and to ensure that distributors remain aligned with the company's strategic objectives. For instance, companies like Cisco and Microsoft offer extensive support programs that include training, marketing resources, and performance incentives to their top-performing partners.

However, managing distributor networks also involves addressing underperformance. Distributors that consistently fail to meet their commercial expectations are flagged for intervention. This process begins with a detailed performance analysis to understand the root causes of the underperformance. Companies may then offer targeted support and resources to help these distributors improve. This could involve additional training, revised marketing strategies, or even changes in operational processes. The goal is to bring the underperforming distributor up to the desired performance level. If these efforts fail, the company may need to consider replacing the underperforming distributor to maintain the overall health of the network.

An essential component of this approach is maintaining a "bench" of potential new distributors. Leading companies proactively identify and cultivate relationships with potential distributors who can step in when a current distributor is underperforming or when market conditions warrant expansion. This bench of potential partners ensures that the company can quickly and effectively replace poor performers, minimizing disruption and maintaining market momentum. For example, Procter & Gamble maintains a robust pipeline of potential distribution partners, allowing them to swiftly respond to changes in market dynamics and ensure continued product availability.

This strategic approach to distributor management is underpinned by several key principles. First, it requires a commitment to continuous improvement, both for the company and its distributors. By regularly assessing performance and seeking opportunities for enhancement, companies can ensure that their distributor networks remain competitive and effective. Second, it emphasizes the importance of clear and open communication. Distributors need to understand the company's expectations, and companies need to be receptive to feedback from their distributors. This two-way communication fosters a collaborative relationship that benefits both parties.

Furthermore, leading companies recognize that distributor management is not a one-size-fits-all process. Different markets and products may require different approaches, and companies need to be flexible and adaptive in their strategies. Customizing support and expectations based on the specific needs and capabilities of each distributor ensures that the management process is both fair and effective.

The successful management of distributor networks involves treating distributors as a dynamic and integral part of the salesforce. By establishing structured workflows, supporting high performers, addressing underperformance, and maintaining a bench of potential partners, leading companies can optimize their distributor networks for sustained success. This comprehensive and strategic approach not only enhances distributor performance but also drives overall market growth and Commercial Excellence.

The Risks of Making a Change

Leading companies recognize the importance of treating their distributors as both customers and partners in sales efforts. This dual perspective is essential for maximizing the effectiveness of distributor networks. Distributors, while buying products, also represent the manufacturer's brand and are responsible for engaging with the end-users. Therefore, fostering a productive relationship involves clear expectations and continuous performance management.

A structured workflow for managing distributor networks can significantly enhance the performance of these partners. For instance, manufacturers should establish performance metrics and regularly evaluate distributors against these benchmarks. Those meeting expectations can be further supported with training, resources, and incentives to drive even better results. Conversely, distributors failing to meet their targets should be identified for improvement or, if necessary, replacement.

Continuous assessment is key. Leading companies maintain a "bench" of potential new distributors ready to step in if current ones underperform. This approach ensures that the network remains robust and capable of meeting sales targets. It also signals to all distributors that high performance is expected and rewarded, while poor performance has consequences.

However, the decision to terminate a distributor's contract should not be taken lightly. There are often significant contractual implications that require careful consideration. Legal and financial repercussions can arise, and manufacturers must navigate these complexities carefully. Additionally, distributors often act as stewards of the manufacturer's relationship with end-users. Disrupting these relationships can have unintended consequences on customer satisfaction and brand loyalty.

For example, in the consumer electronics industry, a manufacturer might rely heavily on a network of regional distributors. If a particular distributor consistently fails to meet sales quotas or provide adequate customer service, the manufacturer must weigh the potential benefits of replacing the distributor against the risks. These risks include potential legal battles, the time required to onboard a new distributor, and the impact on customer relationships during the transition period.

Effective communication is needed throughout this process. Manufacturers should ensure that distributors understand performance expectations from the outset and receive regular feedback. Transparent communication helps to foster trust and aligns the distributor's goals with those of the manufacturer. When performance issues arise, having a documented process for improvement can help to mitigate disputes and provide a clear path forward.

A case in point is the approach taken by leading automotive manufacturers. They often conduct annual reviews with their distributors, providing detailed performance reports and setting clear targets for the coming year. These reviews are not just about identifying problems but also about celebrating successes and planning for future growth. By engaging distributors in this manner, manufacturers can enhance their overall sales performance and strengthen their market position.

Many Manufacturing Companies are Passive

Leading companies are characterized by their proactive approach in managing these networks, consistently setting clear expectations and taking decisive actions to upgrade or replace underperforming distributors. In contrast, less successful manufacturers often maintain passive relationships with their distributors, failing to set clear commercial targets and being slow to address performance issues.

Effective management of distributor networks begins with setting clear and measurable performance targets. Leading companies understand the importance of aligning their distributors' goals with their own strategic objectives. By establishing performance metrics and regularly reviewing distributor performance against these benchmarks, manufacturers can ensure that their distributors remain focused and motivated. This alignment not only enhances sales performance but also strengthens the overall relationship between the manufacturer and its distributors.

A case in point is the approach taken by leading consumer electronics manufacturers. Companies like Apple and Samsung conduct regular performance reviews with their distributors, providing detailed feedback and setting clear targets for improvement. These reviews are not merely a formality but a strategic tool for ensuring that distributors are aligned with the company's goals and are equipped to meet market demands.

On the other hand, manufacturers that adopt a passive approach often struggle with distributor management. These companies tend to lack clear performance metrics and are slow to intervene when issues arise. This can lead to a decline in sales performance and a deterioration in the overall distributor relationship. For example, in the automotive industry, manufacturers that fail to set clear expectations and provide regular feedback to their distributors often find themselves facing declining sales and market share.

Leading companies are not afraid to take decisive action when a distributor fails to meet expectations. This may involve upgrading the distributor's capabilities through training and support or, in some cases, replacing the distributor altogether. By maintaining a "bench" of potential new distributors, manufacturers can ensure that they have the flexibility to make changes quickly and effectively. This approach not only safeguards sales performance but also signals to all distributors that high performance is expected and rewarded.

The pharmaceutical industry provides a pertinent example. Leading companies like Pfizer and Johnson & Johnson regularly evaluate their distributor networks, ensuring that only those distributors who meet their high standards remain part of the network. This proactive approach has enabled these companies to maintain a strong market presence and drive consistent sales growth.

By contrast, poorer performing manufacturers often fail to take such proactive measures. These companies may hesitate to replace underperforming distributors due to concerns about disruption or a lack of potential replacements. This inertia can lead to prolonged periods of suboptimal performance and missed opportunities in the market.

Learning to Walk the Tightrope

Managing distributors effectively requires a skillful and delicate balance. On one hand, manufacturers must provide sufficient support and engage fully to understand the needs and challenges of their distributors. On the other hand, manufacturers must be prepared to revisit distributor relationships if mutually agreed expectations are not met. This balancing act is a critical element of Commercial Excellence, and mastering it is essential for achieving true commercial success.

To cultivate successful business partnerships, manufacturers need to invest in understanding their distributors' unique market conditions, operational challenges, and strategic goals. This understanding enables manufacturers to provide tailored support that addresses specific needs, whether through training programs, marketing assistance, or logistical support. By demonstrating a commitment to their distributors' success, manufacturers foster a collaborative environment that promotes mutual growth and profitability.

For example, Procter & Gamble (P&G) is known for its robust distributor support programs. P&G invests heavily in training and development, equipping its distributors with the knowledge and tools needed to effectively market and sell P&G products. This approach has resulted in strong, long-lasting partnerships that drive significant sales growth and market penetration.

However, support alone is not sufficient. Manufacturers must also set clear, achievable expectations and hold distributors accountable for meeting these standards. Regular performance evaluations, based on predefined metrics, help ensure that distributors remain aligned with the manufacturer's strategic objectives. When distributors consistently meet or exceed these expectations, the relationship is strengthened, and mutual trust is built.

An example of this balanced approach can be seen in the practices of technology giant Cisco. Cisco employs a comprehensive performance management system for its distributors, incorporating regular reviews and feedback sessions. This system not only helps identify areas for improvement but also recognizes and rewards high-performing distributors. Such practices ensure that distributors are continually motivated to excel and align their efforts with Cisco's broader business goals.

Despite everyone's best efforts, there will inevitably be times when a distributor fails to meet the mutually agreed expectations. In such cases, manufacturers must be prepared to take decisive action. This might involve providing additional support to address specific issues or, if necessary, terminating the relationship and seeking new partners. Although this can be a challenging decision, it is critical for maintaining the overall health and effectiveness of the distribution network.

In the automotive industry, Toyota exemplifies this approach. Toyota sets high performance standards for its distributors and conducts thorough evaluations to ensure compliance. When a distributor falls short, Toyota works collaboratively to address the issues. However, if improvements are not made, Toyota does not hesitate to make changes, ensuring that its distribution network remains strong and capable.

Balancing support with accountability requires a strategic and nuanced approach. Manufacturers must walk a tightrope, providing the necessary resources and assistance to help their distributors succeed while also being firm in their expectations and ready to take corrective actions when needed. This delicate balance is a hallmark of Commercial Excellence and a critical factor in achieving sustained business success.

In conclusion, the effective management of distributors hinges on the ability to balance support and accountability. Manufacturers that master this balancing act can foster strong, productive partnerships that drive commercial success. By understanding and addressing the needs of their distributors, setting clear expectations, and being prepared to make tough decisions, manufacturers can achieve true Commercial Excellence and secure a competitive advantage in the market.

Chapter 9

Feedback is a gift

"Observance is the best divinity"

— *Shakespeare (King Henry VIII)*

Closing the Customer Feedback Loop

Companies that engage effectively with their customers and close valuable feedback loops can use the information they gather to improve their customer service quality and refine their go-to-market approaches. This process is essential for companies to maintain their competitive edge and foster long-term customer loyalty.

Customer engagement is the cornerstone of understanding client needs and preferences. Companies that actively engage with their customers are better positioned to deliver products and services that meet or exceed expectations. For instance, Apple's success can be attributed to its continuous engagement with its customer base. Through various channels, including surveys, focus groups, and social media interactions, Apple gathers valuable insights that inform product development and marketing initiatives.

Effective customer engagement goes beyond collecting feedback; it involves analyzing the data to identify trends and areas for improvement. For example, Starbucks uses its loyalty program and mobile app to gather data on customer preferences and purchasing habits. This information helps Starbucks tailor its offerings and promotions to better meet customer demands, resulting in increased customer satisfaction and loyalty.

Closing the feedback loop is a critical aspect of customer engagement. It involves not only collecting feedback but also taking action based on the insights gathered and communicating those actions back to the customers. This process demonstrates to customers that their opinions are valued and that the company is committed to continuous improvement.

A prime example of this is how Dell Inc. transformed its customer service through effective feedback loops. By actively soliciting feedback and implementing changes based on customer suggestions, Dell was able to significantly enhance its customer support operations. This approach not only improved customer satisfaction but also bolstered Dell's reputation for responsive and attentive service.

Engaging with customers and closing feedback loops are also necessary for refining a company's go-to-market strategies. By understanding customer needs and preferences, companies can develop more targeted and effective marketing campaigns. This leads to better market positioning and higher conversion rates.

For instance, Procter & Gamble (P&G) utilizes customer feedback to refine its product launch strategies. By closely monitoring customer reactions and gathering feedback during the initial phases of a product launch, P&G can make necessary adjustments to marketing messages, packaging, and even product formulations. This iterative process helps ensure that new products meet market expectations and achieve greater success.

The goal of engaging with customers and closing feedback loops is to foster a culture of continuous improvement. Companies that consistently seek out and act on customer feedback are more agile and responsive to market changes. This proactive approach allows them to stay ahead of competitors and maintain a strong market presence.

For example, Toyota's commitment to continuous improvement, known as "kaizen," is deeply rooted in its corporate culture. By encouraging employees at all levels to identify and suggest improvements, Toyota continuously enhances its products and processes. This philosophy extends to customer engagement, where feedback is meticulously analyzed and incorporated into ongoing improvements.

Engaging with customers and closing feedback loops are indispensable practices for companies aiming to achieve continuous improvement in customer service and refine their go-to-market strategies. By actively listening to customers and acting on their feedback, companies can enhance customer satisfaction, build loyalty, and drive business success.

The Importance of Customer Feedback

Engaging with customers is necessary for companies striving to enhance their service quality. This engagement is not a one-time effort but an ongoing commitment to understanding and addressing customer needs and preferences. Companies that fail to prioritize customer engagement often find themselves at a significant disadvantage.

Customer engagement involves actively interacting with customers through various channels, collecting feedback, and using that feedback to make informed decisions. This process helps companies identify areas for improvement, develop new products or services, and refine their overall approach to customer service. Engaging with customers ensures that companies stay aligned with their customers' expectations and can quickly adapt to changing needs.

For example, Amazon excels in customer engagement by leveraging data from its vast user base to personalize recommendations and improve the customer experience. Through continuous interaction and feedback collection, Amazon can make swift adjustments to its services, maintaining high customer satisfaction levels and loyalty.

On the other hand, companies that neglect customer engagement risk alienating their customer base and damaging their reputation. One notable example is Nokia, which once dominated the mobile phone market. Despite its early success, Nokia failed to adapt to the rapidly changing smartphone market due to inadequate customer engagement and feedback loops. This oversight allowed competitors like Apple and Samsung to capture market share by better understanding and responding to customer needs.

Another example is the decline of Sears. Once a retail giant, Sears struggled to maintain its market position as it failed to effectively engage with its customers. The company's inability to adapt to the digital age and address customer preferences led to a steady decline in sales and store closures. This case underscores the importance of staying attuned to customer needs and the consequences of failing to do so.

Effective customer engagement goes beyond collecting feedback; it requires closing the feedback loop by acting on the insights gained and communicating those actions back to customers. This process demonstrates a company's commitment to improvement and builds trust with its customer base.

Toyota provides an exemplary model of closing the feedback loop through its Kaizen approach. This philosophy emphasizes continuous improvement and involves everyone in the organization, from top management to frontline workers. By regularly soliciting and acting on feedback, Toyota has maintained high standards of quality and customer satisfaction.

Customer engagement is also vital for refining go-to-market strategies. Companies that understand their customers' preferences can tailor their marketing efforts more effectively, leading to better market positioning and higher conversion rates.

For instance, Procter & Gamble (P&G) uses customer insights to guide its product development and marketing campaigns. By engaging with customers through surveys and focus groups, P&G can identify trends and preferences, allowing the company to launch products that resonate with its target audience.

Continuous Feedback Loops

Engaging with customers and closing feedback loops is vital for companies aiming to achieve continuous service improvement and refine their go-to-market approaches. This practice ensures that organizations stay aligned with customer expectations and rapidly adapt to evolving market demands.

Closing feedback loops involves more than just gathering customer feedback; it requires analyzing the feedback, implementing necessary changes, and informing customers about the actions taken based on their input. This comprehensive approach builds trust and demonstrates a company's commitment to continuous improvement.

For instance, Dell Inc. successfully revitalized its customer service by actively closing feedback loops. By collecting customer feedback through various channels, analyzing it for actionable insights, and making targeted improvements, Dell significantly enhanced its customer support operations. Additionally, communicating these changes back to customers helped to reinforce their perception of Dell as a customer-centric company.

Continuous improvement is a cornerstone of successful businesses. Companies that leverage customer feedback to drive enhancements in their products and services often outperform their competitors. Toyota, renowned for its Kaizen philosophy, exemplifies this approach. By encouraging employees to contribute ideas for improvement and systematically acting on customer feedback, Toyota maintains high standards of quality and customer satisfaction.

This iterative process of collecting feedback, making improvements, and communicating those changes is necessary for maintaining a competitive edge. It ensures that companies can swiftly adapt to new challenges and opportunities, thereby fostering customer loyalty and long-term success.

Procter & Gamble (P&G) provides a notable example of how closing feedback loops can drive continuous improvement. P&G regularly conducts customer surveys and focus groups to gather insights into consumer preferences and needs. These insights inform product development and marketing initiatives, ensuring that P&G's offerings remain relevant and appealing to its target audience. When P&G introduced its Tide Pods, the company relied heavily on consumer feedback to refine the product. Feedback regarding packaging, ease of use, and performance was meticulously analyzed, leading to enhancements that contributed to the product's success. By closing the feedback loop, P&G was able to deliver a product that met customer expectations and gained significant market traction.

Effective feedback loops are also essential for refining go-to-market strategies. By understanding customer preferences and behaviors, companies can tailor their marketing efforts more precisely, leading to better market positioning and increased conversion rates. For example, Starbucks uses data from its loyalty program to gain insights into customer preferences and purchasing habits. This information allows Starbucks to personalize its marketing campaigns and promotions, enhancing customer engagement and driving sales. By closing the feedback loop, Starbucks continuously refines its approach to meet customer needs better.

Strategy Refinement based on Customer Feedback

Effective customer engagement can play a pivotal role in refining many companies' go-to-market strategies. Companies that prioritize understanding and interacting with their customers are much better placed to tailor their offerings and market positioning.

Customer engagement goes beyond mere interactions; it encompasses building meaningful relationships that foster loyalty and trust. By actively engaging with customers, companies gain valuable insights into their needs, preferences, and pain points. This information is instrumental in shaping go-to-market plans that resonate with target audiences.

For instance, Netflix has mastered customer engagement by leveraging data analytics to understand viewing habits and preferences. By collecting and analyzing vast amounts of user data, Netflix can recommend personalized content, enhancing user experience and satisfaction. This customer-centric approach has allowed Netflix to refine its content strategy, ensuring it remains a leader in the streaming industry.

Feedback loops are essential for continuous improvement and refinement of go-to-market efforts. Companies that effectively gather and act on customer feedback can make informed decisions that enhance their service quality and product offerings. This iterative process ensures that businesses remain agile and responsive to changing market demands.

Amazon exemplifies the power of feedback in refining its go-to-market strategy. The company continuously solicits customer reviews and ratings, which provide insights into product performance and customer satisfaction. By incorporating this feedback into product development and service enhancements, Amazon can swiftly address issues and capitalize on opportunities, maintaining its competitive edge.

Procter & Gamble (P&G) provides a notable example of how customer engagement can refine go-to-market strategies. P&G regularly conducts consumer research to gather insights into customer preferences and behaviors. These insights inform the company's product development and marketing initiatives, ensuring that its offerings meet consumer expectations. When P&G launched its Tide Pods, the company relied heavily on consumer feedback to refine the product. Insights regarding packaging, ease of use, and performance were meticulously analyzed and led to significant enhancements. By engaging with customers and closing feedback loops, P&G successfully introduced a product that quickly gained market acceptance and drove sales growth.

Effective customer engagement also enables companies to adapt their go-to-market plans in response to market changes. By maintaining a close connection with their customer base, businesses can anticipate shifts in preferences and adjust their strategies accordingly.

Starbucks is a prime example of a company that adapts its go-to-market strategy through customer engagement. By using data from its loyalty program, Starbucks gains insights into customer purchasing habits and preferences. This information allows the company to personalize its marketing efforts and tailor promotions to individual customers, driving increased engagement and sales.

Aligning Commercial Strategy with Customer Feedback

Customer feedback serves as a vital source of information for companies aiming to understand their market better. It provides insights into customer preferences, pain points, and expectations, allowing businesses to make informed decisions. By systematically collecting and analyzing feedback, companies can identify areas for improvement and tailor their offerings to better meet customer needs.

Apple Inc. exemplifies the effective use of customer feedback. Through various channels, including online reviews, surveys, and social media, Apple gathers extensive feedback on its products. This feedback informs product development and innovation, ensuring that each new release addresses the needs and desires of its customer base. The consistent alignment of Apple's market strategies with customer feedback has been a key factor in maintaining its market leadership and customer loyalty.

Closing the feedback loop involves not only collecting and analyzing customer feedback but also acting on it and communicating back to customers. This process demonstrates to customers that their opinions are valued and leads to continuous improvement in products and services. Companies that close the feedback loop effectively can foster stronger customer relationships and drive higher levels of satisfaction and loyalty.

Starbucks provides a notable example of closing the feedback loop. Through its My Starbucks Idea platform, the company invites customers to submit ideas for new products, store improvements, and customer service enhancements. Starbucks regularly reviews and implements popular suggestions, updating customers on the status of their ideas. This transparent approach has helped Starbucks maintain a loyal customer base and continually improve its offerings.

Integrating customer feedback into go-to-market strategies enables companies to adapt to changing market conditions and customer preferences. By understanding what customers value most, businesses can tailor their marketing, sales, and distribution efforts to align with customer expectations, thereby increasing the effectiveness of their strategies.

Procter & Gamble (P&G) has effectively refined its go-to-market strategies by leveraging customer feedback. The company uses extensive consumer research to gather insights into customer preferences and behaviors. These insights guide P&G's product development and marketing initiatives, ensuring that its offerings resonate with consumers. For example, the launch of Tide Pods was based on thorough feedback analysis, leading to a product that met customer demands for convenience and efficiency.

Aligning market strategies with customer feedback is a fundamental aspect of achieving Commercial Excellence. Companies that prioritize customer insights in their strategic planning can enhance their competitive advantage, drive revenue growth, and improve overall business performance. By consistently refining their approaches based on customer feedback, businesses can ensure they remain relevant and responsive to market needs.

Amazon's success underscores the importance of aligning strategies with customer feedback. The company continuously analyzes customer reviews and purchasing data to refine its product offerings and enhance the customer experience. This customer-centric approach has enabled Amazon to expand its market share and maintain a leading position in the retail industry.

Data and Analytics for Customer Satisfaction

Leading companies continuously assess and enhance how they serve their customers. Employing advanced analytics and customer metrics, such as the Net Promoter Score (NPS), these organizations can significantly improve customer experience and advocacy. This approach not only drives customer satisfaction but also fosters loyalty, ultimately contributing to sustained business success.

Advanced analytics play a pivotal role in understanding customer behaviors and preferences. By leveraging data from various touchpoints, companies can gain deep insights into customer journeys, identify pain points, and predict future behaviors. This data-driven approach allows for more personalized and effective customer interactions.

For example, Netflix utilizes advanced analytics to analyze viewing habits and preferences of its users. By doing so, it can recommend personalized content, enhancing the user experience and increasing engagement. This level of personalization has been a key factor in Netflix's ability to retain customers and maintain its position as a leading streaming service.

Customer metrics, such as NPS, are essential tools for measuring and improving customer satisfaction and loyalty. NPS provides a clear indication of how likely customers are to recommend a company's products or services to others. By regularly measuring NPS, companies can track changes in customer sentiment over time and identify areas for improvement.

Apple Inc. is a prime example of a company that effectively uses NPS to enhance customer experience. Apple consistently achieves high NPS scores, reflecting its commitment to customer satisfaction. By actively monitoring these scores and acting on customer feedback, Apple can address issues promptly and maintain high levels of customer loyalty and advocacy.

Leading companies understand that the quest for customer excellence is ongoing. They continually refine their customer service practices based on insights gained from advanced analytics and customer metrics. This commitment to continuous improvement ensures that they stay ahead of customer expectations and adapt to changing market conditions.

Amazon exemplifies this approach. The company's focus on customer feedback and data analysis allows it to continually improve its services. Amazon's use of advanced analytics to optimize its delivery processes and customer service interactions has resulted in a consistently high level of customer satisfaction and loyalty.

Customer advocacy is a powerful driver of business growth. When customers have positive experiences, they are more likely to become advocates for the brand, recommending it to friends and family. This word-of-mouth promotion can be more effective than traditional marketing efforts.

Tesla's success can be partly attributed to its strong base of customer advocates. By delivering exceptional customer experiences and leveraging customer feedback, Tesla has built a loyal following that actively promotes the brand. The company's high NPS scores reflect this advocacy, contributing to its rapid growth and market penetration.

In conclusion, leading companies that assess and continuously improve how they serve customers through advanced analytics and customer metrics can significantly enhance customer experience and advocacy. By leveraging data-driven insights and metrics like NPS, these companies can refine their customer service practices, foster loyalty, and drive business success.

Assessment Methods

Leading companies understand that continuous assessment of how they serve customers is paramount to maintaining a competitive edge. By employing a range of surveys, analytical methods, and tools, these companies can gain insights into customer experiences, enabling them to enhance service quality and foster customer advocacy. This data-driven approach not only boosts customer satisfaction but also strengthens loyalty, which is necessary for long-term success.

Surveys are a fundamental tool in understanding customer satisfaction and identifying areas for improvement. They provide direct feedback from customers, offering a snapshot of their experiences and expectations. Companies like Microsoft regularly use customer satisfaction surveys to gather insights. By asking specific questions about their products and services, Microsoft can pinpoint areas that need enhancement and quickly address any issues, ensuring that customer needs are met effectively.

In addition to surveys, leading companies employ various analytical methods to delve deeper into customer data. Advanced analytics, such as predictive modeling and sentiment analysis, allow companies to understand customer behavior and preferences on a granular level. For example, Starbucks utilizes predictive analytics to personalize its marketing efforts. By analyzing purchase history and customer preferences, Starbucks can predict which products a customer is likely to purchase next, enabling them to tailor their promotions and offers accordingly. This level of personalization significantly enhances the customer experience, making customers feel valued and understood.

Net Promoter Score (NPS) is a widely used metric that helps companies gauge customer loyalty and satisfaction. NPS categorizes customers into promoters, passives, and detractors based on their likelihood to recommend the company to others. Companies like Apple have successfully leveraged NPS to maintain high levels of customer satisfaction. By continuously monitoring NPS, Apple can identify detractors and address their concerns promptly, converting them into promoters. This proactive approach ensures that customer issues are resolved before they escalate, fostering a loyal customer base.

Feedback loops are essential for continuous improvement. By closing the loop on customer feedback, companies can demonstrate that they value their customers' opinions and are committed to making necessary changes. Amazon exemplifies this approach with its robust feedback system. Customer reviews and feedback are actively monitored and analyzed, leading to rapid adjustments in product offerings and services. This continuous improvement cycle not only enhances customer satisfaction but also drives innovation, keeping Amazon ahead of its competitors.

Netflix is a prime example of how data-driven customer engagement can lead to commercial success. By employing a combination of surveys, advanced analytics, and customer feedback, Netflix continuously refines its service. The company analyzes viewing habits and customer ratings to recommend personalized content. This not only improves the user experience but also increases viewer retention and engagement. Netflix's commitment to understanding and serving its customers through data has been a key factor in its growth and success.

A Commitment to Continuous Improvement

Leading companies understand that the key to sustaining customer satisfaction and loyalty lies in their commitment to gathering and acting on customer feedback. This dedication to continuous improvement not only enhances the quality of products and services but also solidifies customer trust and advocacy. Employing advanced analytics and customer metrics, top firms transform feedback into actionable insights, driving their success in a competitive market.

Customer feedback is invaluable in identifying strengths and weaknesses in a company's offerings. It provides direct insights into customer experiences, preferences, and expectations. For example, Apple consistently seeks feedback through various channels, including customer surveys and product reviews. By meticulously analyzing this data, Apple can refine its products and services, ensuring they meet or exceed customer expectations. This relentless pursuit of excellence has contributed significantly to Apple's reputation for quality and innovation.

In addition to traditional feedback methods, leading companies leverage advanced analytics to gain deeper insights into customer behavior and preferences. Predictive analytics, Machine Learning (ML), and big data technologies enable these companies to anticipate customer needs and tailor their offerings accordingly. Netflix exemplifies this approach. By analyzing viewing habits and feedback, Netflix recommends personalized content, enhancing the user experience and increasing viewer retention. This data-driven strategy not only improves customer satisfaction but also drives growth by keeping subscribers engaged and loyal.

Net Promoter Score (NPS) is a helpful metric that helps companies measure customer loyalty and satisfaction. NPS categorizes customers based on their likelihood to recommend the company to others, providing a clear indicator of overall customer sentiment. Companies like Amazon rely on NPS to gauge their performance. By continuously monitoring and responding to NPS data, Amazon can address customer concerns promptly, turning detractors into promoters. This proactive approach ensures high levels of customer satisfaction and fosters long-term loyalty.

Effective feedback management involves not just gathering data but also closing the feedback loop. This means acting on the insights gained and communicating the changes made back to the customers. Microsoft, for instance, has a robust feedback system where customer input directly influences product development and updates. By visibly incorporating customer suggestions, Microsoft demonstrates its commitment to customer satisfaction, building a stronger relationship with its user base.

Toyota's commitment to continuous improvement, or Kaizen, is a prime example of how feedback can drive excellence. The company encourages feedback from all levels, including customers, employees, and suppliers. This feedback is systematically analyzed and used to implement incremental improvements across all processes. Toyota's dedication to this philosophy has resulted in high-quality products and exceptional customer satisfaction, solidifying its position as a leader in the automotive industry.

Advanced Analytics and Artificial Intelligence

Leading companies are increasingly turning to advanced analytics, Artificial Intelligence (AI), and Machine Learning (ML) to extract the maximum value from customer feedback data. This approach is not just about collecting information; it is about transforming it into actionable insights that enhance customer experience and advocacy. The integration of AI and ML into customer feedback processes allows businesses to gain deeper understanding and make more informed decisions, driving continuous improvement in products and services.

One prominent example is Amazon, which uses AI to analyze customer reviews and feedback. By employing Machine Learning (ML) algorithms, Amazon can identify trends, sentiment, and specific areas for improvement. This process helps the company to personalize recommendations, refine product offerings, and enhance customer satisfaction. The use of AI enables Amazon to process vast amounts of data quickly and accurately, ensuring that feedback is not only collected but also effectively utilized.

The power of AI in this context lies in its ability to identify patterns and predict future behavior. For instance, AI can detect recurring issues in customer feedback that might not be immediately apparent through manual analysis. This predictive capability allows companies to proactively address potential problems before they escalate, thereby improving customer retention and loyalty. Additionally, AI-driven sentiment analysis can provide real-time insights into customer opinions, helping companies to stay agile and responsive.

Another example is IBM, which has implemented Watson AI to analyze customer service interactions. Watson's natural language processing capabilities allow it to understand and interpret the nuances of customer conversations. This understanding enables IBM to identify common pain points and areas where the service can be improved. By continuously learning from customer interactions, Watson helps IBM to enhance the quality of its support services, leading to higher customer satisfaction and advocacy.

AI and ML also facilitate more personalized customer experiences. Companies can use these technologies to tailor their communications and offerings based on individual customer preferences and behaviors. For example, Netflix uses AI to analyze viewing habits and recommend content that aligns with user interests. This level of personalization not only improves the customer experience but also drives engagement and loyalty.

Advanced analytics and AI are also useful for measuring the effectiveness of customer engagement initiatives. Metrics such as Net Promoter Score (NPS) and Customer Satisfaction (CSAT) can be analyzed in conjunction with AI-driven insights to provide a comprehensive view of customer sentiment. This holistic approach ensures that companies are not only gathering feedback but also using it to drive meaningful improvements.

For companies looking to leverage AI and ML in their customer feedback processes, it is essential to ensure data quality and integrity. Clean, accurate data is the foundation of any successful AI initiative. Additionally, companies should invest in the necessary infrastructure and expertise to implement and manage these technologies effectively. This includes training staff to interpret AI-generated insights and integrate them into decision-making processes.

Net Promoter Score and Other Approaches

Many leading companies have recognized the importance of accurately measuring customer satisfaction and loyalty to drive continuous improvement. To this end, many have adopted the industry-standard Net Promoter Score (NPS) as their core metric. NPS, a straightforward yet powerful tool, asks customers to rate their likelihood of recommending the company on a scale of 0 to 10, categorizing respondents into promoters, passives, and detractors. This method provides a clear, actionable measure of customer sentiment and loyalty.

However, while NPS is widely used, some companies have opted for other standardized methods to gauge customer satisfaction. For example, Customer Satisfaction Score (CSAT) and Customer Effort Score (CES) are also popular metrics. CSAT measures satisfaction with specific interactions, while CES evaluates the ease of customer experiences. These metrics offer different insights into customer interactions and overall satisfaction, allowing companies to tailor their improvement efforts accordingly.

Beyond these standardized metrics, many leading companies have developed proprietary surveys and analytics to gain deeper insights. These custom tools often complement standardized scores like NPS by providing more granular data. For instance, Amazon utilizes a combination of NPS and its own extensive feedback mechanisms to continuously refine its customer service and product offerings. This dual approach allows Amazon to maintain its reputation for exceptional customer experience and rapid responsiveness to customer needs.

Advanced analytics and algorithms play an important role in extracting maximum value from customer feedback. Companies leverage Machine Learning (ML) and artificial intelligence to analyze large volumes of feedback data, identifying patterns and trends that might not be immediately apparent. This advanced analysis helps companies to understand the underlying drivers of customer satisfaction and dissatisfaction. For example, AI can analyze sentiment in customer comments, providing insights into the emotions behind customer feedback.

The integration of AI and Machine Learning (ML) in customer feedback analysis is becoming increasingly prevalent. These technologies enable companies to automate the feedback analysis process, making it more efficient and scalable. By automating sentiment analysis, topic modeling, and predictive analytics, companies can quickly identify areas for improvement and take proactive measures. This approach not only enhances customer satisfaction but also allows companies to stay ahead of competitors by anticipating customer needs and preferences.

Additionally, companies are using their proprietary analytics to create personalized customer experiences. By understanding individual customer preferences and behaviors, businesses can tailor their interactions and offerings to meet specific needs. This personalization fosters stronger customer relationships and increases loyalty. For instance, Netflix uses sophisticated algorithms to analyze viewing habits and preferences, recommending content that aligns with individual tastes, thereby enhancing user engagement and satisfaction.

The commitment to gathering and analyzing customer feedback reflects these companies' dedication to continuous improvement. By combining standardized metrics like NPS with proprietary tools and advanced analytics, they can achieve a comprehensive understanding of customer satisfaction. This holistic approach enables them to address issues promptly, refine their products and services, and ultimately enhance customer experience and advocacy.

Fostering Customer Advocacy

Many leading companies recognize the critical importance of continuously assessing and improving their customer service to foster stronger customer advocacy and enhance overall customer experience. By employing advanced analytics and customer metrics, these companies can obtain actionable insights that drive meaningful improvements in their products and services.

A cornerstone of this approach is the use of customer satisfaction measures. Net Promoter Score (NPS) is one such metric that has gained widespread acceptance. It gauges customer loyalty by asking how likely customers are to recommend the company to others, categorizing them into promoters, passives, and detractors. This straightforward question provides a clear indication of customer satisfaction and loyalty, enabling companies to identify areas that require attention.

However, leading companies do not rely solely on NPS. They often complement it with other metrics such as Customer Satisfaction Score (CSAT) and Customer Effort Score (CES). CSAT measures customers' satisfaction with specific interactions, while CES evaluates the ease of their experience. These additional metrics provide a more nuanced understanding of customer interactions, helping companies to address specific pain points and improve the overall customer journey.

For example, Apple uses a combination of NPS and its own internal customer satisfaction surveys to gather comprehensive feedback. This data-driven approach allows Apple to continuously refine its product offerings and customer service. By understanding what customers value most, Apple can prioritize features and services that enhance user experience and foster brand loyalty.

Incorporating advanced analytics into customer feedback analysis is another hallmark of leading companies. Machine Learning (ML) and artificial intelligence technologies enable businesses to process vast amounts of feedback data quickly and accurately. These technologies can identify patterns, detect sentiment, and uncover emerging trends that might otherwise go unnoticed. For instance, AI can analyze customer comments for sentiment, providing deeper insights into customer emotions and motivations.

Google leverages AI and ML to analyze feedback from its diverse user base. By processing this data, Google can identify common issues and areas for improvement across its products and services. This real-time analysis allows Google to respond swiftly to customer concerns, enhancing user satisfaction and fostering stronger customer advocacy.

Additionally, leading companies use these insights to personalize customer experiences. By tailoring interactions and recommendations based on individual preferences, businesses can deliver a more engaging and relevant experience. Amazon is a prime example, utilizing sophisticated algorithms to recommend products that align with customers' browsing and purchase histories. This personalized approach not only enhances the shopping experience but also builds customer loyalty and advocacy.

Furthermore, companies' commitment to continuously improving customer satisfaction reflects these companies' dedication to maintaining a competitive edge. They understand that satisfied customers are more likely to become advocates, promoting the brand through word-of-mouth and social media. This organic advocacy is invaluable, driving new customer acquisition and reinforcing the company's market position.

A Data-Driven Commitment to Excellence

Many leading companies continuously assess and enhance their customer service, employing advanced analytics and customer metrics to improve customer experience and advocacy. The valuable insights derived from analytics drive continuous improvement efforts, which reflects these companies' unwavering commitment to product and service excellence.

Companies like Amazon and Apple have set benchmarks in leveraging customer feedback to refine their offerings. Amazon, known for its customer-centric approach, employs a sophisticated feedback loop where every interaction is analyzed to improve service. By using customer data, Amazon continually optimizes its delivery processes, enhances its product recommendations, and improves overall customer satisfaction. Similarly, Apple uses customer feedback to drive innovation and refine its product line. The introduction of features like Face ID and advanced camera systems in iPhones are results of meticulous customer feedback analysis.

Advanced analytics play a pivotal role in these processes. By utilizing tools like Machine Learning (ML) and Artificial Intelligence (AI), companies can identify patterns and trends in customer feedback that would otherwise be missed. For instance, sentiment analysis tools can process vast amounts of customer reviews and social media interactions to gauge customer sentiment. These insights help companies address issues proactively, tailor their services to meet customer expectations, and ultimately foster stronger customer advocacy.

Customer metrics such as the Net Promoter Score (NPS) are widely used by leading companies to measure customer satisfaction. NPS provides a clear, quantifiable measure of customer loyalty and satisfaction by asking customers how likely they are to recommend a company's products or services to others. Companies that consistently score high on NPS, such as Tesla and Netflix, often have a robust feedback mechanism in place. These companies use NPS data to identify promoters and detractors, understand their concerns, and take actionable steps to improve the customer experience.

Leading companies do not solely rely on standardized metrics. They also complement these with proprietary surveys, tailored analytics, and customized algorithms to gain deeper insights. For example, Microsoft uses a combination of NPS and its own Customer Satisfaction Index (CSI) to get a holistic view of customer satisfaction. This dual approach allows

Microsoft to capture nuanced feedback and make informed decisions that enhance customer satisfaction and loyalty.

The commitment to continuous improvement is evident in the iterative processes adopted by these companies. They regularly review and refine their customer engagement strategies based on analytical insights. This approach not only improves the quality of their products and services but also demonstrates their dedication to meeting customer needs. For instance, by continuously analyzing feedback and implementing improvements, Starbucks has enhanced its mobile ordering system, which reduces waiting times and increasing customer satisfaction.

Chapter 10

Breakfast like a king

"Do not conform to the pattern of this world, but be transformed by the renewing of your mind"

— *Romans 12:2*

Every Strategy Starts with Culture

Peter Drucker, the well-known management consultant and author, famously said, "Culture eats strategy for breakfast." This observation underscores a profound truth: without a strong, supportive culture, even the most well-conceived strategies will struggle to succeed.

In the context of Commercial Excellence, this means that companies must build and nurture a robust cultural foundation to achieve their strategic goals. Therefore, to truly embrace the power of organizational culture, companies must be prepared to "eat breakfast like a king," and focus relentlessly on embedding a culture of Commercial Excellence that permeates every level of the company.

Achieving Commercial Excellence requires a cultural shift towards customer-centricity. This shift involves more than just a superficial change in policies or procedures; it necessitates a fundamental transformation in how the organization views and interacts with its customers. Every employee, from the C-suite to the front lines, must embrace a mindset that prioritizes customer satisfaction and loyalty. For example, Amazon's customer-centric culture is well-documented. Jeff Bezos' focus on customer obsession has driven Amazon to innovate continually and deliver exceptional service, leading to high customer satisfaction and loyalty.

Embedding a customer-centric culture also means fostering an environment where feedback is actively sought and valued. Organizations should implement mechanisms to capture customer insights and use them to inform decision-making processes. This approach not only improves the customer experience but also encourages employees to take ownership of customer satisfaction. For instance, Zappos, an online shoe retailer, empowers its customer service representatives to go above and beyond to delight customers, fostering a culture of exceptional service that is integral to its brand identity.

Engaging all levels of the organization in this cultural shift is crucial. Leaders must model the desired behaviors and values, setting the tone for the entire company. Middle management plays a pivotal role in translating the strategic vision into actionable plans, while front-line employees execute these plans in their daily interactions with customers. Training programs, workshops, and continuous learning opportunities can help embed the principles of Commercial Excellence throughout the organization. Salesforce, for example, invests heavily in training and development to ensure its employees are equipped to deliver outstanding customer experiences.

In an evolving competitive market, the ability to meet and exceed customer expectations is a significant differentiator. Companies that excel in this area understand that customer needs are not static; they evolve over time. Therefore, organizations must be agile and responsive, continually adapting their offerings and strategies to align with changing customer preferences. Apple's success in consistently delivering innovative products that anticipate and fulfill customer needs exemplifies the importance of staying ahead of market trends and customer expectations.

Building a culture of Commercial Excellence also involves recognizing and rewarding behaviors that contribute to this goal. Incentive programs, public recognition, and career advancement opportunities for employees who demonstrate a commitment to customer-centricity can reinforce the desired culture. Google's practice of celebrating innovative ideas and rewarding employees who contribute to product improvements underscores the value of recognition in fostering a culture of excellence.

The journey towards Commercial Excellence is intrinsically linked to the cultural foundation of an organization. Companies must prioritize creating and sustaining a customer-centric culture that supports their strategic objectives. By engaging all levels of the organization, continually adapting to customer needs, and recognizing contributions to Commercial Excellence, companies can ensure that their strategic initiatives are underpinned by a robust cultural framework. This holistic approach not only drives business success but also fosters a sustainable competitive advantage in an increasingly customer-focused marketplace.

Aligning Culture with Commercial Excellence

Achieving strategic change within an organization often necessitates a substantial cultural shift, especially when striving for Commercial Excellence. A significant transformation in organizational culture is essential to align all activities with customer needs. This alignment ensures that every aspect of the business is geared towards meeting and exceeding customer expectations. In essence, to attain true Commercial Excellence, companies must embed customer-centric values deeply within their organizational culture.

A critical component of this cultural shift is fostering a deep understanding of customer needs across all levels of the organization. This requires comprehensive training programs and a commitment to continuous learning. Employees must be equipped with the skills and knowledge necessary to anticipate and respond to customer demands effectively. For example, Apple Inc. has consistently demonstrated the importance of understanding customer preferences by continually innovating its product offerings based on detailed customer feedback and market research. This approach not only enhances customer satisfaction but also drives long-term loyalty.

Leadership plays a pivotal role in steering this cultural transformation. Leaders must exemplify the customer-centric values they wish to instill within the organization. They should actively engage with employees, encouraging them to adopt a customer-first mindset. This engagement can be facilitated through regular communication, where leaders share success stories and customer feedback. By doing so, they create a shared vision and reinforce the importance of customer-centric practices. A notable example is Amazon, where Jeff Bezos has long championed the principle of customer obsession, making it a core part of the company's ethos.

Furthermore, fostering a collaborative environment is critical for embedding customer-centric values. Cross-functional teams should work together to ensure that customer insights are integrated into all aspects of the business. This collaboration can lead to the development of innovative solutions that address customer pain points and enhance the overall customer experience. Google's approach to innovation through its cross-functional teams, such as the Google X lab, underscores the importance of collaboration in driving customer-focused innovation.

Performance metrics also need to be aligned with customer-centric goals. Traditional financial metrics should be complemented with customer-focused metrics such as Net Promoter Score (NPS) and Customer Satisfaction (CSAT) scores. These metrics provide valuable insights into customer perceptions and help identify areas for improvement. Companies like Netflix use these metrics to refine their offerings continuously, ensuring that they remain aligned with customer preferences and expectations.

Investing in technology is another vital aspect of this cultural shift. Advanced analytics and Artificial Intelligence (AI) can provide deeper insights into customer behavior and preferences. These technologies enable companies to personalize their offerings and deliver exceptional customer experiences. For instance, Starbucks leverages AI to personalize customer interactions through its mobile app, enhancing customer satisfaction and loyalty.

Ultimately, the journey to Commercial Excellence is an ongoing process that requires unwavering commitment. It involves embedding customer-centric values deeply within the organizational culture and continuously refining practices based on customer feedback. By aligning all activities with customer needs, companies can achieve sustainable growth and long-term success.

Achieving strategic change through a cultural shift towards customer-centricity is essential for attaining Commercial Excellence. This shift requires strong leadership, collaborative efforts, aligned performance metrics, and investment in technology. Companies that successfully embed these values within their culture can meet and exceed customer expectations, driving sustained growth and profitability.

A Hard Pivot for Manufacturing Companies

Achieving Commercial Excellence often requires a significant cultural shift within organizations, especially for manufacturing companies deeply rooted in an engineering-centric culture. This shift involves reorienting the entire organization to focus on customer satisfaction, engaging all levels to meet and exceed customer expectations. It is a challenging transformation but essential for companies aiming to thrive in a competitive environment.

For many manufacturing firms, the traditional emphasis has been on optimizing engineering and plant operations. Although these aspects certainly remain important, there is a growing recognition that understanding and addressing customer needs is equally important. This requires a pivot towards a customer-centric culture, where every employee, from top executives to frontline workers, is aligned with the goal of delivering exceptional customer experiences.

One prominent example of such a cultural shift is seen in the transformation of General Electric (GE). Under the leadership of former CEO Jeff Immelt, GE undertook a significant shift towards digital and customer-centric strategies. Immelt recognized that to remain competitive, GE needed to focus not only on its industrial capabilities but also on understanding and meeting the needs of its customers. This shift involved significant investments in digital technology and data analytics, allowing GE to offer more tailored and responsive services to its customers.

To achieve a similar transformation, companies must start by clearly communicating the importance of customer-centricity to all employees. This can be achieved through regular training programs, workshops, and internal communications that emphasize the value of customer satisfaction. Leadership must play a pivotal role in driving this change, setting an example by prioritizing customer needs in decision-making processes and rewarding customer-focused behaviors.

Furthermore, companies need to implement systems that enable better customer insights. This involves leveraging data analytics and customer feedback mechanisms to understand customer preferences, pain points, and expectations. By doing so, organizations can tailor their products and services to better meet customer needs, leading to higher satisfaction and loyalty. Amazon is a prime example of a company that has successfully implemented this approach. Through its sophisticated use of data analytics, Amazon continuously monitors customer behavior and feedback, allowing it to offer personalized recommendations and improve the overall shopping experience.

Another critical aspect of this cultural shift is fostering a sense of ownership and accountability among employees. When employees feel responsible for customer satisfaction, they are more likely to go the extra mile to ensure that customers are happy. This can be encouraged through recognition programs that reward employees who demonstrate exceptional customer service and through creating cross-functional teams that collaborate to solve customer issues.

Implementing these changes can be challenging, but the rewards are substantial. Companies that successfully adopt a customer-centric culture often see significant improvements in customer satisfaction, loyalty, and ultimately, financial performance. For instance, Toyota's commitment to customer satisfaction and continuous improvement has been a key factor in its success. The company's "Customer First" philosophy ensures that every decision and action is taken with the customer's best interests in mind, leading to high levels of customer loyalty and trust.

Achieving Commercial Excellence requires a cultural shift towards customer-centricity, engaging all levels of the organization to meet and exceed customer expectations. For manufacturing companies entrenched in an engineering-centric culture, this shift may be challenging but is essential for long-term success. By prioritizing customer needs, leveraging data analytics, fostering employee ownership, and learning from industry leaders, companies can transform their operations and achieve true Commercial Excellence.

Everyone has a Role to Play

Engaging all levels of an organization in a desired cultural change is essential for the successful implementation of any major strategic initiative. This necessity becomes even more critical when the focus is on prioritizing customer expectations. Achieving a cultural shift that emphasizes customer-centricity requires a concerted effort that permeates every tier of the organization, ensuring that customer satisfaction becomes a shared objective from the C-suite to the frontline employees.

A prime example of successful cultural transformation can be seen in the journey of Apple under the leadership of Steve Jobs. When Jobs returned to Apple in 1997, he embarked on a mission to shift the company's culture towards innovation and customer focus. This transformation involved engaging all levels of the organization, from designers and engineers to retail staff, in a unified effort to create products that delighted customers. The result was a series of groundbreaking products, such as the iPod, iPhone, and iPad, that revolutionized the tech industry and cemented Apple's reputation for excellence in customer satisfaction.

For a cultural change to be effective, it must begin with strong leadership commitment. Leaders must not only articulate a clear vision that emphasizes the importance of customer-centricity but also embody this vision in their actions. This involves setting clear expectations, providing the necessary resources, and continuously reinforcing the message through consistent communication. For instance, Satya Nadella, CEO of Microsoft, has been instrumental in shifting Microsoft's culture towards innovation and customer focus since taking the helm in 2014. Nadella's leadership has fostered a culture of empathy and customer obsession, leading to significant improvements in Microsoft's product offerings and customer relationships.

Furthermore, middle management plays a very important role in translating the leadership's vision into actionable steps that resonate with frontline employees. These managers act as the bridge between the strategic objectives set by senior leaders and the daily operations carried out by employees. By empowering middle managers with the tools and authority to make customer-focused decisions, organizations can ensure that the cultural shift is effectively implemented across all levels.

Engaging frontline employees is equally important, as they are often the primary point of contact with customers. Providing training and development opportunities that equip these employees with the skills to understand and meet customer needs is essential. Companies like Starbucks have excelled in this area by investing heavily in employee training programs that emphasize customer service excellence. Starbucks' commitment to engaging its baristas in the company's customer-centric culture has been a key factor in its global success and high levels of customer loyalty.

To sustain a cultural shift towards customer-centricity, organizations must also implement mechanisms for continuous feedback and improvement. This involves regularly soliciting feedback from employees and customers, analyzing data to identify areas for improvement, and making necessary adjustments to processes and practices. Google, for example, has built a culture of continuous improvement by encouraging employees at all levels to share ideas and feedback. This open and inclusive approach has enabled Google to stay ahead of customer expectations and continuously enhance its products and services.

Engaging all levels of the organization in the cultural change is essential for achieving strategic success. This requires a unified effort, starting with strong leadership commitment and cascading through middle management to frontline employees. By fostering a culture of customer-centricity, providing necessary training and development, and implementing continuous feedback mechanisms, organizations can create an environment where customer satisfaction is a shared priority and a driver of long-term success.

Culture and Strategy are Moving Targets

Markets rarely stand still, and neither should corporate strategies. In a rapidly evolving competitive landscape, companies must maintain a dynamic approach to both strategy and organizational culture. This adaptability is needed for meeting changing market demands and staying ahead of competitors. Organizations that succeed in this arena are those that recognize the importance of a flexible culture that can pivot in response to new challenges and opportunities.

One prime example of a company that has effectively adapted its culture and strategy is Netflix. Originally a DVD rental service, Netflix anticipated the shift towards digital streaming and transformed its business model accordingly. This strategic shift required a fundamental cultural change within the organization. Netflix embraced a culture of innovation and risk-taking, empowering employees to experiment and develop new ideas. The result was a seamless transition to a streaming giant, continuously evolving its content and delivery methods to meet consumer preferences and technological advancements.

To remain competitive, companies must ensure that their organizational culture is not static. This requires fostering a culture of continuous learning and improvement. Employees at all levels should be encouraged to stay informed about industry trends, customer preferences, and emerging technologies. Google exemplifies this approach through its "20% time" policy, which allows employees to spend 20% of their work hours on projects they are passionate about, even if they are not directly related to their core job responsibilities. This policy has led to the development of innovative products like Gmail and Google News, demonstrating how a culture of continuous learning and experimentation can drive business success.

Furthermore, organizations must be prepared to evolve their strategies in response to external changes. The COVID-19 pandemic, for instance, forced many companies to reevaluate their business models and operational strategies. Companies like Microsoft quickly adapted by enhancing their remote work capabilities and accelerating their cloud services offerings. This agility was supported by a culture that values flexibility and rapid response to market changes, allowing Microsoft to meet the increased demand for remote collaboration tools and maintain its competitive edge.

Leadership is Everything

Leadership plays a critical role in driving cultural adaptability. Leaders must set the tone for flexibility and openness to change. They should communicate the importance of adaptability to their teams and model behaviors that support a dynamic organizational culture. Satya Nadella's leadership at Microsoft is a testament to this. His emphasis on a "growth mindset" culture has encouraged employees to embrace change, learn from failures, and continuously seek improvement. This cultural shift has been pivotal in Microsoft's resurgence as a leader in the technology sector.

In addition to leadership, companies must implement structures and processes that support cultural and strategic agility. This includes establishing cross-functional teams that can quickly respond to market shifts, leveraging data analytics to make informed decisions, and creating feedback loops to gather insights from customers and employees. Amazon's use of data-driven decision-making and its agile approach to innovation have enabled it to continuously adapt its strategies to meet evolving customer needs and market conditions.

The dynamic nature of markets necessitates a similarly dynamic approach to strategy and organizational culture. Companies that succeed in this environment are those that foster a culture of continuous learning, encourage flexibility, and are willing to adapt their strategies in response to external changes. By cultivating an adaptable culture and embracing strategic agility, organizations can navigate the complexities of a changing

249

competitive landscape and achieve sustained success.

Chapter 11

The end of the beginning

"La acción es la clave fundamental para todo éxito"

— Pablo Picasso

An idea whose time has come

The concept of Commercial Excellence is increasingly gaining traction in manufacturing sectors such as chemicals and oil & gas. After dedicating two decades to achieving Operational Excellence, these industries are now well-positioned to pivot towards Commercial Excellence. The transition leverages the core capabilities honed during their operational focus, creating a solid foundation for enhancing commercial practices.

Operational excellence initiatives have instilled a culture of continuous improvement, data-driven decision-making, and efficiency in manufacturing companies. These competencies are directly applicable to Commercial Excellence, which similarly demands meticulous attention to detail and a commitment to excellence. For instance, the rigorous process optimizations that have been perfected can now be applied to customer relationship management and sales processes.

We've been here before

One of the critical advantages that companies in the chemicals and oil & gas industries possess is their robust analytical capabilities. Over the years, these industries have developed sophisticated data analytics systems to monitor and enhance operational performance. These same systems can be adapted to analyze customer data, predict market trends, and optimize pricing strategies, thus driving commercial success.

The cultural shift towards Operational Excellence has also fostered a mindset of accountability and precision among employees. This mindset is crucial for Commercial Excellence, which requires a disciplined approach to managing customer relationships, executing sales strategies, and delivering value to customers. Companies can leverage this established culture to ensure that their sales teams and customer service representatives are aligned with commercial objectives.

A practical example is the oil & gas industry's experience with process safety management, which involves meticulous planning, risk assessment, and continuous monitoring. This experience can be transferred to managing customer portfolios, ensuring that the most valuable customers receive tailored attention and resources. Similarly, the chemicals industry's focus on product quality and compliance can be extended to maintaining high standards of customer service and satisfaction.

Catching a fever

Embarking on the journey to achieve Commercial Excellence demands a strategic approach that prioritizes early successes. These initial wins are hugely important, as they serve as a catalyst for broader transformation efforts, helping to build momentum and secure buy-in across the organization.

To set the stage for these early successes, companies should identify high-impact areas where quick improvements are possible. This might involve refining pricing strategies, enhancing customer engagement, or optimizing sales processes. For example, implementing advanced analytics to identify and prioritize high-value customers can quickly demonstrate tangible benefits, such as increased sales and improved customer satisfaction.

Securing early successes also helps in building confidence and fostering a culture of continuous improvement. When employees see the positive outcomes of their efforts, they are more likely to embrace the changes and contribute proactively. This aligns with the principles of Operational Excellence, where small, incremental improvements pave the way for larger, transformative gains.

It's also important for companies to communicate these early successes effectively. Sharing stories of initial wins across the organization can inspire and motivate teams, reinforcing the value of the transformation journey. This communication should highlight the specific actions taken, the challenges overcome, and the measurable benefits achieved.

If speaking is silver, listening is gold

Investing carefully and deliberately in customer priority data is essential for developing an effective commercial strategy. This information forms the foundation upon which Commercial Excellence is built and becomes a critical component of the commercial team's data analytics framework.

When companies prioritize collecting and analyzing customer data, they gain valuable insights into customer preferences, needs, and behaviors. These insights enable companies to tailor their products, services, and marketing efforts to better meet customer demands, thus enhancing customer satisfaction and loyalty. Accurate and comprehensive customer data is instrumental in identifying high-value customers, optimizing pricing strategies, and improving overall customer experience.

The eyes have it

A robust data analytics framework leverages this customer priority data to inform commercial decision-making. By integrating advanced analytics tools and techniques, companies can uncover patterns and trends that would otherwise remain hidden. This analytical approach supports more informed, evidence-based decisions, allowing companies to respond swiftly to market changes and customer needs.

The data analytics framework will also become a linchpin of commercial decision-making, guiding strategic initiatives and operational adjustments. It ensures that decisions are not based on intuition or incomplete information but on a thorough analysis of accurate data. This shift towards data-driven decision-making enhances the agility and competitiveness of the organization.

Companies must be meticulous in their approach to data collection, ensuring that the data is not only accurate but also relevant and timely. Investing in the right tools and technologies for data management and analysis is equally important. These investments pay off by providing a clear, actionable understanding of customer priorities, which, in turn, drives commercial success.

Good ol' supply and demand

Once a company has developed a reliable understanding of the market and customer behavior, the next step is to conduct a thorough analysis of the optimal mix of customers and product sales. This mix will serve as the guiding principle for the commercial teams, directing their efforts towards the most profitable and strategic objectives.

The optimal customer mix should be combined with optimized product mix planning from the company's manufacturing facilities. This alignment ensures that the company is producing the right products for the right customers at the right time. It allows the company to meet customer demands effectively while maximizing profitability. By matching the customer mix with the product mix, companies can better balance supply and demand, avoiding both overproduction and stockouts.

This process of matching customer mix and product mix is dynamic and iterative. It requires regular review and adjustment to respond to changing market conditions and customer preferences. Regular analysis helps companies to stay agile and adaptable, ensuring that they can navigate towards sustainable and profitable growth. It involves continuous monitoring and fine-tuning, with feedback loops that incorporate new data and insights into the planning process.

Successful implementation of this strategy depends on the collaboration between commercial teams and manufacturing units. Clear communication and coordinated efforts are essential to align goals and actions. The commercial teams need to provide insights and data about customer preferences and market trends, while the manufacturing teams must ensure that production capabilities can meet these demands efficiently.

The habit of duty without pain

Companies must pay close attention to the complexities of managing their salesforce and distributors to avoid commercial underperformance. Many firms that excel in engineering and manufacturing often fall short in commercial results due to common failure modes. These include passive management of distributors and poor discipline within client-facing sales teams.

Poor discipline within client-facing sales teams is a critical issue that can derail Commercial Excellence. Salespeople may enjoy relationship-building aspects of their jobs but often neglect essential administrative duties or challenging tasks like price negotiations. This neglect can lead to significant gaps in customer data and insights, which are necessary for informed decision-making. Leading companies develop an organizational discipline within their sales teams, emphasizing that each salesperson's primary responsibility is the company's financial well-being. Tasks should be prioritized based on their relative importance to the company's success.

The distributor tightrope walk

Passive management of distributors can also severely hinder a company's commercial success. Distributors, or channel partners, should not be left to operate without clear guidance and active engagement from the manufacturer. Companies must establish robust workflows and processes for managing their distributor networks, treating them as an evolving team whose performance needs regular monitoring and support. Distributors meeting expectations should receive continuous support and evaluation to identify improvement areas. Conversely, those failing to meet agreed-upon commercial targets should be highlighted for improvement or replacement. Maintaining a "bench" of potential new distributors ready to replace underperforming ones is a strategic approach that leading companies adopt to ensure sustained performance.

The most successful companies set clear commercial targets and expectations for their sales teams and distributors. They do not shy away from taking corrective actions when performance falls short. This proactive approach contrasts sharply with less successful companies, which often maintain a passive relationship with their salesforce and distributors, failing to set clear targets and slow to intervene when performance issues arise.

Feedback is a gift

As companies transform their commercial capabilities, gathering customer feedback becomes necessary for ensuring that their portfolio of initiatives delivers the intended market impact. Customer satisfaction serves as a reliable indicator of commercial success and can act as an early warning signal if strategic adjustments are necessary.

Regularly engaging with customers to understand their experiences and satisfaction levels provides valuable insights into the effectiveness of commercial strategies. This feedback loop allows companies to fine-tune their approaches, ensuring they meet and exceed customer expectations. By actively seeking and analyzing customer input, businesses can identify areas of improvement and swiftly address any issues that may arise.

Customer feedback also helps companies to validate the success of new initiatives. It offers a direct measure of how well these initiatives resonate with the market and whether they achieve their desired outcomes. This data-driven approach ensures that the Commercial Excellence team remains aligned with customer needs and market dynamics, fostering a customer-centric culture that prioritizes continuous improvement.

In addition to serving as a performance metric, customer satisfaction also highlights potential challenges before they escalate. If customer feedback indicates dissatisfaction or unmet needs, it signals the need for a strategic pivot. Companies can then proactively adjust their strategies, reallocating resources, or modifying initiatives to better align with customer expectations and market demands.

Incorporating customer feedback into the Commercial Excellence framework ensures that strategies remain relevant and effective. It empowers companies to adapt quickly to changing market conditions and maintain a competitive edge. By prioritizing customer satisfaction and leveraging it as a key performance indicator, businesses can drive sustainable growth and achieve long-term commercial success.

Breakfast like a king

Companies must recognize that company culture is critical to the pursuit of Commercial Excellence. The larger the strategic shift required to achieve this change, the greater the required cultural adjustment. Commercial Excellence teams should closely examine the cultural prerequisites and monitor the evolution of company culture continuously to ensure alignment with the behaviors necessary for the transformation's success.

The connection between strategy and culture cannot be overstated. An effective cultural pivot often involves a fundamental change in how employees perceive their roles, interact with customers, and prioritize their daily tasks. A misalignment between the new strategic objectives and the existing cultural attitudes can hinder progress and lead to resistance within the organization. Therefore, it is essential for Commercial Excellence teams to identify and address any potential cultural barriers early in the transformation process.

Monitoring the evolution of company culture is an ongoing task. It requires regular assessments of employee engagement, feedback, and alignment with the new commercial objectives. This can be achieved through surveys, focus groups, and performance metrics that highlight areas where cultural resistance may be occurring. By staying attuned to the cultural climate within the organization, leaders can make informed decisions to reinforce the desired behaviors and attitudes.

Communication plays a vital role in facilitating this cultural shift. Clear and consistent messaging from leadership about the importance of Commercial Excellence and the behaviors that support it can help to build a shared understanding and commitment across the organization. Leaders should also lead by example, demonstrating the new cultural norms in their actions and decisions.

Training and development programs are another critical component of supporting a cultural pivot. By equipping employees with the skills and knowledge they need to succeed under the new strategic framework, companies can reduce resistance and foster a more adaptable and resilient workforce. These programs should emphasize the connection between individual roles and the broader commercial objectives, helping employees see the value of their contributions.

The end of the beginning

Winston Churchill once remarked, "Now this is not the end. It is not even the beginning of the end. But it is, perhaps, the end of the beginning." This sentiment also applies to the conclusion of any strategic planning phase. The final chapter in any transformative journey marks the conclusion of discussions, of learning, and of planning. What follows is the critical phase of implementation, which is *the fundamental key to achieving success.*

Planning and strategizing are essential components of any significant initiative. They lay the groundwork, establish objectives, and identify the resources necessary for success. However, the value of even the most meticulously crafted plans remains theoretical until they are put into action. Action is the bridge between potential and reality. It transforms aspirations into tangible results and drives progress.

The shift from planning to execution requires a different mindset and skill set. Whereas planning involves analysis, forecasting, and decision-making, execution demands focus, determination, and adaptability. It is during this phase that challenges are confronted, unforeseen obstacles are navigated, and adjustments are made in real-time. The ability to adapt and respond swiftly is critical to maintaining momentum and ensuring that the strategic goals remain on track.

Furthermore, execution necessitates accountability. Clear roles and responsibilities must be established to ensure that everyone involved understands their part in the process. Regular monitoring and evaluation are essential to track progress, identify areas for improvement, and celebrate milestones. This not only keeps the team motivated but also provides opportunities to recalibrate efforts as needed.

Action is also about leadership. Leaders must inspire their teams, foster a culture of commitment, and provide the support necessary to overcome challenges. Effective leadership ensures that the vision and objectives remain clear, even when the path forward becomes difficult.

Although planning and strategizing are undoubtedly critical, the true test of any initiative lies in its execution. The end of the planning phase is merely the beginning of the journey. Success hinges on the ability to translate plans into action, to navigate challenges with agility, and to remain steadfast in the pursuit of goals. Now is the time for action, the fundamental key to turning vision into reality.

Writing the next chapter

Embarking on the journey toward Commercial Excellence is a significant endeavor, and this book is designed to be a trusted companion throughout that process. The success stories shared within these pages aim to inspire and motivate, highlighting the tangible benefits of committing to Commercial Excellence. Learning from others' experiences, both their triumphs and their missteps, offers invaluable insights that can guide your path and help you avoid common pitfalls.

I wrote this book to serve as more than just a source of information; it is intended as a call to action. The principles and practices discussed are not merely theoretical; they are practical tools that can be implemented to drive real change. This final chapter signifies the beginning of your own personal efforts to transform your company's commercial practices. Now is the time to apply what you have learned, to make informed decisions, and to take deliberate steps toward achieving your goals.

As you move forward, remember that the journey to Commercial Excellence is gradual and never-ending. It requires ongoing commitment and a willingness to adapt and evolve. The lessons learned and the actions that you take today will lay the foundation for your future success. So stay focused on your goals, but remember to remain open to new opportunities and challenges as they arise.

I hope this book has provided you with the knowledge and confidence that you need to embark confidently on your own Commercial Excellence journey. May you find the process rewarding, not just in terms of business success but also in personal growth and development.

The pursuit of Commercial Excellence is not a solitary endeavor. Rather, it is a collective effort that benefits from shared wisdom and mutual support. Remember that the ultimate measure of your success will be your growing ability to guide others. Remain open to future opportunities in which you can use your experiences and insights to mentor others, to share what you have learned, to help others achieve their own success, and to foster a culture of continuous improvement within your organization. By doing so, you contribute to a larger community of professionals dedicated to Commercial Excellence.

May this book serve as the beginning of a new chapter in your professional life. Embrace the principles of Commercial Excellence with enthusiasm and determination. Your success will not only transform your organization but also inspire others to strive for their own achievements. You are now equipped with the knowledge and the confidence you need to create a future where Commercial Excellence can become the standard, and where your success is measured not just by financial gains but by the positive impact you can have on the people and the world around you.

Made in the USA
Columbia, SC
12 August 2024

231046c4-57bb-463d-aeab-e9c1abe7367eR01